The Kingdom Manifesto

An exploration of the Sermon on the Mount

for today

Steve Wilmshurst

EP BOOKS
Faverdale North,
Darlington, DL3 0PH, England

web: www.epbooks.org
e-mail: sales@epbooks.org

First published 2012

British Library Cataloguing in Publication Data available
ISBN 13: 978-0-85234-826-0

Printed and bound in Great Britain by the MPG Books Group, Bodmin and King's Lynn.

Contents

Preface   5

Introduction   7

1. The ladder of light: Matthew 5:1-3   15

2. First steps on the ladder: Matthew 5:4-6   27

3. Just like Jesus: Matthew 5:7-9   49

4. What happens when you're different: Matthew 5:10-16   71

5. Jesus and the Law: Matthew 5:17-20   87

6. You have heard it said... Part 1: Matthew 5:21-32   101

7. You have heard it said... Part 2: Matthew 5:33-48   125

8. Giving up hypocrisy: Matthew 6:1-4   147

9. Spiritual reality: Matthew 6:5-18   157

10. Where is your heart? Matthew 6:19-34   179

11. Life in the family: Matthew 7:1-12   197

12. Decision time: Matthew 7:13-29   211

Notes   233

Preface

Like my two previous books published by EP (*The Final Word* and *A Ransom for Many*), this one began as a sermon series preached at Kensington Baptist Church in Bristol. The difference this time was that it was preached in collaboration with others and across the three sites where the church now meets. Each Sunday, three of us were preaching on the same passage as we worked our way through the Sermon on the Mount. That meant that we were able to encourage each other in preparation and listen to one another's messages afterwards – along with some of our congregations! This enriching experience has helped me to fill in gaps and think through some of the issues more fully. So I should particularly acknowledge my preaching colleagues, especially Andy Paterson and Mark Detzler. An additional note of gratitude is due for all the support and encouragement I've received from Andy, who as I write is on the point of moving on from the ministry at Kensington, where he has been the faithful pastor for twenty-three years.

Whenever we explore any section of Scripture in depth, we invariably find that the treasures to be mined are far more extensive than we could ever have guessed from the surface. That has certainly been my experience with the Sermon on the Mount. To an extent that I had never realised, these three chapters of Matthew draw together the whole biblical story. Time and again an exposition of a verse or paragraph would take us all the way from the Law and the Prophets through to the new heavens and the new earth. But then, that should not be surprising when we recall that this is truly the manifesto of the kingdom of heaven, and the story of the whole of Scripture is the story of the King!

This book is dedicated to my family, Andrea, Sarah and Anna: with my love.

Steve Wilmshurst
2012

Introduction

The manifesto we need

On 21st February, 1848, a document was published in London which would change the course of history. The document, written in German by Friedrich Engels and Karl Marx, was the Communist Manifesto. Their idea was to explain exactly what was wrong with the world and what should be done to put it right. According to Marx and Engels and their followers, the world is divided between two groups of people. There is the ruling class, who own everything; and there is the working class, who actually do everything. It's the workers who do all the work, who produce all the useful stuff. But the problem is, they have no power. The ruling class, who own everything, exploit the workers. They crush them. So the workers suffer; and however hard they work, they never get anywhere.

The answer, according to those early Communists, is to create a 'classless society', where everyone is on the same level. Then the conflict will cease; no-one will have the chance to exploit other people; and everyone will be treated fairly. That was the vision. The Communist Manifesto set out a ten-point plan, a list of ten steps to be taken before this perfect, classless society could come into being. One of those, revolutionary in 1848, was free education for every child. But most of the points were about ownership. No-one should be allowed to own any land; no-one should have the right to inherit from their parents; and the State should take over all financial resources and all the means of production, fields and factories alike, so they would belong to everyone. This was radical change. Get all this right, and all the rest will follow. The Manifesto closes with the immortal words: *Workers of the world, unite!*

Some thought this vision was glorious; some believed it was outrageous, over the top, diabolical. But over the next century, the Communist Manifesto would change the lives of millions of people. Ultimately, it was the work of Marx and Engels that led to the Communism of the Soviet Union and Eastern Europe. It lies somewhere behind the ideology of China today. It has informed hundreds of revolutions and uprisings across the world. Most people would say that where it has been seriously pursued, the result has not been justice and equality; rather the opposite. But whether that's true or not, its vision of a perfect, classless society has never materialised. The reason for that is simple. It's not that Marx and Engels went too far with their ideas and their theories. The problem was that they did not go nearly far enough. They saw that the world was full of appalling injustice and inequality; and of course it is. But they thought that if you only give everyone a fair share, if you take out the people who exploit the poor, then you can make everyone happy. Everyone will be well-off; and everyone will behave themselves.

They were wrong, of course. You can't put people right just by correcting their circumstances. Our worst problems don't come from outside, they come from within. If we want to see a community of real peace and justice, we have to deal with what's inside us – we have to deal with the state of our hearts. No laws, and no amount of external rules, can do anything about that. In fact, we can't do anything about it at all – it is only God who can change people's hearts and create this new community of justice and peace where people can live in harmony. And that is exactly what he has done. This new community is what the Bible calls 'the kingdom of heaven' or 'the kingdom of God'. This kingdom also has a manifesto. It had already been in existence for 1800 years by the time Marx and Engels published theirs. The kingdom manifesto is called the Sermon on the Mount. It's not a rule book. It's not a ten-point plan for creating a perfect community. No, God has already done that! The Sermon on the Mount is the manifesto for the people who are already part of the kingdom. It's radical – and it is Jesus' clearest and most extensive presentation of what the kingdom looks like. If we want to see what God's new community is supposed to look like, and catch the vision for how he wants us to live as his people, this is an excellent place to start.

Introduction

The Sermon on the Mount: introductory issues

Matthew's gospel

For most of Christian history, it was assumed that Matthew's gospel was the first to be written. A minority of commentators today do hold that view, but most now believe that Mark came first and that Matthew and Luke used Mark's gospel, along with other material, as they wrote their own. That question of priority, however, is of little importance when we consider the Sermon on the Mount, because Mark has nothing remotely like it! And although the basic order of the narrative in the two gospels is very similar, it is immediately obvious that Matthew structures his material very differently. Whereas Mark has a primarily Gentile audience in mind, Matthew is clearly writing for Jews. He is thus concerned to show very explicitly how the life and ministry of Jesus fulfils the Old Testament. Rather than leaving the references to prophecy (about sixty of them) for his readers to work out for themselves (as Mark does), Matthew constantly uses a formula like that in 4:14: '...to fulfil what was said through the prophet Isaiah'. Matthew emphasises that Jesus is the promised kingly Messiah, the fulfilment of Israel's hopes and longings.

One of the major features of Matthew is the five great teaching discourses which between them occupy eight out of twenty-eight chapters. Unusually in the gospels, the teaching content is almost unbroken, with little narrative material. That is certainly true of the Sermon on the Mount, the first and longest of these, which is framed by only two verses of narrative at either end (the 'narrative frame'). In general, Matthew arranges Jesus' teaching more systematically than Mark or Luke, who have their own distinctive methods of ordering their material[1]: hence the reputation of the 'teacher's gospel'. This systematic arrangement is clearly seen in the Sermon on the Mount itself, where we find eight Beatitudes, six case studies of Jesus fulfilling the Law and three instances of 'religious observance' – often framed in a repeating formula that would be easy to teach and to remember. We cannot be certain exactly how much of this structuring is due to Matthew's editorial activity, but from the fact that much of the material is paralleled in the other synoptic gospels (especially Luke) it is clear that Matthew has had a major part in it.

The kingdom of heaven

When Matthew uses the expression 'kingdom of heaven', as he frequently does (including five times in 5:1-20), he means exactly the same as Mark and Luke do by 'kingdom of God'. Jewish sensitivities to the use of the name of God led Matthew to favour the former term, though he does use 'kingdom of God' occasionally. The kingdom must be understood as both an activity – God is reigning there, through Christ – and as a 'space' – it consists of people and places where the name and rule of God in Christ are clearly and gladly acknowledged.

Clearly, the kingdom is a key term, and I will discuss it more extensively in the commentary where it arises. But it is perhaps worth warning now against two ways in which the word has been abused in our own day. The first comes from liberal theology, which is prone to regard the kingdom of heaven as everywhere where good things are happening in the world (and only in *this* world). Thus any acts to relieve poverty, to feed the hungry, to establish justice, to raise the status of women or to restore damaged eco-systems is freely badged as 'kingdom activity'. In other words, the kingdom is understood to embrace anything that God is thought to approve of. I say this is an abuse of the word because it completely disregards the New Testament teaching, which is implicit in the term anyway, that the kingdom involves submission to the king. The good deeds just listed are kingdom activity only if they are done in the name of the king, which implies that they are done by his people and accompanied by a call to submit to him.

The second abuse, which will be closer to home for most of my readers, is to make the kingdom entirely 'other-worldly'. Typically this is justified by Jesus' words in John 18:36 – 'my kingdom is not of this world'. I have written about this elsewhere[2], but suffice it to say that Jesus, in that fascinating dialogue with Pontius Pilate about the nature of power and truth, is referring to the *source* of his kingdom and, therefore, his power. If we used the literal translation 'my kingdom is not *from* (Greek *ek*) this world' there might be less confusion about this. The problem about believing in a kingdom which is *only* 'other-worldly' is that it will prevent us from doing very much to build the kingdom here and now. We will tend to a rather defensive mentality and confine ourselves to recruiting souls for heaven. This is not what Jesus calls us to in the Sermon on the Mount (see 5:13-16, in particular).

The Sermon on the Mount, like the rest of the New Testament, speaks of the kingdom with a present and a future sense. The Beatitudes refer to the kingdom primarily in its present aspect (5:3, 10) – Jesus is saying, This is what kingdom people are like *now*. In 7:21, however, Jesus is speaking of the Day of Judgment, and the kingdom referred to is the completed, perfected eternal kingdom. In theological language, the kingdom of heaven is therefore eschatological – it relates to the new age, the eternal age, but it is already present in some measure now. At the outset of his ministry Jesus proclaims that 'the kingdom of heaven is near' (4:17, echoing John the Baptiser in 3:2). The sense of the Greek is that the kingdom has come near and is now present in the vicinity, waiting to be populated by the members Jesus will call into it. In that context, 11:12 ('the kingdom of heaven has been forcefully advancing') is like a progress report. The kingdom is here and now, and the Sermon on the Mount calls us to make it visible, both individually and corporately.

The people of this kingdom are to be clearly, radically different from the world around them. The message runs through every paragraph of the Sermon. It is a distinctiveness that begins with a changed heart, which inevitably produces in turn a transformed life. We will no longer think, feel or behave like anyone else – people from the secular world, followers of the religions of the world, or nominal Christians. The Sermon on the Mount marks us out from them all.

The setting of the Sermon
We don't know for sure whether the Sermon was preached on a single occasion, perhaps even on a single day, or whether Matthew has assembled material from many different occasions. The fact that the teachings in the Sermon on the Mount are distributed at many different points in the other gospels does not necessarily mean that Matthew has made a deliberate collection. It is very likely that, like any travelling preacher, Jesus used similar material many times in his ministry. Personally, I think it is truest to the Scriptures to say that the Sermon on the Mount was a single event. Matthew 5-7 reads like teaching that has been given its basic structure by the original teacher. I am happy to accept that Matthew has paraphrased the words of Jesus and quite certain that he has greatly abridged the original message. Beyond that, we cannot say.

On the specific question of the parallels with Luke's so-called 'Sermon on the Plain' (Luke 6:17-49), opinions are divided as to whether this is an account of the same occasion or a different one. I think the latter is much more likely, not so much because Luke describes the setting differently as because the thrust of the teaching itself is so different – not least in Luke's equivalent of the Beatitudes. For example, in Luke there are just four Beatitudes; they are all explicitly addressed to 'you'; and they are balanced by four corresponding 'woes'. In the first three of both blessings and woes, the note is more 'physical' and less 'spiritual' than in the Sermon on the Mount. I think the two Sermons are best read (and obeyed, which is after all the point!) separately and on their own merits. For this reason, I have hardly cross-referenced to the Sermon on the Plain at all. The technical commentaries on Matthew and Luke discuss these issues in greater depth.

A debt to the past master

Every expositor of the Sermon on the Mount is (or should be) indebted to the masterly work of Dr Martyn Lloyd-Jones. Indeed, it seems to me that the only justification for producing any new book on this passage of Scripture is the passage of time. Over fifty years have passed since 'the Doctor' preached those sermons at Westminster Chapel. Inevitably, the culture and politics of the world have moved on a great deal. In many other ways, of course, we have not, and there are few places where I have ventured to differ from Lloyd-Jones' analysis of the biblical text[3]; but there are many points where the message calls for different application today. There are other good treatments of the Sermon on the Mount, some of which are mentioned below, but most of them date from the nineteen-seventies and are also beginning to show their age.

Further reading

I have already mentioned Martyn Lloyd-Jones' published sermons (*Studies in the Sermon on the Mount*). I have also been greatly helped by Don Carson's *The Sermon on the Mount: an evangelical exposition of Matthew 5-7*, John Stott's *Christian Counter-Culture* and John Blanchard's book on the Beatitudes, *The Beatitudes for Today*. There are numerous helpful commentaries on Matthew's gospel. The shorter ones are necessarily too brief to be really helpful on the Sermon on the Mount, so I will not mention them; but among the more substantial commentaries, those of

Introduction

Leon Morris (*The Gospel according to Matthew*, in the Pillar series), Dick France (*The Gospel of Matthew*, in the NICNT series) and John Nolland (*The Gospel of Matthew*, in the NIGTC series) should certainly be noted.

Structure of the Sermon on the Mount

5:1-2 Narrative introduction: the setting

5:3-12 The Beatitudes: the character of the kingdom and its consequences
       5:3 The poor in spirit
       5:4 The mourners
       5:5 The meek
       5:6 The passionate for righteousness
       5:7 The merciful
       5:8 The pure in heart
       5:9 The peacemakers
       5:10-12 The persecuted

5:13-16 The kingdom's impact on society: salt and light

5:17-20 Jesus and the Law: introduction to the main body of the Sermon

5:21-46 Living by the Law fulfilled by Jesus: six case studies
       5:21-26   Murder
       5:27-30   Adultery
       5:31-32   Divorce
       5:33-37   Oaths
       5:38-42   Retribution
       5:43-47   Enemies
       5:48   Conclusion: be perfect!

6:1-18 Genuine devotion: living for God without hypocrisy
       6:1-4 Giving to the needy
       6:5-15 Prayer
       6:16-18 Fasting

6:19-34 The priorities of the kingdom
       6:19-24 Earthly treasure versus heavenly treasure
       6:25-34 Worrying versus confident faith

The Kingdom Manifesto

7:1-11 The relationships of the kingdom
        7:1-6 Sound judgment of those inside and outside
        7:7-11 Relating to God as Father

7:12 Summing up Law and Prophets: conclusion of the main body of the Sermon

7:13-27 Responding to the kingdom
        7:13-14 Two ways
        7:15-23 Discerning true and false
        7:24-27 The test of authenticity: obedience

7:28-29 Narrative conclusion

Chapter 1
The ladder of light
Matthew 5:1-3

In this chapter we will start looking more closely at the text of the Manifesto. We will begin by looking at the first two verses of Matthew 5, where our gospel writer sets the scene for the Sermon on the Mount. Then we will take an overview of verses 3-12, which are known as the Beatitudes. After that we will look at the first and most crucial of these eight magnificent sayings.

Setting the scene

The end of Matthew 4 places Jesus in the region of Galilee. That's in the north of the territory around the lake of the same name. He is near the start of his ministry; he has been moving around from place to place teaching, proclaiming the coming of God's kingdom, and healing. The short passage in 4:23-25 summarises this early phase of the Galilean ministry. As a result, massive crowds are flocking to him, not just from Galilee itself but from every direction, as we read in 4:25.

But Jesus never follows the crowds. He never seeks them out. We see this in 8:18 and even more clearly in Mark 1:35-39, where Jesus deliberately refuses to return to the place where he is already famous and the crowds are swarming; he insists on moving on. So at this point Jesus decides he will station himself away from habitation and start to give his disciples some basic teaching about the kingdom he's announcing and what it's going to look like. Hence verses 1-2. Probably what follows in the next three chapters is a condensed summary of what Jesus says in the course of one full day; it's certainly set out as if it's spoken on a single occasion. I have discussed this issue a little further in the Introduction.

When Matthew says 'mountainside', he doesn't mean that Jesus is perching halfway up a crag somewhere. The rolling hill country of Galilee fits the bill nicely. Possibly calling it a mountain may be intended to connect us with other times when God has spoken to his people on a mountain, as at Sinai; there may be just an echo of that here, but we shouldn't read too much into that.

The Kingdom Manifesto

'Sitting' is the traditional posture for teachers: the fact that Jesus is sitting down underlines the fact that his words are really intended for just a small group. Then if the crowds want to follow and listen in, that's fine. The 'disciples' here are not the familiar group of twelve – in fact Jesus seems not to have settled on a group of twelve at this point – but they are the people who are serious about following him. They are the insiders; they are the citizens of the kingdom; they are *us*, if we are Christians. So the picture is of Jesus speaking to an inner group while the crowds listen in – if you glance over to 7:28 you can see that they do. The Sermon on the Mount is mainly for people who are in the kingdom, or at least for those who are serious about exploring the implications of joining it. This is for Christians first and foremost. But if you are not a Christian, I am delighted you are reading this book! I hope you, like those crowds, will listen in and understand what it will mean if you *become* a Christian.

The biggest mistake we can make about the Sermon on the Mount is to think that this is what will make you a Christian – that if you can make your life look like what Jesus describes here at the beginning, if you can try your best to obey the teaching that follows – don't swear, turn the other cheek and all the rest of it – that will *make* you a Christian. It's often been read that way. And people who think of Jesus as a great teacher will usually quote the Sermon on the Mount. They'll say, That's the bit of the Bible I can really relate to; that's the bit I will pick up; that's how I try to live my life.

But in fact (and we will need to keep repeating this) the Sermon on the Mount is nothing of the kind. It's not 'Do this and you'll be a Christian'; it's 'because you *are* a Christian, be like this'. We can only follow the Kingdom Manifesto if we are already in the kingdom, because it is only God who can give us the new heart we need to live like this. The way to become a Christian is not to meet Jesus in the Sermon on the Mount. To become a Christian today, you have to meet him first at the *cross*, dying for your sins, dying to give you new life, dying to create a new person with a new heart, a new direction, a new ambition. Become part of the kingdom. *Then* you come to the Sermon on the Mount and see what living in the kingdom is all about.

Introducing the Beatitudes

The Sermon on the Mount begins with this series of eight sayings in 5:5-12 known as the *Beatitudes*. They are called that because they all begin with 'Blessed' and the Latin for 'Blessed' is *beatus*. By the way, if you are counting them and you reckon the total comes to nine, verses 11-12 are really an expansion of verse 10, not a new saying, so eight is the number! And these Beatitudes appear at the beginning for a very good reason. They describe *the character of the kingdom*. They tell us what a Christian *is*; and then the rest of the Sermon on the Mount tell us what a Christian *does*. So it's first *character*, then *conduct*.

The ladder of light

As we look through the Beatitudes, there are two key words that spring out: the word 'blessed' (Greek *makarios*) and the word 'kingdom' (Greek *basileia*). Let's think about 'blessed' first – it's clear that we can't make much sense of the Beatitudes if we don't know what Jesus means by 'blessed'. When Jesus says these people are 'blessed', he is saying they are in a good place, they are well-off, they should be congratulated. Sometimes the word is translated 'happy', but that makes it sound as if it's about how you feel. You might feel happy this morning and unhappy this afternoon. Being blessed should *make* us happy, but no-one is happy all the time, and that's not what Jesus is saying[4]. No, if you are 'blessed' it means that God has put you in a good position; and that doesn't change with your mood swings! You are *well-off*. People ought to look at you and say, I wish I was you!

As soon as you look down the list of Beatitudes you can see how unexpected that is. Many of these descriptions don't sound like being in a good place at all – but Jesus says they *are*; and as we work our way through them we will find out why.

The second word to look at is 'kingdom'. You see that both the first and the last Beatitudes say 'theirs is the kingdom of heaven'. When you see an expression like that topping and tailing a passage in the Bible, it means it's important. What does it mean? We see the word 'heaven' and we might think, This is about some place that we go to when we die. But actually, 'kingdom of heaven' is just Matthew's alternative form of 'kingdom of God'. All the other gospels call it the 'kingdom of God'; Matthew *usually* calls it the 'kingdom of heaven', because he is writing for Jews and they are very cautious about using the name of God. But they mean exactly the same[5].

When we talk about a 'kingdom' in normal conversation, we mean a geographical area, a territory that's ruled over by a king or queen; my own country is called the United Kingdom, and that's what it means: an area of land ruled over by a monarch. The kingdom of God, or kingdom of heaven, is not a geographical area. You can't draw God's kingdom on a map. You would have to draw it in people's hearts, because God's kingdom is all the people, all the places, where God's rule is gladly accepted. It consists of all the people who say, God is my King, I acknowledge him, I live under his rule and authority. The kingdom of God is God reigning in the hearts of his own people[6].

For now, that kingdom is largely unseen as it grows quietly, almost stealthily, drawing in one person after another and growing within us – think of all those parables where Jesus talks about the kingdom being like a growing seed or a crop in a field (13:1-43). But one day, when Jesus the King comes back, these days will be over, his kingdom will be seen by everyone, and it will be clear exactly who is in the kingdom and who has been left outside. Here and now, you are either *in* the kingdom, or you are *outside* it; and the Sermon on the Mount, the Kingdom Manifesto, is for people who are inside.

The Kingdom Manifesto

These Beatitudes, then, are about people God says are fortunate, or in a good place; and they are about what God is doing among his people in the kingdom. Before we move on, let's look at three brief points which will help us when we come to examine them more closely.

1. They are a set meal, not a buffet[7]. The Beatitudes are describing the Christian's character, so *all* of them should describe *all* of us who are Christians. We are not supposed to look down the list and think: ah, blessed are the merciful, yes, I can see that's important, I'll work on that one, I'll have some of that; but 'pure in heart', no, that's a bit heavy for me, I think I'll leave that on the table. This is not a buffet, where you pick and choose whatever you like the look of – it's a set meal, you need it all. Jesus doesn't mean that some Christians are blessed because they're meek and a completely different group are blessed because they are persecuted. If it helps to think of it this way, the Beatitudes are more like the *fruit* of the Spirit (Galatians 5:22-23), which we should all show, rather than the *gifts* of the Spirit (1 Corinthians 12:4-6), where we are all different.

2. They are a ladder, not a pile of sticks. By which I mean, they are not simply a random heap of sayings that start anywhere and lead nowhere and which you could pick up in any order. They are not like a pile of sticks, they are much more like the rungs of a ladder – a 'ladder of light' as C.H. Spurgeon described them. A ladder is something you climb up; and if you are climbing a ladder up the side of your house, it is fairly important to take the rungs in the right order. You don't try to step on the seventh rung before you've stepped on the first one – or at least, you won't make much progress if you do! And again, you'll need *all* the rungs of the ladder, not just the ones you like the look of! So with the Beatitudes, there is a logical order and you have to start at the beginning. When we come to unpack them all, we'll see why that is; but just by glancing through, perhaps you can already see that the Beatitudes begin by understanding properly what we are like, where we stand; they move on to the character that develops from that; and they conclude with what happens to you when you live this way. That will become clearer as we go on.

3. They are a demand, not a tick-list. This is not a list for us to work through, ticking off one item after another and deciding at the end that we must be OK because we have ticked all the boxes. If you find yourself doing that, let me warn you, you are simply proving that you don't belong to the kingdom at all. This is not a list that you can tick off. These are *spiritual* characteristics that only a child of the kingdom can show.

In fact, the way we react to the Beatitudes says a lot about us. How do you respond – how *will* you respond – to these words as we study them? Will you contentedly tick them off, or say, well, I can do three out of eight, so that's

The ladder of light

OK? If you're thinking like that, it's a sign that you are spiritually dead and you need to repent and turn to Christ – and *then* come back to this passage. Or can you recognise, from these words, that this is how you *should* be, but you're not because you know you're incapable of living this way?

Martyn Lloyd-Jones puts it like this: 'Nothing shows me the absolute need of the new birth, and of the Holy Spirit and his work within, so much as the Sermon on the Mount. These Beatitudes crush me to the ground. They show me my utter helplessness. Were it not for the new birth, I am undone.'[8] You see, without knowing Christ and having him in our life, the uncompromising demand of the Beatitudes is simply beyond us. The Beatitudes tell us, This is how you must be. This is how you are called to live. God *demands* it. But without Christ, it's impossible. If you can read through the Beatitudes and respond, I see that's how I should be. I know I'm not there, but I *long* to be like that, I *wish* I was like that – that's a very good sign. Be encouraged! It shows you're alive!

To look ahead for a moment, here's a quick taste of what that will mean. 'Blessed are the poor in spirit' – the people who *know* they are no-hopers, that if we're not born again we are helpless – is that you? Or are you still saying, No, I'm working my way through life quite nicely, thank you? 'Blessed are those who mourn' – does the thought and the sight of sin in your own heart and life horrify you, does it make you want to weep that you are still failing, you still have relapses into sin? Or are you not bothered? Yes, I have good days, I have bad days, on average I'm not too bad? If so, you are probably still outside the kingdom. 'Blessed are the meek' – the people who aren't proud, who aren't arrogant, who don't push themselves forward, because they know where they come from, they know what they are made of, and whatever they have, they owe it all to the Lord. Is that you? 'Blessed are those who hunger and thirst for righteousness' – are we people who yearn to be better, whose passion is to be more like Jesus? Or are you happy with the state of your heart? 'Blessed are the merciful' – what do you want to do when you have the chance to get your own back? Do you want to get even? Do you want to 'give them what they deserve'? Or are you merciful – as the Lord has been to you?

'Blessed are the pure in heart' – does the thought of being innocent and clean excite you, or does it turn you off? 'Blessed are the peacemakers' – who go out of their way to create peace. Just like Jesus, who came all the way to this earth, and all the way to the cross, to preach peace to those who were far away, and peace to those who were near. Do you want to be like that? Or do you prefer to stay comfortably out of trouble? And 'blessed are those who are persecuted because of righteousness – because of *me*'. Are you willing to face trouble and pain because you belong to Jesus? If you belong to the kingdom, you *will* be willing – because the people of the kingdom love Jesus that much.

The Kingdom Manifesto

Blessed are the no-hopers

Imagine you are eighteen years old and you are applying to university. You have filled in your UCAS forms and now you are up for interview. You're nervous; but you're looking your best and you feel prepared. You sit down and the man behind the desk asks you what makes you think they should admit you to this university. 'Well', you say, 'I've got these GCSEs and AS-levels, you see – in fact my grades are really rather good – look, I've even brought my certificates. I've been working hard and I'm predicted really good A-levels. I think I'll do well here.' 'A-levels?', he says. 'Certificates? Working hard? Oh no, this university is only for people with *no* qualifications. I'm afraid we won't be admitting *you!*'

You want to open a bank account, so you go down to the High Street to join the bank. You sit down with the bank manager and she asks you, 'Right, so you want to open an account with us. How much money do you have to start with?' 'Well', you say, 'It may not be much to you, but I've been saving up and I've got £1000; and I think that should be enough to open my account.' '£1000?', she says. 'Saving up? Oh no, to open an account here you have to be in *debt* – a million pounds, we usually say. I'm afraid there's no chance we could sign *you* up!'

You fancy a holiday and you've heard of one particular place that sounds fantastic. A holiday island in the sun: clear blue waters, white sand, palm trees; it's absolutely idyllic, in fact you can imagine spending all the rest of your days there. So you decide to go. You pack everything you think you'll need: sunscreen, Hawaiian shirt, spending money, passport; and off you go with your suitcase. You arrive at the airport; and they ask, 'Hello, what have you got there?' 'Well', you say, 'I've got one suitcase, which I have packed myself, and here's my passport. I'm ready for my trip of a lifetime.' 'Suitcase?', they say. 'Passport? Oh no, we don't accept people who bring their own luggage. And we certainly can't accept people with a passport! I'm afraid you won't be allowed in.'

Now those three scenarios may be hard to imagine; but they illustrate exactly what Jesus is talking about when he says, at the beginning of the Sermon on the Mount, 'Blessed are the poor in spirit, for theirs is the kingdom of heaven' (5:3). If you want to get in to this amazing place called the kingdom, if you want to sign up, if you want to be allowed in, the entry requirement is to arrive with absolutely *nothing*. Anyone who comes along with more than nothing will be turned away. *Blessed are the no-hopers!*

To use the image I described just now, we are now about to put our feet on the first rung of the ladder. This is the starting point. We know what 'blessed' means; and we have an idea what the 'kingdom of heaven' means; but what in the world does 'poor in spirit' mean? We won't get far until we know.

The ladder of light

Poor in spirit – what it's NOT
Let's first see what it doesn't mean. Often people have read this verse and thought: Jesus is saying you are blessed if you are poor – *materially* poor. You haven't got much money, you haven't got a roof over your head – you are poor. And Jesus is pronouncing a special blessing on people like that. After all, surely Jesus cared for the poor, so isn't this the sort of thing he *might* have said to them? That would mean that if we decide to live a very simple life, give up our luxuries and so on, God will bless us. In the past, this kind of thinking encouraged people to become monks and hermits; it encourages many people who advocate a simple lifestyle today.

But actually that just doesn't make sense. There is no blessing in being poor. If you don't agree with me, I suggest you go and try it for a while. But before you go, remember that when the New Testament uses this word 'poor', it doesn't mean someone who can't afford a new car or a foreign holiday. This word means really poor. The equivalent for us would be someone who sleeps every night under a bridge somewhere, because they have nothing. So if you'd like to go and do that, and then come back and tell me how blessed you are, that's fine and I'll wait to hear from you! There is nothing romantic, nothing privileged, nothing blessed about being really poor. The 'parallel passage' (if it really is a parallel) in Luke 6:20 might lead us to think otherwise, because there Jesus simply says 'blessed are the poor'. But the thrust of that passage is quite different. For one thing, Jesus is comparing the actual situation of his disciples (*materially* poor, *physically* hungry) in contrast to the well-off (currently rich and well-fed, Luke 6:24-25): the message is that the disciples will ultimately be vindicated, their fortunes will change – *because* they are members of the kingdom, not because they are poor!

It's worth quoting Leon Morris' commentary at some length on this, especially given the experience from which he speaks:

'There are strong protests... against 'spiritualising'... this beatitude, and it is insisted that it must be seen for what it is, a radical reversal of the world's values. We are told that it is the poor and distressed as such of whom Jesus speaks. But... Jesus is not saying that poverty is a blessing in itself; to canonise a state of life in which people find themselves against their will (real poverty does not mean voluntarily choosing to live simply) and from which they would escape if they could is scarcely Christian. Now it is true that it is easy for the interpreter smugly to transfer the meaning of what Jesus says into an understanding of which the interpreter approves and avoid any real contact with the poverty-stricken. A rediscovery of Jesus' interest in the poor is long overdue. But I cannot rid myself of the feeling that much modern writing proceeds from the comfortable, people for whom poverty is an interesting subject for discussion but who have never themselves experienced what real poverty is. I have. And poverty is not a blessing, nor is powerlessness... Jesus is pronouncing a blessing on those empty of any spiritual resources, poor as they often were in material things as well.'⁹

Yes, Jesus most certainly *cared* for the poor; and so should we. Yes, God is most certainly concerned about injustice, the way the poor of this world are oppressed and ground down; and so must we be. Yes, many of us should certainly be living more simply, though that is not the same thing as poverty. Many Scriptures, many Bible verses tell us about all that – but this is not one of them! There is no blessing in being materially poor, and Jesus never says there is.

Poor in spirit – what it IS

If Jesus is not talking about ordinary poverty, what does this expression mean? Jesus is talking about people who have *no spiritual resources* – and they know it. People who in spiritual terms are no-hopers. So that you know this is not just me putting my own spin on a difficult phrase, let's have a look at a couple of places in the Old Testament which talk about the same theme. Look at Isaiah 57:15 and 66:2b. Here is God saying that although he is so great and holy, although he is a God 'up there' and 'out there', he also comes near to anyone who is lowly in spirit, who is contrite – words which parallel Matthew 5:3 almost exactly. The Lord says he values the one who is humble and lowly and trembles at his word.

Or, in other words, Blessed are the poor in spirit: the ones who have nothing to offer, the no-hopers. This verse is describing God's invitation to those who are at the bottom. And that's where we have to begin. The kingdom of heaven, the kingdom of God, is for no-hopers – and for no-one else. This, you see, is quite the reverse of what Jesus' contemporaries, the religious people of his day, believed was the case. They believed they *did* have something to offer – they had their obedience to God's Law to offer, and they thought that God would be pleased with them for that. They came, as it were, to open an account at the bank with money in their pockets. They didn't realise that with God we have *nothing* to offer, that when we encounter God, we bring nothing to the table except our debts – our sins.

Jesus told a parable about exactly this. It comes in Luke 18:9-14. Of these two men, which one was accepted? Which one was justified? Which one was *blessed*? Not the Pharisee, who came proud of his outstanding record, his qualifications; but the tax-collector, the outcast, who brought only his sins and asked for mercy. He was poor in spirit.

This idea that God counts our qualifications is not confined to New Testament times. It didn't finish with the Pharisees. It's what people of every age and culture have thought. It's precisely what Islam teaches its followers. Your good deeds and your bad deeds are being counted, all through your life; the angels are noting it all down. On judgment day, when you stand before God, if your

The ladder of light

good deeds weigh more than your bad deeds, there is a good chance that he will admit you to the kingdom of heaven, which Muslims call paradise. If your bad deeds weigh more, you won't get in.

Muslims are not alone in holding that kind of belief about counting good deeds. This idea that God accepts or rejects us, loves or hates us, admits or excludes us, according to our performance, is the default setting of all of fallen humanity. It's how we all instinctively feel. It offers us something to be proud of. Jesus says no, that is totally misguided, there is no entry to the kingdom that way. Jesus tells us that the golden ticket for the kingdom is handed to you by God and by no-one else. This is how you get your foot on the ladder. Only the no-hopers need apply. *Blessed* are the no-hopers! So if it is only the no-hopers who can enter the kingdom, what does it mean? Let's see.

The kingdom is open to everyone

You may never have had the qualifications to go to university – no such place may ever have opened its doors to you. You may never have had the money to open a bank account or the funds to take a dream holiday – but even if your whole life has been about doors closed in your face, the kingdom of heaven is open to you. How? Because Jesus has bought your ticket. He has sat and passed the exams for you, he has earned the entry fee that you need. We were no-hopers, but Christ died for us. This is what his death on the cross has achieved. Jesus lived a perfectly good life from beginning to end; you and I, from beginning to end, have messed up our lives in every way we could find: offended God, outraged his goodness, rebelled against his generosity, flouted his purposes, spat in his face. We have all done that. But Jesus took our place, condemned to die for our crimes instead of us, so that he gets the 'credit' for our sins and we get the credit for his perfect life. So because of the cross, the door of the kingdom is open to everyone.

You come to the kingdom with nothing

We have to recognise that we have absolutely nothing to offer. Anything we think might give us a better chance with God, anything we think might be to our advantage, we need to forget about. Your parents might be Christians – that's great – but it won't buy you any favours with God. You might be very bright, or you might think you live a very good, very moral life – but don't try to offer that to God. Only no-hopers can apply to the kingdom. If you think you have qualifications, read Philippians 3:7-9a. The apostle Paul was someone who had all sorts of advantages – he could boast about his family background, his religious activities, in fact all kinds of qualifications – that was some CV! – but this is what he concludes. Here was a member of the religious elite, a man who had everything, but who knew he had nothing to offer. And he says, In order to gain Christ, in order to get into the kingdom, I have to recognise that all that is worthless. It's not even worthless, in fact it's a loss. As Toplady's hymn puts it, 'Nothing in my hand I bring, simply to thy cross I cling'.

The Kingdom Manifesto

So what about you? Have you come to that point where you can let go of everything you think is credit? The point where you can look at God, and look at yourself, and see that you have *nothing* to bring? And then look at Jesus, and see what he has done for you, that he has bought you in to the kingdom, if you will come. Are you ready to come with *nothing* – to begin the life of the kingdom, and be 'blessed'? Don't try to live by Jesus' teaching until you have come to Jesus' cross. Don't come to the Sermon on the Mount unless you have come through this verse first. You must come with nothing.

The kingdom is the best place, now

Most people reading this book are Christians already. We *are* the kingdom people. And you may well be thinking, I know all that. I know about coming to Christ with nothing, and I have, I belong to him. Well then, take a look around. If we have come to Christ like this – empty, weak, offering nothing – we have the kingdom. We *are* the kingdom. It's already begun. Eternal life begins not when you die, but when you first find Christ, when he first finds you. We are living it today, and we are *blessed* because the kingdom belongs to us – we are in the best possible place, right now. But here's what we need to see. This is not just about how we *enter* the kingdom. It's also how we *live* in the kingdom – the Beatitudes are the character of the kingdom people. The people of the kingdom are *still* poor in spirit. We *still* depend on his grace.

How long have you been in the kingdom? A year? Five, ten, twenty – fifty years – more? As we travel further on through the Christian life, we become more and more keenly aware of how much we need that grace, how far we are in debt, how much we owe to Christ. We begin to understand that when the Bible talks about people being in darkness, or dead in their sins, or under the wrath of God, it's not exaggerating. We begin to see our life without Christ just a little bit in the way that God saw it. And more and more we realise how desperately we still fall short of what he's called us to – even after many years of living in the kingdom. We see how poor we are, and we see how magnificent Christ is.

We *still* don't boast of ourselves. In the Christian life, we can never be self-reliant. The world honours people who are strong and stand on their own feet – but in the kingdom, we can never do that. We are no-hopers – we have to rely on Christ. We still need the cross; we need to come back to the cross every single day. The Christian life is still 100% grace. We still don't push ourselves forward. Kingdom people don't point to themselves. They point to Christ (2 Corinthians 4:5).

Let me ask you this, if you are a Christian. As the days go by, as the years pass, do you find yourself thinking less of yourself and more of Christ? Comparing today with a year ago today, are you seeing him more clearly, are you loving him more, do you find yourself wanting to please him more and finding your joy and delight with him? (By the way, Jesus doesn't love *you* more than a year ago

The ladder of light

today! He couldn't!) Compared with a year ago, is there more of Jesus in your life and less of your old, stinking self? Do you look more like a citizen of the kingdom? What is the honest truth?

Whatever you have come through in the past year or may still be going through now, God's will for you is that you should grow, and growing means being more and more like Jesus. Praise God if that's happening in you, because it's his Spirit who is making it happen! But if not, if your view of Christ is dimmer and more distant than it used to be, if your Christian growth has stalled, then don't stay there – why would you want to? Tell him about it. Seek his face and pray this: Lord, I want to remember I am poor in spirit. I brought nothing when you saved me: I came spiritually bankrupt; it was all from you. Whatever good I have now, whatever good there is in me, is all from you. Now I want to know you more. I want to love you more. I want to see Jesus more clearly so that I can be more like him.

Questions to reflect on or discuss

1. Having worked through this chapter, how do you feel about being part of the kingdom of heaven – assuming that you are? What does it mean to you?

2. Are you convinced, in your heart of hearts, that you have nothing good in yourself to offer to God? What kind of things are you tempted to be proud of, to boast about?

3. Look back over your Christian life so far. How does being 'poor in spirit' show itself in your life? Do you 'find yourself thinking less of yourself and more of Christ'?

Chapter 2
First steps on the ladder
Matthew 5:4-6

Now, having placed our feet on the first rung of the ladder, we move onwards and upwards with Beatitudes numbers two to four.

Blessed are the mourners

The funeral procession moves slowly forward to the graveside. Following close behind the coffin comes Mavis, the widow, her face tear-stained. It is just ten days since her beloved husband passed away and she is devastated. She has never known such pain, such loss. In line behind her, the family and the few close friends, their faces intent; while the undertaker watches calmly. They arrive at the graveside and gather round. The usual words are spoken and the coffin is lowered into the ground. A few moments of silence, a few unspoken thoughts, and Mavis turns away. One by one the other mourners approach her – some because they feel they ought to, some because they care. They fumble for the right words. They want to help. What can they say? They say what people always say. 'He had a good innings.' 'You've got so many happy memories.' 'Don't worry, dear – time is a great healer.' And then, with an arm round her shoulders, 'Come back to the house and have a cup of tea.'

When Jesus said, 'Blessed are those who mourn, for they will be comforted' (Matthew 5:4), is this what he had in mind? Mourning is what people do at funerals, that is where you 'mourn'; and 'comforting' is what you do for people who are upset. Mourners get comforted – so does Jesus have this kind of picture in view? Does that make it *good* to be a mourner? Does that make sense? Or is there any other possible meaning to these strange words? How can we get to the bottom of it?

The Kingdom Manifesto

We've seen that these Beatitudes are no haphazard collection of sayings, arranged in random order. Reading through the Beatitudes is more like climbing a ladder, one rung at a time. Jesus speaks these words, in this order, for a very deliberate reason. We have begun with the first rung, being poor in spirit: that is how we enter the kingdom, and it is the only way in. Now we come to the second rung. So what does this mean? Is it something to do with funerals? Is it about losing a loved one? What kind of 'mourning' *is* this that means we are blessed? We tend to read these words to mean something like this: If you've been going through hard times – if unfortunately you have lost someone, or a relationship has broken up, if you happen to be feeling very low for some reason like that – well, don't worry because things will get better. Every cloud has a silver lining. Time is a great healer.

That's the way we might read it. But that can't be what Jesus means, because as well as being very trite, it simply isn't true. We know that from experience. There are many, many people who never break free of misery, who live their whole lives in despair or on the edge of it. That's true in a Western city just as it is true on the streets of Calcutta. They are not blessed – and the Bible doesn't ever say so!

We might think, since this is about *kingdom* people, that perhaps Jesus means that when *Christians* have a hard time, when we are mourning, we have hope and comfort because we know that God is with us and we can trust him even in the darkest of days. Now, that is true and wonderful. As God's people we *do* know that the Lord stands with us in every dark and painful experience – praise God, it's true. But is it what Jesus is talking about *here*? Actually, it can't be – because as we've already seen, the Beatitudes are meant to be a description of us all. This is about the character of the kingdom, not just for times of special difficulty or pain. And just as we are *all* to be poor in spirit, and we are *all* to be meek, and we are *all* to be merciful, Jesus says we are *all* to be mourners. Jesus says, it is in the character, it is in the nature of my blessed people, that they will be mourners. But then of course, as we still struggle to pin down exactly what Jesus means here, that only raises another problem. Surely Christians are supposed to be happy, cheerful people? Doesn't Jesus want us to be happy? How can he be saying that kingdom people are mourners – and that if we *are* mourners, we are in a good place, blessed? But that is just what he is saying! Of all the Beatitudes, for us, in our day, this I believe is the most unexpected. So as we look closely at this very surprising verse, we are going to ask two simple questions: Why should we mourn? and, Where does mourning end?

Why should we mourn?
The passage itself doesn't directly tell us why we should mourn. That's what confuses us. Let's see what clues we can find. Clue number one comes from the rest of the passage. If the Beatitudes are like a ladder, we should expect that this one leads on from the first one. Being 'poor in spirit', remember, is about standing before God with nothing – it's about our *status* in the sight of God. So we should expect that this 'mourning' has something to do with how we relate to him.

Clue number two comes from the example of Jesus. If we are the people who belong to him, let's see if *he* mourned over anything. Was there anything that caused Jesus real distress when he saw it? Yes, there was. What distressed Jesus was the horrible effects of sin in people's lives. Do you remember the time when he was in the synagogue one Sabbath? The story is at the beginning of Mark 3. There is a man there with a disabled hand; and Jesus' enemies are there too, watching like hawks to see if Jesus will heal him on the Sabbath. Quite possibly it's a set-up; they have actually planted him there as a trap. Mark 3:4-5 tells us that as Jesus' gaze sweeps the room there are two emotions in his heart: there is anger and there is distress. The Greek word means he is filled with *grief* – because they are hard and blind to the truth and grace of God. He is mourning at the blindness of sin. Or do you remember the scene Luke describes, as Jesus rides on the donkey, over the Mount of Olives, and the sight of Jerusalem the beloved city reaches his eyes, and the sun gleaming off the marble and gold of the temple – Luke 19:41-44. If only they had known – if *only* they had recognised him as their king – if only they had not been blinded by sin! And he weeps over the city – he *mourns*. Do you remember the tomb of Lazarus and Jesus weeping there (John 11:32-36)? Why is Jesus weeping – in ten minutes' time he is going to raise Lazarus from the dead! What does he have to weep about? He weeps because sin has done *this* to the human race – because he can see the misery and the dread that sin has brought through death. And he *mourns*.

Do you get the picture? Why should we mourn? We mourn *because of our sin*. Jesus had no sin of his own to mourn over, but we do! We come to God with nothing; we are poor in spirit, we have nothing to offer, and we are blessed because of it; only no-hopers can enter the kingdom. But then we begin to see ourselves as God sees us; and when we do that, when we look at our life story through his eyes, what strikes us most powerfully and most horribly is our *sin*. We see how our lives appear to a God who is pure and holy: how offensive, how hideous, how ugly we appear to One who cannot look upon evil. And here I am with my pride and my cowardice and my lust and all the rest of it.

When the respectable front that I like to show to others is stripped away; when I abandon the idea that I am the centre of the universe and that everything revolves around me, and I look down on myself from the perspective of heaven; when I see that in my whole life I have performed not one single deed that is truly and purely good; when I recognise that every thought, every attitude, every action of mine has been shot through with the corruption of sin; when I know that even those times when people around have praised me, when people have thought well of me, in my very best moments my heart has still been full of poison – when all that finally becomes clear to me, what do I do? Can I be indifferent? Can I simply wave it away? No, I hate my sin. I *mourn* over it. And still more when I remember that because of my sin, I stand condemned by God, that I am an object of his wrath. We mourn because of our sin. Have you ever done that? Do you know what this means? Can we really remain dry-eyed when we contemplate our sin? There is no true repentance until we have grasped the reality of our sin. There is no entry into the kingdom, there is no knowing Jesus, without mourning over sin.

We mourn because of our *own* sin; and we mourn because of the *effects* of sin – as Jesus did. When we look at the world we live in, and we see what sin has done to people, and we see the wreck and ruin in their lives because they are rebels against God, how do we feel? The psalmist says, 'Streams of tears flow from my eyes, for your law is not obeyed' (Psalm 119:136). When you, as a Christian, look at your friends who are still outside the kingdom, and you see their lives step by step being ruined as they refuse God's claims on them – don't you mourn over that?

When we look at our country and we see things that are appalling and disgraceful being accepted as normal – don't we mourn over that, whether it is the cheapening of sex, or the idea of gay marriage, or the casual selfishness of the company boardroom? We live in a world that is ruined and laid waste by sin. We cannot be at home with that. We need to mourn. We're kingdom people and we need to mourn. Of course our response to sin and evil doesn't *end* with mourning – but it certainly has to start there.

Now this idea of mourning is a very unpopular one today. It's an unpopular idea in our *world*, which has gone pleasure mad. People have been saying that for a very long time, but there has been nothing to touch the last twenty years for the pleasure mania which has swept over us. Life has become an endless quest for entertainment and self-fulfilment – in the well-known words of Neil Postman, we are 'amusing ourselves to death'. We don't have time to go much further into that now; I am sure you will recognise the picture.

It's not that people today think the world is a wonderful place where everyone is kind and no-one gets into trouble. People are not so stupid as to imagine that. But their way of dealing with it, very often, is to escape it instead of facing it. And that escape from reality is easier than ever before. Two weeks ago, as I write this, the new Xbox 360 video game *Halo Reach* was launched. The concept is that you, the player, are fighting a war, on a different planet, in a different age, against an alien race. If that's not escapism, I don't know what is! On the first day in Britain alone, *Halo Reach* sold 300,000 copies. Globally, on the first day, sales were worth two hundred million dollars. And within one week *two thousand man years* had already been spent playing it!

Now, *Halo Reach* may be a very fine game. It sounds fun, actually – and I can shoot up aliens with the best of them! But the point is that people are devoting their lives to this *imaginary* deadly alien world in order to escape the deadly *reality* of this familiar one. Just as they are through a hundred other escapist doorways, whether it's drugs, legal or illegal; whether it's an addiction to shopping, or sex, or Facebook – all these become ways of denying reality, so that they do not have to mourn. Who wants to hear a message like 'blessed are the mourners' in a world like this?

It's a message that's unpopular in *churches* as well, where often the focus is to create a 'worship experience' that will be emotionally intense and uplifting, that will give you a buzz and send you away feeling on top of the world. An experience that claims to bring you into an encounter with God – but seems to have forgotten that a *true* encounter with God has to begin with the grim reality of our sin in the face of his awesome holiness – which should bring us to tears. Where church is about entertainment, where the church is drinking deep of the pleasure mania of the world, where the church has forgotten to mourn, we are heading for disaster.

How different it should be with us! According to Jesus, kingdom people don't need to escape the reality of this world. We don't need to pretend, we don't need to play running away games, and we don't need to turn church into yet another theme park. We can be real. Kingdom people can face the dreadful worst of what this world is like and we can even face the rotten core of our own hearts; and we can mourn over it. We must! In fact, if we don't mourn over our sin, we are not blessed! Now to find out *how* we can mourn without despairing, let's ask our second question.

Where does mourning end?
'Blessed are those who mourn, *for they will be comforted*', says Jesus. So where does mourning end and comfort begin? The answer is that mourning ends when we see the Saviour. Look at Isaiah 61:1-3. Here's a picture of people in mourning. And the promise is that their mourning will turn to gladness. Their despair will turn to praise. Who are these people? They are *God's* people who are grieving over sin and suffering from its consequences. The promise is comfort for the mourners. These are wonderful words. Blessed are the mourners! Now, how is this prophecy fulfilled? Who is the 'me' in Isaiah 61:1 who makes it all happen? Luke 4:16-21 tells us the answer: Jesus goes into the synagogue, opens the scroll of Isaiah, reads these very words, looks round the crowded room and says '*Today* this scripture is fulfilled in your hearing'.

Jesus the Saviour has come to bring comfort to the mourners. Jesus has come to bring joy! Look what happens to the mourners in Isaiah. They become – God *makes* them – a planting of the Lord, oaks of righteousness, to show off his splendour. Don't you love that picture? The mourners, bowed down with grief and desolation, lost in their grief, become a forest of majestic trees, standing tall and displaying the beauty of their Saviour. That's us! That's *you*, if you've met the Saviour! Why? – because once you have recognised your position before God, your emptiness; once you have seen your own sin; once he has forgiven you through the cross, he has dealt with it all. He has taken away your ugliness, the horrible ugliness of sin, and crowned you with beauty. He has clothed you in a garment of praise and he says that from now on you will be showing off his glory. Who needs an escape to the fashion store when you are already dressed like that? We see the Saviour; and we are comforted. And how!

For now, of course, we still live in a messed-up world, with a sinful nature that still hangs around our neck and with an enemy who is out to get us. And so we still sin – this is terrible – even *after* we have met the Saviour. So again, as soon as we realise that, we mourn once more as we remember what our sin has cost to put right; and we are driven back to the cross, and again we come to the Lord with nothing but our sin, and again we find his love and forgiveness and mercy, and again there is comfort.

That's the comfort we can find now. It's good! But the final comfort lies ahead. And the mourning finally ends – when we SEE the Saviour! Not by faith only, now, but by sight, face to face. The day will come when Christ will return to the earth in glory and judgment. When he has finished his work of judgment, the earth will no longer be a place overrun with terror and injustice. The tyrants and oppressors, the rebels great and small will be put in their place and evil will be banished for good. Revelation 21:3-4 describes the glory of the heavenly city: no more mourning over sin, for there will be no sin, and its power and influence will no longer exist. Death and pain, which are the results of sin, won't be there either. No mourning over sin, no mourning over anything at all, in the new heavens and new earth. And that's the home we are heading for. Comfort now – final comfort and peace to come.

God's Word calls us to get serious about sin. In a world that takes everything so lightly, we dare not take this lightly. If you have never glimpsed the appalling reality of sin, it's doubtful whether you can claim to be saved at all. In that case, I would urge you to shut yourself in a very quiet room for an hour, get on your knees before the Lord, and ask him to show you your heart in all its deceitfulness and pride and its deep, deep selfishness. It is not a pretty sight. And then look at your Saviour and his deep, deep love for you.

Finally, may I urge you to make a habit of examining yourself. The medics are always urging us to examine various parts of our bodies to look for the early signs of cancer, so that there is the best possible chance of treatment. It's obviously a good idea. Isn't it even more obvious that we should constantly examine our hearts for any sign of sin? The time-honoured way is at the end of every day to think back and examine what you have done, and what was in your heart, right through the day – and confess, and mourn, and come back to the cross.

Blessed are the meek

Like many of you, I'm sure, we have a drawer at home full of greetings cards, ready for any greetings emergency – sudden birth of a child, unexpected driving test pass, that kind of thing! And somewhere in this drawer sits a mother's day card, several years old, and never used. I bought it: why did I never send it to my mum? It seems fine – it ticks all the boxes for a mother's day card – it has flowers, a tea-pot and the word 'Mum' after all – so what's wrong with it? Well, the problem is that when I got home and looked at it properly, I discovered these words at the bottom, 'You're so nice'! The question in my mind was, Is that the message I want to send to my mum? I don't think so. It's not that my mum *isn't* nice. The problem is the whole image that goes with the word 'nice'. What does 'nice' suggest? It makes me think, 'eager to please': that's all right. 'Rather spineless': not so good. 'A bit weak': not good at all, not the message I want to send to my mum. I can't send her this card. So because I'm not very good at throwing anything away, it stays in the drawer. Every so often I find it again: every so often I bury it!

That's what we tend to think when we hear the word 'meek'. It's actually not a word we use very often these days. It even sounds funny, 'meek'. If we use the word at all, we probably mean something like eager to please, rather spineless, and a bit weak – in short, nice, but not very strong. It doesn't sound very appealing and it certainly doesn't sound like the kind of character that will ever rise to the top. Meek people, surely, are likely to stay at the bottom. But here is Jesus saying, 'Blessed are the meek, for they will inherit the earth' (5:5). How can he be so naïve? Doesn't Jesus know how the world operates? The meek are the very last set of people we would expect to take over the earth. Whatever is he talking about?

With this strange word *meek*, and its even stranger reward, we reach the third rung of the 'ladder of light'. To try to understand it, we will

First steps on the ladder

tackle it under three headings: first, the unexpected meaning; second, the improbable prize; and third, the inescapable challenge.

The unexpected meaning
We need to get at the meaning of this word 'meek'. What does the Bible mean by the word? Let's cut out a few things that it really doesn't mean. 'Meek' does not mean being a doormat, so that you invite people to trample all over you. And it doesn't mean the natural characteristic we call being 'nice'. A person can be naturally nice; in fact even a cat or dog can be nice. My dog is very nice – he's very eager to please and he is a complete coward. He's terrified of the vacuum cleaner, even when it's switched off. That may be nice, but it's not meek!

To understand the meaning, we need to look at the example of Jesus himself; and we immediately see that meekness is something very powerful. In the gospels Jesus does not say a great deal about his own character, but look at Matthew 11:28-29 where he does speak of himself. That word translated 'gentle' is the same word 'meek' that we find in Matthew 5 (Greek *praus*). This is what it means to be meek: it means to be gentle, to be humble; it means not asserting your own rights. For the Lord Jesus, being meek meant that he left the glory of heaven, his home from eternity past; it meant he set aside the privileges of God-hood and was born as a baby, to a peasant woman, in an obscure village, in an occupied country. It meant growing up here, sharing his perfect life with sinners; it meant dealing with people of all kinds – the best who misunderstood him and the worst who accused him, the friends who all abandoned him and the enemies who hated him, who schemed against his life and ended up rigging his execution – and still going on loving them. This is what it means to be meek.

If we look at the way Jesus dies we see this most clearly of all. We see him in that moving scene in Gethsemane, the night of his arrest, grappling with the prospect of the hideous death he must face, and all that goes with it, praying (Matthew 26:42). Submitting to the will of his Father, trusting himself to God's loving purposes – *that's* meekness! And a few minutes later, as they come to arrest him, as Peter strikes out with his sword and injures one of the arresting party, see how Jesus responds (Matthew 26:52-54). Jesus is about to face the most absurdly unjust trial in human history – yet he never once strikes back. He knows that is not the way.

The Kingdom Manifesto

Look at the famous words in Isaiah 53:7, speaking about Jesus seven hundred years in advance. Is this weakness? Could anyone read the story of Jesus and say he was weak? No – it is *meekness*. If you want to see it lived out and personified, look at Jesus. And this is what we are called to be, as people of the kingdom! What Jesus was in his life here on earth, *we* are called to be. Paul makes this clear and explicit in Philippians 2:6-8. Your attitude, my attitude, should be the *same*, the Bible says. Humble, not clinging to our rights, not provoked to anger – in a word, *meek*.

Returning to the Beatitudes, can you see how this fits in to the sequence? How this meekness becomes the third rung of the ladder? Once we have recognised we are poor in spirit, once we have seen our sin and failure and *mourned* over it and found the comfort we need in Christ – once we know we are fully accepted by God because of Christ, loved so much as we see at the cross – we can be meek. We aren't going to worry what anyone else thinks of us! Because if *God* declares we are accepted, it really doesn't matter what people think. Only someone who knows that their true identity is in Christ can be truly meek – and therefore truly blessed.

Now, this idea of the meek being blessed is not what people expect – especially when Jesus goes on to say that they will inherit the earth, as we'll see. It wasn't what the Jews of Jesus' own time would expect their Messiah to say: far from it. The Messiah they expected was anything but meek. They expected a conquering king who would unleash a holy war against their enemies, the Romans. In fact, for Jesus' original audience, this is probably the most counter-cultural of all the Beatitudes. But it's unexpected today, as well. Popular wisdom is perhaps best summed up by what the Emperor Napoleon said. 'I have noticed that God is on the side of the big battalions.' In other words, battles are won by the strongest armies and it's the general with the heaviest artillery who will conquer the earth. And certainly, people who refuse to push themselves forward will never get anywhere. Jesus says, no. In actual fact, it is the *meek* who will inherit the earth. That brings us on to the second point.

The improbable prize
'Blessed are the meek, *for they will inherit the earth'*. It seems *highly* improbable, but it's true. As so often, it turns out that what Jesus is saying has its roots in the Old Testament. Look at Psalm 37. This is a

psalm that David wrote, and if you glance through it you can see that it is a song of *security*. It's tempting to worry about the way that bad people seem to get on so well; it's tempting to fret. But David says, Don't worry (verses 1-7 and continuing along much the same lines). Then we get to verses 10-11. And verse 22 says 'those the Lord *blesses* will inherit the land' – put those together and you've pretty much got the Beatitude of Matthew 5:5.

The message of Psalm 37 is that the Lord is in charge and as his people we don't need to worry. Meek people trust and don't fret. That's a message we need to hear, because most of us are desperate worriers. David says here, Don't worry – whether it's the neighbouring farmer, then, who wants to steal your land, or the office bully or gossip, today, who wants to crush you, or the family member who accuses or abuses you – don't fret because, ultimately, it is the meek who will inherit the earth. It is the meek, the people who are secure in God, the ones who trust in him, who come out on top in the end. That's God's promise.

Now, what has happened to that promise? Under a good king like David, there was justice in the land. The weak and defenceless would be protected and evil men would be dealt with. But even then, the promise would never be completely fulfilled. It never is. Under the evil kings, and in the chaos that would follow, Psalm 37 must have seemed like a mockery. Where *is* this peace? Where *is* this end to evil? But it's not a mockery. In fact, the ultimate fulfilment of these promises lies in the age to come. The Bible talks about the day when God will bring about something completely new – a new heavens and a new earth where justice and peace will reign. We read about it even in the Old Testament (Isaiah 65:17-19). There is plenty more about this new world in Revelation 21 and 22. It's a vision of a world at peace, a world under the rule of God where there is no more conflict and where evil people no longer hold sway, where the humble people of God live and thrive. An earth, in fact, inherited by the *meek*. That is the ultimate prize of the meek – the ultimate blessing – and the Lord will bring it about. It's our inheritance. It's his promise.

But perhaps you are thinking, That's just pie in the sky. Perhaps you're thinking, This is the usual Christian claptrap about a wonderful world in the future somewhere, that says nothing about real life, no help for the life I have to live here and now. What about the grim reality of my work-place, my difficult family, my debts – and all the other worries that keep me awake at night? In fact, the first reward of meekness comes right now. It's *contentment*. To see how that works, come back to Paul's letter to the Philippians. In Philippians 4:10-13 Paul is saying thanks to his friends in Philippi for some gifts they have sent him. We must remember that Paul is not sitting in some comfortable suburban home as he writes this. He's in prison and facing the real possibility of imminent execution. Yet he's content! How can that be? Paul is content because he is trusting the Lord to supply everything he needs. He knows the Lord has accepted him, he knows the Lord is with him, so whatever happens – whatever accusations are flung at him in court, however empty his stomach may be, however many of his friends may desert him and turn against him (and many of them have) – he is completely secure and therefore he can be content. Even the prospect of death doesn't shake that profound contentment. That is the prize of the meek. Blessed are the meek!

It's this that explains some slightly odd language that Paul uses in his other letters, where he says for instance 'all things are yours' (1 Corinthians 3:21) or about himself, 'having nothing, yet possessing everything' (2 Corinthians 6:10). It's as if he has inherited the earth *already*! But if you're really content, that's exactly what it feels like! And do you see how sharply this idea of meekness and contentment cuts across the outlook of the world we live in? The world where we are encouraged, sometimes by the media, sometimes by the law, sometimes just by popular opinion, to assert our own rights, to get even, to claim compensation: when we suffer any injustice, to sue the offenders for every penny! Now, there are times when it's right to defend ourselves and our families, of course there are. But there's a world of difference between that and the instinct to complain, to become a victim, to scrabble for whatever could be due to us. As the meek people of the kingdom, we can be content. The Lord Jesus calls us to trust and be content.

The inescapable challenge

We need to make sure that this Beatitude is earthed in reality. Saying we should be meek sounds tough. We may well feel – I know I am a sinner in the sight of God, I've accepted that. I can accept it when *God* tells me my life is a mess – he has every right to say so. But to have *other people* tell me I'm a mess, or I've failed – people who are just as screwed up as I am, or more – that's hard! But that's just what this is asking of me. I agree

First steps on the ladder

– it's not natural. I get riled even when someone yells at me when I am out cycling or driving, never mind when anything more serious happens! No, it's not natural – this is something that God does in us, by the Holy Spirit. Meekness, or gentleness, is part of the fruit of the Spirit, the evidence that he's at work inside us. If you belong to the kingdom, he is doing this in your life right now.

Let's put some flesh on that. *Being meek means we can trust and not fret.* That will show itself in the ordinary events of life. When people in your office are complaining bitterly about their pay, or that their pension contributions are going up, you won't need to join in. You will be content because you know it's really the Lord who provides for you and gives you all you need. And your colleagues will see the difference it makes. When our friend's children seem to be doing much better than ours, and we start to feel envious – why are my kids a mess while hers are so beautifully scrubbed, why is my Johnny so slow while their Mary is winning those awards? – or we're fretful about schools or exam results or university places, we'll remember that all of this is in the Lord's hands – and of course we'll do our best for them, but we'll be content because we can trust *him.* It will show itself in the times of real struggle as well, when the issue is not just your pay, but losing your job – to trust, on that day, that the Lord has your times, and your needs, in his hands. When it's not your children's GCSE grades at stake, but your child's life that's in danger – or when the result you dread comes back from the clinic or the doctor – to trust the Lord *then,* to rest, to know that his purposes for us are good even when we do not understand them – that is the power of meekness.

What about the way we deal with difficult people? *Being meek means we won't be provoked.* When you face cutting remarks or abuse, at work or at home or wherever it may be, you won't strike back, you won't retaliate, because in the end, it really doesn't matter what they think of you. We should actually be impossible to provoke! Even if it's a fellow Christian who turns against you – even if your friends desert you or your family rejects you and you feel completely alone, you know where your real security is. We have a Saviour who loves us – who experienced exactly that opposition, and worse – and still loved us all the way to the cross. That's the only opinion that counts! Contentment in Christ here and now; and one day, perfect contentment *with* Christ, in the new world which is our inheritance.

The Kingdom Manifesto

Blessed are the desperate

As I write, the sequel to the 1980s film *Wall Street* is out and it is topping the ratings in British cinemas, though the reviews are not very flattering. But the original 1987 film was unforgettable. The wonderfully-named Gordon Gekko, played by Michael Douglas, was a corporate raider who would do anything it took to achieve his goals. His hunger for money and his passion for power were such that he would trample over anyone, manipulate the most vulnerable, work any hours and generally be as ruthless as necessary in order to satisfy them. The way that he dressed – the suits and those braces! – even his hair style – so epitomised his thirst for dominance that they became trendsetters for the boardrooms of the *real* world. It was all summarised in his famous saying that 'Greed is good' – it is *good*, says Gekko, because it represents the drive that has brought humanity to the place where we stand today. Perhaps the 2010 version of Gordon Gekko, in the sequel, has softened a little – or maybe not: I won't give the story away! But certainly, the original Gekko set the standard for the ruthless extremes that a hunger for wealth can take us to.

We know that people are motivated by all kinds of drivers. For some, like Gordon Gekko, it is wealth and power that drives them. For others it's material security – the longing to arrive at that safe middle-class moment where you have everything you need and a little bit more. For others, the drive is about their family, whether it's the hunger to see their children get on in life, or the wife who's ambitious for her husband. Meanwhile, many people are driven by *pleasure* – whether that comes out through cruising the world, or their appetite for sex, or gourmet dining. Olympic athletes would tell us of the hunger for success that drives them to train for hours each day and put their bodies through all kinds of stress and strain.

We all have drivers, we all have goals that we long for. Here in the Sermon on the Mount, Jesus comes up with yet another one. 'Blessed are those who hunger and thirst for *righteousness*, for they will be filled' (5:6). The people who are blessed, the people who are in a good place, are the ones who are desperately longing for *righteousness* – whatever that is exactly, Jesus is saying this is the best longing that anyone can have! As we explore what Jesus is getting at, we will discover that this little saying, this fourth rung of the ladder, poses us a particularly searching question.

First steps on the ladder

The desperation

What is Jesus talking about here? What is the *goal* of this longing, this 'righteousness'? It's another of those words that doesn't get used very much in everyday language today, so we need to see what it means in the pages of the Bible. The New Testament uses the word 'righteousness' in two senses. Sometimes, it refers to our *right standing* with God. This is what every Christian has. Because Jesus has paid the penalty for our sins, when he died on the cross, God has declared us righteous in his sight – we are no longer under judgment, we are counted as innocent, as righteous. Another word for this is *justification*. Everyone who has put their faith in Jesus Christ and his dying for them is *justified*, counted as *righteous*. This is wonderful, it's the central truth of the Christian gospel, that guilty sinners are set free because of what Jesus has done for us! When Paul talks about righteousness, for instance in Romans 3:21-26, this is what he means. Technically this is called 'forensic' or 'legal' righteousness because it concerns our legal standing with God.

That is one meaning of righteousness – but it's not what Jesus is talking about here. That first meaning of righteousness is not something that we have to hunger and thirst for! If we belong to the kingdom, if we belong to Jesus, we already *have* this righteousness – it is ours, it is done, it belongs to us, and nothing can change that – ever. So we don't hunger for it, we *celebrate* it!

The righteousness which Jesus is talking about here relates to what happens *after* we enter the kingdom. To use another theological word, this is about *sanctification*. It is about living a life that is righteous, a life that pleases God. This is 'ethical' righteousness, which is the way that Matthew generally uses the word[10]. It's about our *character* – just like the other Beatitudes, it's about the character of the kingdom. A life that pleases God – or to put it another way, it means being like Jesus. That's the goal. As the people of the King, we long to be *like* the King we love.

We want to be like the Jesus we read about here. The Jesus who walks the dusty hills of Galilee, reaching out to people of every kind – reaching the weak and downtrodden, the people society has written off; opening his arms to children when his own disciples think he is wasting his time; giving dignity and honour to women, bringing in

41

outcasts, caring even for those tax-collectors like Zacchaeus who are detested as collaborators. The Jesus who loves all of those. The Jesus who challenges the hypocrisy of religious leaders, who stands for truth even at the risk of his own life, the Jesus who displays, from beginning to end, perfect integrity in the face of every provocation.

We want to be like the Jesus who is *meek* – who submits to his Father's will and in the end lays down his own life for those he will call his friends. The Jesus who goes on loving them even when they walk out on him, who even calls for forgiveness for his execution squad. The Jesus who never sins: who *never* bends the truth, *never* harbours a grudge, *never* pursues material security (and never has it), *never* abuses or exploits his own position – the Jesus who thinks of his own people first, even in the moments when he is facing a horrifying death. *That* is righteousness. It's beautiful – it's costly – it's Jesus! It's the life of Jesus lived out in us. This follows on very logically, you see, from what Jesus has said in the first three Beatitudes. Because we now understand how sin has so devastated our lives, because we can now see that clearly, we will long to get rid of every last trace of sin in our lives. And because we are meek, not worrying any longer about our own status or position, we are free to pursue what matters most – which is knowing Christ and being like him. That's the goal.

So what is this longing, this 'hungering and thirsting'? Think what those feelings mean for the people Jesus is addressing. Hunger for them is not what you and I feel in the late morning when we think we're ready for a snack. These are peasant farmers who know what it is to be without food sometimes for days at a time – to go out in the morning with an empty stomach and do a full day's heavy work in the fields, and come home again to nothing. Have you ever been hungry like that? I haven't. And it's a dry country where in the long, hot summer the streams disappear, and clean water is hard to find, and the sun is beating down.

The longing Jesus describes combines real hunger and this kind of thirst – this is nothing less than utter desperation. When Jesus speaks of being hungry and thirsty for righteousness, he is not thinking of some vague aspiration. This is not one priority among all the other priorities in our lives. Someone who is hungry and thirsty like this can scarcely even think about anything else. Jesus is talking about an intense passion to live a righteous life, to know God better, to be like Jesus. The psalmists captured this longing, for instance in Psalm 42:1-2 or Psalm 63:1. Think of that image; does it strike a chord with you? That's the longing.

Jesus says, *Blessed* are the people who long so desperately – for they will be filled. At this point in the Beatitudes, we have recognised we are empty: now we need to be filled. And like all the Beatitudes, this one comes with a promise. Notice what Jesus does *not* say. He does not say, You are blessed because if you keep trying, you will make it in the end. He is not saying that if you try really hard to reform yourself, you'll eventually succeed in living a good life. He says 'they *will be* filled' – in other words, *God* will fill them (it's called a 'divine passive'). We don't achieve it by our own struggles – this is what the Holy Spirit of God does in our lives. We meet with Jesus, we come into the kingdom; and the Spirit gets to work in us. It's the work of a lifetime, but it happens. The man who's pursued his own career at all costs begins to make time for his family. The insecure woman who has had a fling with every man who is kind to her becomes secure and content in God. The parents who are eaten up with worry about their children or their finances find peace of mind. Family members who haven't spoken for years call each other and are reconciled. Gossips give up talking behind people's backs. Little by little, we are filled with righteousness. We are satisfied. There's another wonderful Old Testament image of this, this time in Isaiah 55:1-2. Do you hear the invitation – and what a promise! Jesus speaks of this satisfaction in John 6:35.

Yet strangely, the more we are filled with righteousness, the more we are satisfied, the more of it we want – so as long as this life lasts, in a sense, the hunger and thirst will continue! Ask any mature, older Christian that you know, and this is what they will tell you. The closer you come to Jesus, the closer still you long to be. The more we become like him, the more we hunger to be *just* like him. And if we want it – if we long for it – that's exactly where he is taking us. Blessed are the desperate!

The test
This Beatitude asks us a very pointed question, and perhaps you already know what it is. *How does your heart respond to this?* Where do you stand with what Jesus is saying here? Let me quote Martyn Lloyd-Jones at this point. 'If this verse is to you one of the most blessed statements in the whole of Scripture, you can be quite certain you are a Christian; if it is not, then you had better examine the foundations again.' As we said at

the start of this section, people today are longing for all kinds of things. Gordon Gekko types long for power and untold wealth, but the quest for security, or family, or career success, or pleasure, may be closer to home for you. So what is your priority in life? Is it a passion to be like Jesus – to be, as Robert Murray M'Cheyne prayed, 'as holy as it is possible for a redeemed sinner to be'? Let's be clear about this. If we think we have anything good in *ourselves*, anything at all worth offering to God, we are *not* hungering and thirsting for righteousness. If we think we can live a good life by our own determination and will-power, we are *not* hungering and thirsting for righteousness. This righteousness is something God has to work in us; we cannot fill ourselves.

What does this Beatitude say about you? Can you look at these words and say, Yes, that is what I am longing for, that is my goal? If so – keep hungering and thirsting – you are blessed! – the promise is that you will be filled. If not – then you had better examine your foundations. Ask the question, What is my life built on? Have I ever had that life-changing encounter with Jesus Christ, have I made that vital step of abandoning the ruins of my own life, finding forgiveness for my sins and being made new by him? Is there actually a new person in here – is there anything for the Holy Spirit to work with – or am I still stuck in the old ways, the old life, without Christ and without hope?

At this half-way point in the Beatitudes, this is the test. This is the question that faces us. Where do we really stand? Just as a doctor might ask about the state of your appetite, so God's Word is asking you here, Are you hungry? The Lord himself is asking you, Are you hungry for me? That's the test.

The reality
Let's put all this into focus. Suppose you have read these words of Jesus and you are saying, No, to be honest, I can't say that is what my life is all about. I can't say that I have this passion to be like Christ. You have standards that you try to live by, standards that you have set for yourself, but if you are honest you know that you don't keep them. You know you need something more. What Jesus says here is what you need. But please understand: you can't have this hunger for righteousness, this longing to be like Christ, if you don't know him in the first place. If you're not in the kingdom, you won't love the king. Jesus didn't come to the earth merely to share some helpful teachings for us to pick up at our leisure – of

course that's exactly how some people still think of this Sermon on the Mount – but the Sermon on the Mount is the kingdom manifesto – it's for people who are *already* in the kingdom. You need that first encounter with Jesus. You have to meet him first at the cross, the cross where he died to pay the penalty of your failure and make you right with God. At that point, a relationship begins – a relationship where you know God as your Father and Jesus as your Saviour and the Holy Spirit as your powerful mentor and guide. If you want a life that is different and real, that's the way in.

Assuming you are a Christian, you probably hear these words of Jesus and say, Yes, that's what I want but I can see my hunger and thirst are not so strong. I realise that my priorities are not so clear; there is so much that seems to get in the way. Well, let's deal with this. How can we make pursuing Christ the most important thing of all?

Step one is to realise that being like Jesus is the best! Knowing him intimately, becoming like him, is better than anything else you could be offered. If you are a Christian, are you fully convinced that having Jesus is the most precious thing on earth? Is he worth more than your career, your family, your ambitions or whatever might be in your heart? Are you fully convinced that that is true? – because it is!

Step two is to recognise how this longing can be dulled. There are some more questions we must ask. Are you ruthless with sin in your own life? If you are a Christian, you know what I am talking about! There are sins we admit to freely enough, and there are sins that lie half-hidden, like great ugly boulders that don't want to be dug out. Then there are sins that we won't admit to at all. We need to be ruthless with every kind of sin. We need to let the Holy Spirit search our hearts and point us again to where sin still finds a refuge – and then with his help we need to dig them out. Are we prepared for that, even if it means giving up thoughts, attitudes and actions that we relish – because we know Christ offers us a better way?

Then, are you wise in your use of time? There are certain activities that may not be evil in themselves, but you know that in excess they will distract you from following Christ with all your heart. Too much of those TV programmes, too much of that computer, too much of those magazines or novels, and that's what will fill your mind instead of the Lord.

And then, are you actively pursuing God? Let's press the image a little further. If you are hungry, really hungry, and you know where the food is – that's where you go! So you go for the presence of God – in meeting with him every day as you pray and study the Bible, giving him the best time of your day; as you meet with God's people as a priority on Sunday and during the week because you want to get closer to him – pursuing him, cultivating this relationship he has brought you into?

Remember the promise again. Hungering and thirsting for righteousness, we are blessed, because we will be filled. Our lives will be transformed, we will be flagrantly and unmistakably Christ-like. Beyond this life there is the vision of our eternal life with him, the vision of his people in heaven seen in Revelation 7:15-17. In that place, on that day, every kind of hunger and thirst will be satisfied for ever, because he will satisfy them all. On that day, safely home, the Spirit's work completed, we will at last be like him.

Questions to reflect on or discuss

1. Do you have personal experience of mourning over your sin? If not, do you think you have ever grasped the dreadful reality of sin? What do you need to do about this now?

2. Do you agree that our culture, both in society in general and in churches, is very hostile to the idea of taking sin seriously? If this is true, how should we change our church life to help us to reflect Matthew 5:4?

3. Reflect on the meekness Jesus displayed and pray that he will form his character in you.

4. Contentment is one of the prizes of meekness. Which biblical truths explored in this chapter can help you to greater contentment?

5. In what specific ways is the Lord calling you to display greater meekness? Pray for his Spirit's help to obey him.

6. Hungering and thirsting for righteousness... How does *your* heart respond to this challenge? Do you have this passion to be like Christ? Where is the evidence – think of some areas where you are actively pursuing this righteousness.

First steps on the ladder

7. Work through the steps in the closing section. At what point do you need to respond, so that your longing for Christ may increase?

Chapter 3
Just like Jesus
Matthew 5:7-9

In the previous chapter we reached the point of longing for righteousness – longing to be just like Jesus. In this chapter we will look at the next three Beatitudes, which show us supremely what the character of Jesus is like, and what our lives will be like if we long for him with all our hearts.

Blessed are the merciful

A British November would scarcely be complete without the BBC's annual Children in Need appeal, complete with its mascot – the larger-than-life yellow Teddy named Pudsey – and a succession of ever-smiling TV hosts. Fund-raising events typically range from school cake sales to people sitting in baths of baked beans, while our favourite BBC presenters amuse us by humiliating themselves in various interesting ways. Tens of millions of pounds are raised each year, all donated to support hundreds of projects across the UK working with disadvantaged children. And it makes a real difference. Up and down the country, children with disabilities, young people who have to be carers for parents with mental illness, refugee and asylum-seeker children who struggle with English and their school work – all these and more have their lives changed because ordinary people are moved to give to Children in Need.

So when we hear the words Jesus said, 'Blessed are the merciful' (Matthew 5:7), it's action like this that we probably think of. Or perhaps we think of the response to disaster appeals in somewhere like Haiti or Pakistan. We see the devastation and havoc wrought by natural disasters; we see the misery on the faces of suffering people; and we respond by giving money or possibly even by going ourselves to do our bit to relieve such desperate need. Actually, that is not a bad definition of mercy. Mercy is *a generous response to misery*. It's what we feel and do when we see the misery of others. But as we look at what Jesus says here, we will find that the mercy he speaks of goes far beyond giving to charity, however worthwhile that is. This mercy takes us to places we can never hope to reach by ourselves, and to a depth of human need that the TV can never show us.

This is the first in a group of three Beatitudes that in a sense unpack the previous one. Hungering and thirsting for righteousness (5:6) means longing to be like the Lord Jesus. 'Blessed are the merciful, for they will be shown mercy' is easy enough to understand, in that it's not difficult to grasp what each of the words means. But there *is* a difficulty here, and we'd better clear it up before we go any further. If we take this saying on its own, it is very easy to misunderstand it. It sounds as if Jesus is saying something like, If you are merciful – if you give lots of money to charity, or go off and help in a disaster area – then you will get the same kind of mercy shown to you when you need it. Or even, If you are kind to others, God will be kind to you.

This Beatitude has often been misread that way: it is perhaps more open to misunderstanding than any of the others. This illustrates the problem of pulling odd verses out of their context, especially in the Sermon on the Mount, and setting them up as rules to live by. Again, we need to remember that Jesus is setting out his Kingdom Manifesto! This teaching is for people who already belong to the kingdom. This is where it is specially important that the Beatitudes are a set meal (with eight courses!), not a buffet where we can pick and choose what we like. So the Beatitudes work like this. If you are truly poor in spirit, then you are a true member of the kingdom, and therefore you are blessed. If you are a mourner for your sin, then you are a true member of the kingdom, and therefore you are blessed – and so on. If you are part of the kingdom, one of your character traits is that you are merciful – and you are blessed. You are blessed because your being merciful proves that you are on the receiving end of mercy from God. You can be really merciful only when you are receiving *his* mercy. To help us stay absolutely clear on that point, this time we will look at the second part of the Beatitude before the first part.

The mercy we receive
What is the mercy we receive from God? Remember, mercy is essentially a generous response to the misery of others. In one sense, God has mercy on everyone, all the time. Everyone on earth is a sinner, having lived his or her life as a rebel against Almighty God. We deserve eternal death from the moment we are born, or even before. Yet he allows us to live. That's mercy! In fact, the Bible even tells us that it is only through God's will, moment by moment, that we remain in existence (Hebrews 1:3). It is only the power of God's Word that sustains the laws of physics (as we call them) which hold the universe together – laws that he invented and laid down for every atom in the cosmos. Every moment, every breath, is given us by the mercy of God. By God's mercy the sun shines, the rain falls, the earth produces food. By God's mercy we live. This is what theologians call 'common grace' – God's generosity to everyone, to the world in common''.

God shows us that kind of mercy especially to give us the chance to respond to the very special mercy he holds out to us in Jesus Christ. This is the mercy we begin to see in the life Jesus lived on earth. His very appearing among us, entering a broken and screwed-up world, was an act of mercy in itself, that God should come as a man to step into his fallen Creation! We see it too in the way that he lived his life here. Time after time, it is his mercy that people cry out for. Look at these examples, and you will see what I mean: the two blind men who cry for mercy in Matthew 9:27, whom Jesus heals in response; the Canaanite woman in Matthew 15:22, whose daughter he heals; the father in 17:14-15, whose son he heals; and the two blind men in Matthew 20:30-31, whom again he heals.

By the way, these incidents prove that mercy is not just about how you feel. These people were not calling out for Jesus to have nice, warm feelings about them – they needed him to *act*. Jesus' whole life was an act of mercy: as he went about healing diseases, as he shone the light of God with his teaching, as he demonstrated purity and integrity with people, speaking the truth fearlessly – all this was the mercy of God made known to miserable humanity. The character of the kingdom, set out in the Beatitudes, is perfectly seen in the Lord Jesus.

But God's mercy is seen supremely at the cross where Jesus died. Some might think of mercy as turning a blind eye, tolerating evil; that mercy means letting people get away with it, as if mercy were the opposite of justice. The cross proves that idea is wrong. The cross shows us that God is not *ignoring* the problem of evil: he is providing a decisive *answer* to the problem of evil as he intervenes in his mercy to deal with our sin. What we are powerless to do, God does for us. In mercy, the Father sends and the Son goes, willingly, to lay down his life and bear the punishment we deserve. In mercy, the sacrifice is made, our salvation is secured, and now God holds out his hands to us and invites us to accept his mercy. Christians, kingdom people, are simply those who have accepted God's mercy. Paul sums it up in Ephesians 2:3-5. Mercy is a generous response to misery and these verses show the extent of our misery as 'objects of wrath'. But because he is merciful, God made a way for us to come from death to life, from enmity to acceptance, through the cross of Jesus (1 Peter 2:10). Now we have an identity, and now our fortunes have been transformed completely, all through the mercy of God.

The New Testament writers cannot help but be overwhelmed at what God has done for them, as Paul puts it in 1 Timothy 1:15-16. You can hear the amazement in his voice: that someone like me, a guilty rebel against God, should find his mercy; should find, not his anger, but his smile! If we are Christians, we share the amazement: that we were God's enemies, and yet it is God himself who has intervened to make us his friends!

The mercy we display
The Beatitude is 'Blessed are the merciful'; that is what kingdom people are, so how does it happen? Follow through the logic of the Beatitudes: look at the connections. Remember we began with being poor in spirit. That means we know we are spiritually poor, helpless to save ourselves – in other words, we know how much we need *mercy*. From that position, stripped of our pride, having lost all pretensions of being able to put ourselves right, relying absolutely on God's mercy, naturally we shall be willing to show mercy to others. Then, as part of the passion for righteousness, the longing to be like Jesus, we will long to be merciful, to reach out in mercy just as Jesus did. Remember, none of this happens just because we want it to. It is only God who can make us like Jesus. It is only his Spirit who can make us merciful.

Just like Jesus

What does this mercy look like? First, it is *heart-felt*. People might give to charity for all kinds of reasons. It might be because they feel it's their duty, or because they are shamed or embarrassed into giving, or because they feel guilty being so comfortable while others suffer. But the mercy Jesus speaks of comes from the heart. The measure of this mercy is nothing less than the love of God, as John puts it (1 John 3:16-17). God puts his love, his mercy, in our hearts; and then from our hearts we have mercy for others. It is a mark of the kingdom.

Second, this mercy is *practical*. It was true of Jesus, and it is true of us, that this mercy has very practical results. History shows that Bible-believing Christians have made a huge contribution to relieving suffering. Take the story of the treatment of leprosy, for instance. Leprosy was for centuries a terrifying and dreaded disease: incurable, deforming, and an almost total mystery to medical science. Most of the world simply ignored a scourge that afflicted tens of millions of people and left them outcast and destitute. The patient work of understanding it, caring for leprosy sufferers and learning how to put their lives back together, was done almost entirely by Christians who had the mercy of God in their hearts and knew that these forgotten people were made in the image of God.

Or take the story of the great social reformers of nineteenth century Britain. William Wilberforce and his allies with the slavery issues, the seventh Earl of Shaftesbury with factory reform, Elizabeth Fry with the prisons, Thomas Barnardo going out at night to the streets and the rooftops of London where the homeless orphans slept – they were all evangelical Christians who were moved to compassion by the desperate needs and injustices they saw around them and gave their lives to the cause of mercy. In my own adopted city of Bristol, we often recall the incredible work done by George Muller in his orphanages on Ashley Down – moved by the powerful mercy of God. This mercy is not just a warm glow; and it's not just putting a few pounds in a collection tin. To this day, great numbers of kingdom people are active across the world to relieve people's practical needs, often risking or even losing their lives.

It is also vital to see that, thirdly, this mercy is *spiritual*. Patching up people's bodies and putting a roof over their heads are important, most definitely, but they are not enough. In a sense, anyone can do that. Only kingdom people can see that mercy does not stop with people's physical bodies and that true mercy goes far beyond what we think of as charity. Kingdom people understand that there is no point giving someone a few years of comfortable living here on earth while ignoring the endless years of eternity. Those great Christian reformers were motivated by love for the whole person. They knew that the greatest mercy is to care for someone's immortal soul. This is the kind of mercy that shares the good news of Jesus so that they will be saved, that Jude describes so vividly (Jude 22-23). He is talking about caring for believers who are struggling with their faith; we should do the same. He is talking about proclaiming the gospel so people will be saved from hell; we should do the same. And he is talking about hating the sin which is dragging people to hell, even while we love the sinner.

This is why, for example, planting new churches is just as much an act of mercy as giving out food parcels, or more so. Churches are rescue stations: their business is to show mercy, snatching people from the fire and saving them, meeting the greatest need that anyone has, as well as caring for physical needs.

Fourth and last, this mercy is *forgiving*. In Matthew 18:21-35, Jesus tells a very memorable parable. It's the story of a king whose servant owes him a vast debt – millions of pounds, in today's currency. It seems the whole family will be sold into slavery to try and raise something to pay the debt. The servant pleads for more time to pay; the king has mercy and lets him go; but when the servant is faced with a situation where he is begged for mercy, he refuses. When we get on to the Lord's Prayer and its message of forgiveness (6:12) this will come up again – but do you see the point of the parable? The servant who is unwilling to forgive, who will not show mercy, proves that he has never really grasped the mercy of the king. His heart should have been melted by the king's love, but it wasn't! And if we are real kingdom people, who have received the mercy of the king, saved and rescued from a fate worse than death and forgiven for our lifetime of rebellion against God – then will we not forgive those who forgive us?

Stephen Oake was a police detective constable who in January 2003 was stabbed to death by a man he was arresting. Stephen and his parents were committed Christians – in fact I grew up in the same church and Stephen and I were baptised together. At the time of Stephen's murder, his father Robin was chief constable of the Isle of Man. Within twenty-four hours of the murder, Robin Oake gave a press conference and a journalist shouted, 'What do you think of the man who killed your son?' He found himself saying, 'I've forgiven him'. And he *had* forgiven him! Robin speaks of sitting in court at the trial, within twenty feet of the murderer, and feeling no bitterness towards him – in fact, feeling pity. None of this is to minimise the pain the whole family have felt. Mercy does not ignore evil: instead it steps in to heal. And Robin prays every day for the murderer, that he will come to know Christ and find the ultimate forgiveness that only he can give. That is mercy[12].

One measure of mercy is to ask what you do to your enemy when you finally have him in your power. Do you have an enemy? Is there someone who has wronged you deeply in the past? What will you do? Can you find the mercy to forgive? No – but the Lord can *give* you the mercy to forgive. Again, this Beatitude challenges us. That's good: if we are Christians, we know it is good to be challenged by God's Word, it's good to examine what is really in our hearts. So if you know the Lord, have you seen the vision of mercy – heart-felt, practical, spiritual, forgiving? Don't let bitterness keep hold of you. And remember that the greatest mercy you can show is to share the love of Jesus, through words and actions, with people who don't know him.

Blessed are the pure

On the night of 20th April 2010, the oil drilling rig *Deepwater Horizon* suffered a catastrophic blowout. The explosion and fire killed eleven workers and released a vast quantity of crude oil directly into the clear waters of the Gulf of Mexico. For twelve weeks the oil flowed. The heroic attempts to skim and burn off the oil could deal only with the edges of the problem. Within a few weeks, as we saw every night on the News, stinking lumps of oil, balls of tar, were drifting ashore; and every wave and tide only added to the number of birds, turtles and other wildlife that were poisoned by the disaster. For mile upon mile, out in the Gulf, its deep blue water was stained an ugly reddish-brown. But the scope of the catastrophe was even more profound than you could see from the surface. Under the water, the attempts to disperse the oil were creating another problem. Huge underwater plumes of oil and gas were identified, one as big as Manhattan, quite invisible from above. Within these plumes, the bacteria that feed on the gas were draining all the oxygen out of the water in layers hundreds of feet deep, creating a vast zone of death. The water that had been so pure, clear and alive was now ugly on the outside and dead within.

If we want a picture of the human heart as the Bible describes it, the Gulf of Mexico in the worst weeks of that oil spill would be a very good one. According to the Bible, the hearts of men and women are polluted through and through with sin. Wherever you looked you would find, as it were, droplets of sin mixed in. It's ugly, it's impure, and in fact it's spiritually dead. We might recoil from such a description. Surely we are not as bad as all that! But this is the Bible's exact diagnosis of what we are like without Christ.

So what is Jesus doing saying here, in the same Bible, 'Blessed are the pure in heart, for they will see God' (Matthew 5:8)? If the Bible says we are like a polluted death zone, what is the point of telling us that our hearts have to be pure if we want to see God? And that's where the 'blessing' is – seeing God, which is surely one of the greatest and highest aspirations that anyone could have. It's telling us that if we want to see God, we must somehow find the transformation from polluted and impure to clean and pure. It's like going to the Gulf of Mexico and putting the clock right back to before the blowout – which is a tall order, to say the least.

We will tackle this Beatitude by asking three rather obvious questions of it. Firstly, what *is* a pure heart? Secondly, When do we see God? And thirdly, assuming that's what we want, How does a heart *become* pure?

What is a pure heart?
When we hear the word 'heart', we might think mainly of our emotions. An image of Valentine's Day might come into your mind, with those sometimes rather over-the-top cards covered in vivid red hearts! The Bible uses the word with a much wider scope. In Bible language, the heart doesn't mean emotions only; it means what you think, what you want, what your character is made of; in fact, it means your whole personality – the real you. The heart defines you, it says what you are. The Bible also says that when God looks at us, it's the state of our hearts that he is interested in. In 1 Samuel 16, we read how God sends Samuel to an obscure village called Bethlehem to anoint an unknown young man as future king of Israel. Now Samuel knows the family he has to go to, but he doesn't know which member of this family the Lord has

in mind. So he turns up at the house and takes a look at the family. He sees Eliab, the oldest son; and he seems really impressive. And Samuel thinks, Surely this must be the man the Lord has in mind to be king. But he's wrong. It's actually the *youngest* son the Lord wants – whose name happens to be David. The crucial verse is 1 Samuel 16:7.

You see, when we make judgments about someone, it's generally on the basis of what's on the outside. When you meet someone for the first time, you look at how they are dressed; you listen to how they speak; you pick up hints about their background, their education, their family, their job. We all do this, all the time. We say, Actions speak louder than words, so we watch what a person does, and we make judgments from that. But the Lord is not limited to what appears on the surface. He is able to look *below* the surface. He is able to look at the heart; he knows every one of us through and through. As that same David would later write in Psalm 139: 'O Lord, you have searched me and you know me': every thought, every word before I speak it, nothing is hidden from you. That's the reality. The Lord sees right through to the hidden depths of our being – he sees the heart.

So now what exactly does 'pure' mean – 'pure in heart'? Clearly, it follows that Jesus is not talking about our external behaviour. In Jesus' day the Pharisees have become obsessed with external compliance with the Law of Moses. They think the way to please God is to create a rule to cover every tiny eventuality in life and their whole focus is on observing these rules in meticulous detail. And so impurity or uncleanness are about issues like whether you've done the ceremonial hand-washing correctly. Jesus often comes into conflict with the Pharisees, and after one of these encounters he explains it to his disciples (Matthew 15:18-20). In other words, you don't please God by strict compliance with a fat rule-book. He is interested in your *heart* and what comes from there.

In many ways, the Pharisees' teaching is echoed today by Muslims. Islam prescribes just the same sort of meticulous compliance with rules, especially around the issues of prayer and fasting. If you've ever read or studied the rules for *wudu*, that is washing before prayer; or the rules for the Ramadan fast, with its regulations about not swallowing saliva, and what happens if you get a bit of food stuck between your teeth, you will recognise the description! This is so different from what Jesus says about the people of his kingdom. Christians are never defined in terms of the rules they keep. We are defined by the state of our hearts – and our actions, our deeds, good or bad, are the overflow of our hearts.

So purity of heart is not about our external behaviour. But also, and perhaps this will be reassuring, purity of heart is not the same as total sinlessness. When the Bible talks about being pure in heart, and shows us *people* who are pure in heart, it is never claiming that they are completely without sin. There have been various Christian movements that taught that we can reach the point of sinless perfection in this life on earth; but it's not what the Bible says, and ultimately that kind of teaching can only lead to a sense of failure and disillusionment[13].

A pure heart *does* mean cleanness; it *does* imply driving out sin. But it means more than that. The Danish philosopher, Soren Kierkegaard, came up with a famous definition of this – in fact it was the title of a book he wrote on the subject: *Purity of heart is to will one thing*. His book is a painstaking exploration of double-mindedness, the confused and insincere state of mind that is so typical of us. It's a great definition, because it tells us that to have a pure heart is all about what your will, your heart, is set on – having one over-riding desire. It is what David asks God for in Psalm 86:11. One centre: one priority: an undivided heart.

Now what kind of life will a heart like that produce? It will be a life of utter *integrity*, where what you are in public, where you can be seen, is no different from what you are in private. That's what integrity means – a unified personality, where every part of your life is consistent. You don't put on a mask when you go out of the front door. It is a heart that is committed solely to God. The old-time theologians and pastors used to distinguish between our *emotions* and what they called our *affections*. It's an important distinction. Emotions are what we feel, and they can vary wildly depending on circumstances, our state of health and so on: but our affections are what our heart is set on. Our affections are what we love, what we believe, what our life is built around. A heart that is pure and undivided has its affections fixed on God.

The Bible is quite clear that if we want a relationship with God, this pure heart is exactly what we need to have. Again, look at what David writes, this time in Psalm 24:3-5. And in the New Testament we find the same message in a letter written to Jewish Christians (Hebrews 12:14). The problem is the one we began with. God's assessment of our hearts is so negative (Jeremiah 17:9). If we are honest, surely that is a description we recognise! Even our *own* reactions, even our *own* sins, constantly surprise and shock us.

But here is how the Christian message is unique. Only the Christian gospel is so stark and negative about the mess we are in because of our sin. At the same time, only the Christian gospel sets the standard so high. Only the Christian gospel can be realistic about all this, can face our situation honestly – because we have the unique answer! In Jesus Christ we have the answer to the horrible mess that is the human heart, because when Jesus went to the cross, he took all that sin and impurity *with* him, and he paid for it and he dealt with it all. And so for us who have committed ourselves to him, been forgiven and united with him in his kingdom family, there is new life and a new heart. As the apostle Paul puts it, 'If anyone is in Christ, he is a new creation; the old has gone, the new has come!' (2 Corinthians 5:17). That is why we don't have to pretend that everything is really OK. We can be honest about the horrible depths of our sinfulness because Jesus has dealt with it and given us a new heart, a heart that can be pure.

When do we see God?
That's what Jesus says: Blessed are the pure in heart, *for they will see God.* So when does it happen? We've seen with several of these Beatitudes already that the kingdom blessings they promise have a present aspect and a future aspect. That's certainly true in this case. Kingdom people, people whose hearts have been made pure, see God *now*, in a sense. We don't see him with these eyes, of course. But by faith we can see God in all kinds of ways, even now.

We see him in creation. One of my favourite places is the far end of the Gower Peninsula in South Wales. On clear nights there, I love to go out and look at the stars, the stars as you can never see them from the city where the sky is never dark. The crowding constellations and the Milky Way – I look up on such a night and see a little bit of the majesty and the awesome creative power of our God. And the fact that I know something about the stars from my background in physics, and the theories of what makes them shine, does not reduce my wonder at the Creator God – in fact it increases it. It makes me worship. We see God in his rule over our lives. We see him working out his loving plans for our good – sometimes we can see it at the time, often we can only see it afterwards, but we know he is working out his promises for good in our lives. Seeing God now means the fellowship we have with him in our experience day by day. Even though there is still sin in our lives as Christians, the more he grows in our lives, the closer we get to him, the more we enjoy his presence. If you're a Christian, you know that!

But however good the Christian life can be now, it pales into nothing compared to what is still in store for us. The day will come when we are no longer troubled by sin and nothing can get in the way. The Bible closes its long story with a vision of the heavenly city which is the eternal home of God's own people. It is the place where we will spend eternity with God and with Christ if we belong to him now. Revelation 22:4 contains the specific promise that 'they will see his face'. For anyone who has begun to contemplate what God is like, what seeing him would be like, that is an astounding thought. What men and women through the ages have longed for – to see God, to know unbroken and untarnished fellowship with our Maker – will be ours for ever. We don't know what kind of eyes we will have to see – we know we will be in resurrection bodies far better than now – but we will see what no-one in human history has ever been able to see. Seeing the face of God, in all his holiness and his majesty, would instantly destroy us, sinners that we are. Even as we will be then, totally pure and clothed in perfection, the sight will surely overwhelm us. But we *will* see his face!

How does a heart become pure?

If we belong to Christ, we are a new creation, we have a new heart; and yet we still sin. We are far from perfect and we often fall. We've seen that when we are united with Christ, the Holy Spirit gets to work in our lives to change us. It's a process; it's what we call sanctification – God's work within us to make us more and more like Jesus. But the Bible also makes it clear, over and over again, that we have to co-operate with the Holy Spirit. We have a part to play. And in view of what's in store for us, surely this is exactly what we want. As John puts it in 1 John 3:2-3, if we are longing to see him, it will *motivate* us to be pure. We want to prepare ourselves for the perfection of eternity, here and now. Becoming pure, becoming like Jesus, doesn't happen overnight. It doesn't happen through a single dramatic experience, being zapped with holiness or through some easy, fast-track route. But it happens, usually quite slowly and with many struggles. Do you honestly want to be pure? Well then, here are two very clear features which your life will display.

Just like Jesus

The first of these features is *a loathing for sin*. Remember the second Beatitude – 'blessed are those who mourn, for they will be comforted' (5:4). There is a blessing for those who mourn deeply over their own sin. Here's the connection. The one who knows what it is to mourn over their sin is the same person who longs for a pure heart – a heart *free* of sin. They are two sides of the same coin. When you find that you have fallen into some sin, you will be appalled. When you realise that once more you have lost your temper with the kids, or joined in that cynical conversation or risqué banter in the office, or let yourself go on some fantasy, whether it's about sex or the ideal home – when we realise that something or someone has taken centre stage in our life, and it isn't Jesus, we will be horrified. We will hate this ugly thing that has clouded our friendship with the Lord. We'll want to repent, yes, but beyond that we will want the whole idolatrous root of the sin to be removed and destroyed. If we don't feel that loathing for sin, we need to ask God for it. Why should the children of eternity be wading through muck?

The second feature is *a shaping by God's Word*. There's another psalm that answers exactly the question we are asking. In particular, Psalm 119:9-11 makes it clear that it's God's Word that has to shape and mould our lives. The point about the Bible is not that it's a rule-book, so that in every situation we face we look up in the index exactly what to do, turn to page so-and-so and read off the answer. That would be going back to the religion of the Pharisees or the Muslims! The point about this book is that it tells us about God, and his age-long plan to rescue men and women from destruction, and the lengths of love he went to when he brought it about. This book tells us who we really are, what we are like, where we are going if we accept the rescue plan and where we are going if we don't. It shows us how to live in relationship to the God who saved us.

Through this book he speaks to us, he reveals himself to us; and as we read this book prayerfully, getting up with it every morning and taking it with us through the day; and as we study it and as we hear it taught, God uses the Bible to shape our lives and lead us into *purity*. If we want to defeat sin and live pure lives, then as the psalmist says we will hide God's Word in our hearts. Many years ago as a young Christian I heard a man say, This book has turned my life upside down, it has transformed me. Now I can begin to say the same myself. It's true: that is what the Bible can do. How does a heart stay pure? A loathing for sin and a shaping by God's Word.

The Kingdom Manifesto

If you are not a Christian, you need to recognise the true state of your heart. Be honest and admit it: it's not a pretty sight. The most you can do about that yourself is a little bit of cleaning up around the edges. As with the oil spill in the Gulf, you can skim off some of the dirt, maybe; you can do your best to limit the damage. But you can't clean it up! The only way to clean your heart is to come to Jesus Christ. Come to him with all your life story of guilt and failure and ask him to forgive you and put you right, to give you that new heart that you need. Join the kingdom and you will be blessed, for you will see God!

Blessed are the peacemakers

September, 1938. War is threatening to engulf Europe. A resurgent Germany, led by Adolf Hitler, has rebuilt its armed forces and swallowed up Austria, and is now defying the world by threatening to invade Czechoslovakia. Fear of conflict grips the continent. The British Prime Minister, Neville Chamberlain, carries the burden of deciding how to respond to Hitler's aggression. Every concession by the Czech government is being met only by further demands, yet Chamberlain believes that Hitler's ambitions are limited to what he says he wants: just a little bit of Czechoslovakia and he will be happy. On 28th September, Chamberlain calls for an international conference to settle the question. And early in the morning of 30th September, the agreement for which Neville Chamberlain will always be remembered is signed in Munich by the leaders of four nations – not including the Czechs. A relieved Chamberlain flies home to Britain. To cheering crowds he speaks these words: 'My good friends, for the second time in our history, a British Prime Minister has returned from Germany bringing peace with honour. I believe it is "peace for our time". Go home and get a nice quiet sleep.' The British nation, most of it, rejoices. Chamberlain is hailed as a peacemaker. A commemorative plate is issued, with the striking inscription 'Chamberlain the peacemaker'. Meanwhile in Germany, Hitler regards Chamberlain with contempt. Within six months, he has occupied the *whole* of Czechoslovakia. And six months after that, it is Neville Chamberlain who has the task of announcing to the British people that 'we are now at war with Germany'.

'Blessed are the peacemakers, for they will be called sons of God', says Jesus (5:9). Is that what peacemaking means, buying off a tyrant and hoping for the best? If not, what does it mean? We are dealing now with a very popular statement: surely everyone agrees that peacemaking is a good idea. Before going any further, we need to notice a couple of connections. You see how this leads on from being pure in heart. Someone who is genuinely pure in heart is not envious or full of his own agenda; and to be a peacemaker, you must have the right motives, that pure sincerity. But also, if we look at the whole series of Beatitudes, there's a bigger structure in place. There's a connection between the first three and the set of three which verse 9 concludes. People who are poor in spirit know they deserve nothing; so naturally they will be merciful. People who mourn over their own sin will long to see it banished from their hearts – to be pure in heart. And people who are meek, who are secure in the love and approval God gives them, will be strong enough to reach out and make peace. These Beatitudes don't describe eight different people. They describe just *one* person – one complete, integrated personality – the man or woman who knows God, who belongs to the kingdom.

So with that in mind, let's come to this statement of Jesus. We will look at this in four stages: the peace we can make; the problem we must face; the peacemaker we follow; and living as peacemakers.

The peace we can make
What is this 'peacemaking' all about? We'd better say what peacemaking *isn't*. Obviously, it isn't enough to think that peace is a good idea. It doesn't really help the world very much if all we do is watch the news, sigh and say, If only the world was a better place. Wouldn't it be so much better if there wasn't all this fighting? Yes, that's true, but just thinking it is not peacemaking! Good wishes are not enough to make peace. But also, to be a peacemaker it's not enough to have a cheerful character. Clearly, it's true that some people are naturally more peaceable than others. I can think of people I've known who enjoy nothing more than starting an argument. Others have only to walk into a room and a fight breaks out – while others again radiate a natural, calm assurance that no-one wants to argue with. They're nice people to have around – but this is not what Jesus is talking about here. Remember, the Beatitudes are not about our natural disposition; Jesus is not picking out a certain category of people who happen to have friendly characters. He is saying, *kingdom people are peacemakers* – peacemaking is part of the kingdom DNA.

We also need to say that peacemaking is *not* about appeasing or ignoring evil. It is not about letting sleeping dogs lie, about avoiding conflict at all costs. The story we started with is a good example of that. The idea of appeasing Hitler was that if he was given just a little bit more, he would be satisfied – conveniently ignoring the evil and treacherous track record he had already established. Chamberlain staved off war by a year, and was convinced he was doing the right thing, but that doesn't make him a peacemaker.

Moreover, in biblical terms, real peace is not just the absence of war. Many of us grew up in the Cold War, when Europe was divided by the Iron Curtain and was filled with huge armies, ready to go to war at a moment's notice. The threat of nuclear destruction was never very far away. That was peace of a kind – it was certainly better than war – but it's not what the Bible describes as peace. Biblical peace is what's described by the Hebrew word *shalom*. If you have shalom, it doesn't mean only that there's no war. It's positive, it means you're living in harmony with people around you. It means security, it means you are safe in your own place; it means a wholeness and healthiness of life. This kind of peace is what we long for our children to know. As parents, we long for our kids to be able to walk the streets safely and without fear; and to grow up in a world that is secure. We want to be able to trust our neighbours and the people we work with. How much more do you think parents in a place like Afghanistan or Somalia long for peace? Put yourself in their shoes for a moment and think of what you would pray for and long for for your kids there. That the violence would cease. That there would be no more fear of being swept off your land. That you could simply stay put, and build your home and farm your land or run your business without it being stolen, without corrupt rulers grinding you into the dust; and you would long for an atmosphere of harmony and trust. That is *shalom*. That is the peace we are called to make.

The problem we must face

The question that arises from this Beatitude is, *Why* is peacemaking necessary at all? Why is this world of ours the way it is – why is peace not the natural state of play? Good question. James puts his finger on the answer in his letter – look at James 3:16-4:2. James is saying, Peacemaking is great, it produces wonderful results, it's a godly activity: James 3:17 even sounds like an echo of the Beatitudes. But here's the problem, laid out in James 4:1-2. Where does conflict come from? It comes from what's going on inside us. It comes from battling desires, from the relentless, desperate quest to get what we want. In a word, it comes from our *sin*. 'Why can't people just get along?' How often have you heard that said – or even said it yourself? Here's why. It's because of the sin in all our hearts. Now we can see this easily enough on the grand scale: again we can look at the Second World War as an example. That war came about because of Adolf Hitler and his twisted and perverted ideas. But the same is true on the smallest scale too. Why do we have rows at home? Why are there always fights in the school playground? Because of the sin that lives in every heart. None of us is exempt from this. It is *sin* – the relentless quest for self, the monster that puts me at the centre of the universe and will do anything in its power to keep me there – that's at the root of every row, every street fight, every outbreak of road rage and every war!

More disastrous still, it is sin that has made us enemies of God. It's bad enough to have no peace with our fellow men. How much worse to be at war with God himself. But that's exactly the situation. The Bible makes it clear that in our natural condition every one of us is God's enemy – because we sin, and God detests sin; and because every sin violates his commands to us his creatures, we are at war with the Almighty One who made us and who one day will judge us, with the power to send us to hell. We have to understand that our greatest need is not to abolish war between nations, but to make our peace with *God*.

So yes, we should support every genuine effort to bring peace among the nations, and pray for it too. We must certainly take an interest in the valiant attempts to create peaceful solutions in Afghanistan and the Middle East. But we have to recognise that there is no true peace on earth as long as the world is dominated by sin, the greatest problem we all have to face. And it's at this point we move on to the *reason* for the blessing.

The peacemaker we follow

The promise is that as peacemakers we will be called sons of God. Why 'sons' and not 'children'? The reason is that Jesus is not speaking here so much of our *relationship* with God as our *character*. In biblical language, to describe someone as 'son of' is a way of telling you what they are like. There is a character in Acts called Joseph Barnabas. 'Bar-nabas' means 'son of encouragement', but that doesn't mean his father's name was 'encouragement'! 'Barnabas' was a nickname chosen because he was such an encouraging character – he was a 'son of encouragement'. So here in the Beatitude, what Jesus means is that a peacemaker is someone who will be specially recognised as sharing the character of God himself. In fact, that expression 'will be called' is another 'divine passive': it means that God *himself* will acknowledge us in this way on the Day of Judgment; he will see us peacemakers and recognise us publicly as people who share his own character. Now we know that this is what we *are*, if we belong to Christ and we are members of his kingdom. It's not that we have to go and sort out a hundred quarrels and then God will acknowledge us as his own! This Beatitude encourages us to live up to what we already are. That's the point.

Why is it that being a peacemaker is so particularly God-like? Why is peacemaking a specially godly quality? The reason is that he is the supreme peacemaker. We have noted the enmity between God and man, and from man to God, the enmity we are all born into, the distance that separates us fallen, sinful men and women from a pure and holy God. But God has not simply accepted that situation. Ephesians 2:13-18 tells us what he has done about it. The heart of what Paul is saying is in Ephesians 2:16, that statement about Jesus Christ reconciling both of them – he means Jews and Gentiles – to God through his own death on the cross, the cross which brought hostilities to an end and created peace between God and man. The cross deals with our sins – Jesus' death pays the penalty which God's justice rightfully demands. The cross destroys the hostility between God and man; and it also breaks down the barriers of hostility which separate us from one another, race from race, group from group, here on earth. Paul describes that as creating *a single new humanity* in Christ. The people who belong to Jesus are an entirely new race, at peace with our God and at peace with one another. That's how radical the gospel is. The gospel is a peace plan forged in the unimaginable depths of the Father's loving heart for us and paid at the cost of blood and wrath. What an initiative! What love beyond description.

God is, simply, the supreme peacemaker. That's why kingdom peacemakers can best be described as sons of God. The first and foremost 'son of God' is of course the Lord Jesus Christ, the great peace ambassador. And as peacemakers we are counted with him. We are like him and we share in his mission. Paul makes the connection between what Christ has done and what we are to do in 2 Corinthians 5:17-20. *Reconciliation* is simply another word for peacemaking. But now we need to put all this into practice. What does it mean? How can we be peacemakers?

Living as peacemakers
Here we are as people of the kingdom. We are to be known as peacemakers; we trust that as the Holy Spirit does his work in us, that is what we are gradually becoming – people who live in harmony ourselves and who create harmony between others, just like Jesus. So what are the everyday tools of the peacemaker's trade?

The first and most basic is to *live a peaceable life*. This isn't about our natural character; it will be harder for some of us than for others, but for all of us this is what the Lord wants. We live a peaceable life – not causing contention, not adding to the long list of woes and strife which we know all too well. For many of us, that will mean learning to keep quiet when our every natural instinct is crying out to put someone else in his place, or to blast the horn, or to protest our innocence, or to claim our rights, or simply to tell everyone what I am so sure they need to hear! A peacemaker needs to know when to shut up. There is no peacemaking without listening and understanding; and to do that, we have to learn to be quiet and use our ears. I have only limited experience of organised peacemaking, but in each situation I have encountered, success has been possible only by shutting up and listening to the different stories of the injured parties.

But then also, peacemaking means *taking the initiative*. 'Keep yourself to yourself' is part of British culture, but it certainly isn't biblical! We cannot be peacemakers from behind a barricade or a closed door. Peacemaking means taking the initiative – being willing to go into difficult, dangerous and hostile places – which is exactly what the Lord Jesus did. The places he came to were *very* difficult, *highly* dangerous and *extremely* hostile. He knew that, and still he came to be a peacemaker. This is why a peacemaker has to be meek – because the meek person is so secure in God that he is willing to take the risks.

Most important, peacemaking means *prayer*. As Christians, we should of course be praying about every activity we undertake, but there is something about peacemaking that demands special boldness, special insight, special care, special wisdom. It's a spiritual activity. So when we have a conflict to resolve, or we have to enter a tense situation, we will stop first and pray. We will ask the Lord to help us to be agents of his peace. We will pray while we are *in* the situation, that we will know how to speak peace and have the grace to take the shots that may be fired at us; and we will pray when we've come out. Peacemaking must be surrounded with prayer.

Living a peaceable life; taking the initiative; prayer – these are the tools of the peacemaker's trade. Finally, where do peacemakers go? The answer is, peacemakers go anywhere! As people of the kingdom, as sons of God, we are called to bring peace into any and every situation where we find ourselves. Where are you going to be today, or in the next few days? Where can you use the tools of the trade to bring peace? It may be in your work-place. Will you be the one who is willing to listen to the grievances of others instead of pouring out your own? Will you be the one who is bold enough to challenge a hostile atmosphere, or to knock on the boss's door to ask him to put right an injustice? – knowing, of course, that it's quite possible that some of your colleagues will reward you by turning against you instead? But you'll do it because you belong to Jesus, the great ambassador of peace, who laid down *his* life to bring peace into yours.

It may be in your home. Perhaps there is some long-running conflict with your spouse, or with a child. Perhaps it's in your wider family, a branch of the family with whom you may not even be on speaking terms. What can you do to bring peace? It may mean giving up some of your own rights – not to appease evil but to admit where you have pushed yourself forward too far. It may mean doing some serious listening that you have never done before. It can start with a word, or a phone call, or even a friendly text or email – but it has to start with you!

Or it may be in your street, where you know neighbours are at loggerheads – what can you do to sow peace into that situation, to bring about reconciliation? It's risky, but peacemakers take risks, because peacemakers are like Jesus.

Peacemakers go anywhere; but above all, peacemakers go where people need the gospel. The greatest peacemaking of all is to share the good news about Jesus and to heal the hostility between God and anyone who is still without Christ (again, look at 2 Corinthians 5:20).

Just like Jesus

That is what Christians are supremely called to do – to summon men and women to make their peace with God.

Questions to reflect on or discuss

1. Work through the four points about the mercy we are called to show (heart-felt; practical; spiritual; forgiving). In each area, look at yourself. How far does your character and behaviour measure up to these standards? Is there one area where you particularly need to pray for God's help?

2. Do you recognise my description of the state of the human heart without Christ?

3. Has it ever struck you that the Christian message is liberating simply because it allows us to be honest about ourselves?

4. Think about the two features mentioned in regard to purity of heart: a loathing for sin and a shaping by God's Word. What do you need to do to co-operate with the Holy Spirit's work of giving you a pure heart?

5. Do you think you are a peacemaker? If so, do you think that is a natural quality or something that the Spirit has made you? Is there a difference?

6. If the 'tools of the peacemaker's trade' are living a peaceable life; taking the initiative; prayer; and going anywhere, where do you most need the Lord's help to make you more of a peacemaker?

Chapter 4
What happens when you're different
Matthew 5:10-16

Throughout the Sermon on the Mount, Jesus constantly emphasises that his people are to be different from those outside the kingdom. The Beatitudes we have looked at so far – the first seven – often express that difference in terms of an overturning of the world's expectations: that those who mourn are blessed, that it is the meek who inherit the earth, and so on. In this chapter we come to two short passages which focus on the consequences of that distinctiveness and in doing so conclude the introduction to the Sermon on the Mount (though it is a long introduction!). First, in the final Beatitude, we see the consequences for the Christian. The world's standard response to the character of Christ in the believer's life is persecution, Jesus says; yet even in that, you are blessed. It is perhaps the most unexpected blessing of them all! Then we see the consequences for the world. If we are living as kingdom people should, the world will be blessed by us, for we will be both salt, restraining the tendency of the world to fester and decay, and light, shining the goodness of God into the darkness.

Blessed are the persecuted

August 2010: police in China enter a prayer room and throw out the Christians who are praying inside. The Christians then watch as the police demolish the prayer room and training centre owned by the house church they belong to. In China, the government regularly cracks down on unregistered Christian groups, imprisons their leaders or puts them under house arrest, and prevents believers from travelling abroad.

The Kingdom Manifesto

September 2008: a young man named Ahmadey Osman Nur is attending a wedding in Somalia. The sheikh conducting the service identifies him as a Christian and tells him to leave. On his way out he is shot dead by the armed guard. Somalia is the most dangerous country in the world to be a Christian. Most of those who have converted to Christ and stayed in the country have been martyred. May 2010: 45-year-old Said Musa is arrested in Afghanistan, along with dozens of others known to have left Islam to follow Christ. Musa is held for some months in Kabul provincial jail. In a letter from prison to President Obama he pleads for help, detailing his story and the torture he has suffered. Afghanistan is possibly the world's second most hostile country for Christians. Even government ministers have publicly called for the execution of every convert to Christ.

Meanwhile, somewhere in your own home town, a man works in the back office of a small business. His boss is putting pressure on him to conceal certain financial transactions, so that the business can avoid paying tax. But the man is a Christian; he knows this is dishonest; and very politely he says he won't do it. He gently reasons with the boss; but the boss neither listens nor sympathises. Instead. he accuses the man in front of the other staff of trying to ruin the company. They all turn against him; and very soon his life at work becomes impossible and he loses his job, because of Christ.

The first three stories are real. The last is invented; but it happens. None of these stories is in any way exceptional. Persecution of Christians is real. The countries may vary from decade to decade, but the stories remain the same. Around the world, in a hundred different ways and in a thousand different places, followers of Christ are under attack for their faith. It has always been this way. It was like this in the days of the apostles, who faced all kinds of opposition. Most of them ended up being executed in one brutal way or another, some of them under Emperor Nero, who was notoriously fond of the most extreme and perverted tortures. Several of the later Roman emperors did the same, in a couple of cases making systematic attempts to annihilate the church altogether. Persecution has continued right down the years, with the twentieth century being the most bloody of all. Huge numbers of Christian believers were slaughtered in Armenia, in the Soviet Union, in Sudan and in many other places: some well-known, some now known only to God. Throughout history, nothing has sustained such intense hatred and persecution as the church of Christ. Persecution is a reality for Christians around the world today; and increasingly, even in Britain and the USA, with the rise of the new atheism, an aggressive gay rights agenda and militant Islam, the church is coming under attack.

We have reached the last of the Beatitudes, these eight sayings of Jesus which form the overture to the Sermon on the Mount and which together describe the character of the kingdom of heaven. Step by step we have seen the character of the Christian described; and all these characteristics have a blessing attached to them. If we are genuine Christians, then all these descriptions are true of us, right now – all of them! They may not be very visible yet, but this is where the Lord is taking us; this is the work of his Spirit in our lives. And now we come to verse 10: 'Blessed are those who are persecuted'. What?! It comes as a shock. How could persecution be a blessing? Occupational hazard, maybe, but blessing? Remember, the Beatitudes are not a buffet where you can pick and choose whatever you fancy. You can't leave any of them on the table, not even this one. It's a description of the Christian just like the rest. As if to emphasise that, the blessing attached to it goes right back to the beginning, echoing the first Beatitude; and we could equally well translate it, '*Only* theirs is the kingdom of heaven'. We will tackle this final Beatitude by asking three simple and direct questions about persecution.

Why does it happen?

Let's look more closely at verses 10-12. This time we have a whole paragraph, not just a single verse. Jesus gives the Beatitude in the style of all the others, and then in verses 11-12 he expands on it. He redirects it from the general 'those' and 'theirs' to say 'you' and 'your'. It's as if he turns away from the listening crowd at this point and faces his disciples directly; and he intensifies the message, saying: yes, this is really how it will be for *you*. We might have thought persecution is about physical violence only, but verse 11 makes it clear that he is taking in persecuting words as well – words of insult, abuse, slander. They are all included with 'persecution' and they are all attached to the blessing.

So why does persecution happen? Let's begin once more with what Jesus does *not* mean. He is not talking about being persecuted because you're obnoxious! Whether you are a Christian or not, if you are generally unpleasant to people, it's not really surprising if they give you a hard time. You are not blessed for being a pain in the neck – which Christians sometimes are, and then claim they are persecuted! Nor is Jesus talking about being persecuted just because you're eccentric or odd; and nor is he speaking of the general trials of life. If your builder overcharges you or your child's teacher takes a dislike to you, that's not persecution; that's just something you have to bear graciously!

No, Jesus is speaking of persecution for one cause only. He says it twice here, but he says it in two different ways. In verse 10 he speaks of being persecuted 'because of righteousness', and in verse 11 he speaks of being persecuted 'because of me'. They are parallel statements and they mean the same. We saw in the fourth Beatitude that 'hungering and thirsting for righteousness' really means longing to be like Jesus; and it's the same here. Jesus is saying that his people will be persecuted *because we are like him*. Persecution happens because your Christlikeness – what you say, what you do – becomes an offence to the world.

Perhaps we need to pause for thought here. We might think, Wait, surely being like Jesus really means being good and kind to everyone; and who's going to persecute me for that? The answer is that no-one will persecute you for being good and kind – and that's not what they persecuted Jesus for either! They didn't persecute him for healing people (unless its timing happened to contravene their religious rules). No, they persecuted Jesus because he showed up their hypocrisy. They hated him because he said their religion was empty and worthless, as we will see him doing in chapter 6 especially. They had him killed because of what he claimed to be. That's why persecution happens to his people too: because we insist that Jesus is the only way to know God, and every other way is empty and worthless; and that if we fail to worship him as God then we can never know God. It happens because we insist on the cross as the only place where God and man can make peace. Christians are persecuted because they will not agree that any other path leads to God, because they will not unconditionally obey the dictates of a godless government, whether that is in China or even in the UK, and because the transparent integrity of their lifestyle challenges and rebukes the lives of those around them.

We are persecuted for taking our faith too seriously, for refusing to keep our beliefs confined inside our heads. And if they persecuted Jesus, the only perfect man in history, why should we think they will not persecute us in the same way? So: didn't Jesus come to make our life easier, smoother, more comfortable? Absolutely not. Welcome to the kingdom! What this tells us is that persecution is *normal*. The word 'when' in verse 11 really has the force of '*whenever* they do this to you' – it is to be expected. Jesus frequently warns his disciples of that. It is part of being a Christian that we are persecuted, just as it is part of being a Christian to be merciful and meek and pure in heart. So here is a test for us, and it's a searching one: if we are never truly persecuted at all, are we truly Christians at all? For if there is this genuine, flagrant, Christ-likeness in us, it is inevitable that sooner or later the world will hate us. Do you ever say or do anything that threatens or disturbs the people you meet every day? Or does being like Jesus, for you, just mean being nice? If you think Jesus was simply nice, you need to go and read the gospels again!

Our message about Christ will not always be accepted or tolerated. People will react with hostility – not just to the message, but also to the messenger. It's normal – because we are like Jesus. There is a very good summary of this in 1 Peter 4:12-16. There's no blessing in suffering for doing wrong – or just for being annoying! – but as we will see now, there is great blessing in suffering for the name of Christ.

Why is it a blessing?
Frankly, suffering for what we believe and live out sounds like a pretty depressing prospect. It's even harder to imagine how it could be a blessing when we live in a world that is obsessed with pleasure and self-gratification. Our culture has trained us to believe that life is one long quest for happiness and fun, so how can we possibly say that persecution is a blessing?

Persecution is a blessing, says Jesus, *because it connects us with the prophets* (5:12). The prophets of the Old Testament were God's spokesmen. One after another, they challenged God's people to be faithful to him, to repent of serving other gods, to live as the beacon of light to the world which he had called them to be. They did that – and almost without exception, they were persecuted. They were abused, rejected and in many cases killed. In Jesus' day, everyone knows about the prophets, everyone knows they were approved and blessed by God, and everyone knows they were persecuted. Jesus tells his followers – you're with them. And if we are God's people today, and we are persecuted, then we too are with them. We are in good company – the company of men and women who stood and spoke boldly and faithfully for God, no matter what opposition they faced. We are part of an unbroken history going back thousands of years before Christ. Being part of that heritage is a *blessing*: it means we're in a good place.

More than that, persecution is a blessing *because it identifies us with Christ* (5:11). Whenever we suffer for Christ, we are standing with him. In a small way, we are sharing in his sufferings; we are enduring what he endured. As Jesus would later put it, 'If the world hates you, keep in mind that it hated me first' (John 15:18). What an honour that is for any of us who belongs to Christ: that we should be disgraced, despised, rejected, because we are identified with the one who loved us and gave himself for us. Soon after Jesus ascended to heaven, the disciples would start to be persecuted. Early on, they faced the Jewish Council, the Sanhedrin, because they refused to stop speaking about Jesus. See how that story concludes (Acts 5:40-41). Being flogged was a *blessing* because it showed they were identified with Christ himself. That is a blessing, because being with Christ is the best place to be.

Then persecution is a blessing *because it proves the kingdom is ours* (5:10). The kingdom of heaven is for the persecuted – so if we are persecuted, genuinely, because of the Lord Jesus, it proves we are part of the kingdom. If you are persecuted in your work-place because you refuse to join in the gossip, or the character assassination, or the dodgy jokes, and they exclude you or gang up on you because you are a Christian, and you accept it with joy – that proves you are in the kingdom. If you are at home or with friends, and they insult you or despise you, not because you're difficult but because of Christ, that proves you are in the kingdom. If you are sharing the gospel, and the only reaction is hostility or mockery, and you receive it cheerfully – that proves you are in the kingdom. That's a blessing! And if we are in the kingdom, there is great reward ahead (5:12a). Jesus is saying there is a particular reward associated with facing persecution. It's not a question of earning your way to heaven through suffering, as some in the past have taught – of course not. Everything here is about grace, God's undeserved kindness to us. But even so, if you face persecution faithfully for the name of Jesus, there is a reward in heaven for that – as if being part of the new world was not blessing enough already!

What happens when you're different

So the blessing in persecution is joy here and now – the joy of knowing we truly are among God's own people, the joy of knowing we are united with Christ himself, and the joy of being sure of a wonderful future ahead. And it's the blessing of total security and the reward in the age to come.

How do we face it?

If persecution is inevitable for the true Christian, this is the practical question we have to answer. When we experience persecution for being like Jesus, how do we respond? In verse 12 we find the only command in the whole of the Beatitudes. 'Rejoice and be glad' – be overjoyed, in fact! When we face persecution, our first instinct is probably to hit back. Our second instinct is probably to be angry. How dare they say that? To come over all 21st century and say, What about my rights, what about respect? That's how our culture trains us to react. It's what we naturally feel when someone does us wrong. Jesus says no. When you face persecution, my people, you rejoice. He does not ask us to rejoice about the persecution itself. Persecution is an evil, it's always bad, of course it is, that someone should insult or hurt someone else. It would be perverted masochism if we claimed to enjoy it! No-one is asking us to enjoy being insulted, still less being beaten up or tortured – for we must never forget that that's what persecution means in many places. But we can rejoice in what it *proves* – that it identifies us with Christ and shows we are his people, and in the unique fellowship with him that only persecution can bring us.

We rejoice, also, because of our eternal home. Non-Christians don't like to think about the world beyond death. In fact, this is another test of where we really stand in the spiritual world. If you never find yourself longing for heaven and the new heavens and earth which lie beyond it, and meditating on what it will be like to live there in the company of Jesus and all God's people – if you never think about that, it's very doubtful if you are really a Christian. Christians focus on our eternal home – or we should! What's in your heart? An ideal home here on earth, or an eternal home to come? Our problem is that we are too much at home here in this present life – for most of us it is so comfortable, and we relish and enjoy so much the delights that this world has to offer, that of course we are upset when that comfort is disturbed. Of course the idea of persecution is a shock. But if our hearts are set on what Jesus is preparing for us, we won't be shaken by what happens to us here!

If we are Christians, the Bible tells us we don't really belong to this world at all. We are people of a new kingdom, which will be seen in all its glory in the age that's to come. The truth is that what happens to us here and now can't really touch us, because this isn't our final destination; it isn't our true home. We can rejoice in the prospect of the amazing, glorious, eternal realm where we belong and where the Lord Jesus will receive us to be with him for ever.

Persecution is a reality in our world today; and given what Jesus says here, that's just what we should expect. Suffering is very real. The stories we began with are true, painful and bitter. In most countries of the world, persecution is far worse than it is in the West; and we must support our brothers and sisters in whatever way we can, as Paul tells us in 1 Corinthians 12:26. We can give financially; we can write letters to our governments; and above all we can pray for individuals and for churches, that they would have strength to endure, that they would know they are suffering for the Name of Christ, that they would remember they have an eternal home in glory; and because of that they would rejoice.

In the West, meanwhile, we must be ready for whatever the future will bring. It is likely to get harder to live a faithful Christian life; in Britain, persecution from official laws, from society at large and from other religions, is already on the rise. We can be confident – we can rejoice – and we can focus on our eternal home with Christ. That will keep us faithful here. Paul sums up this attitude in 2 Corinthians 4:17-18. The troubles and trials of this dark world will soon be forgotten, drowned out in the brilliant light of eternity.

Salt and light

The scene is a first century butcher's shop in Galilee. It's hot. The sun is almost overhead: people and animals seek out whatever shade they can find. In the little, open-fronted shop the butcher has his cuts of meat lined up. The flies are already at work. From the top of a post nearby, a vulture gazes in with interest. As the day goes by, an odour begins to waft from the unsold meat. The flies become more active. There is only one thing for the butcher to do. In a small box on one side of the shop, he keeps a supply of salt. It's valuable, because it comes from a hundred miles away. But he can see that the meat is festering. He can see that if he does not act to preserve it, it will become useless, fit only for the flies and the vultures. So he takes out the salt and starts to rub it into the meat. As a result, decay is staved off: the meat remains edible.

In verse 13, Jesus tells his people, 'You are the salt of the earth'. It's a simple message with a very clear meaning. Coupled with the message of verses 14-16 – 'You are the light of the world' – he is telling us that if we are living as the people he has called us to be, we will make the world a completely different place. It is no accident that this passage immediately follows the Beatitudes. As kingdom people, who demonstrate the character of Jesus in our lives, we are blessed indeed; but we are not simply to sit around and enjoy being blessed, we are to go into action. At the same time, as we noted at the beginning of this chapter, there is an obvious connection between these verses and the final Beatitude. Living a truly and obviously Christian life will have a two-fold outcome: persecution for us, but blessing for the world. The persecution Jesus has just spoken of might make us feel that the Christian life isn't worth all the trouble it costs us; in that case, verses 13-16 will act as a powerful antidote.

These are, in fact, very challenging verses for us. As Christians (at least in the UK), we are fond of complaining about the state of society, the way that moral standards have slipped in recent decades and the widespread acceptance of evil around us. But if we are not fulfilling our calling to be salt and light, as Jesus describes us, what right do we have to blame a decaying world? Just as with the Beatitudes, the 'you' in verses 13-14 is emphatic. Jesus is telling us that *no other salt or light is available*. If we don't do the job, no-one else will. If the salt is not in contact with the meat, or (as Jesus says here) it has lost its saltiness; or if the light is concealed or dim, the responsibility can only be ours.

As we study this passage, we will break it down in the obvious way, looking first at salt and then at light. Then we will see how the two images combine.

Salt of the earth

'He's the salt of the earth' is an expression that is still used today, one of many that the Sermon on the Mount has passed into the English language. The way it is used colloquially is not quite the same as what Jesus means here. We tend to use the expression simply to mean that someone is a solid, dependable character, though perhaps with harmless eccentricities! Here in verse 13, Jesus means more than that. In a world where there is no refrigeration or air-conditioning, and where ice is a rarity unless you live on the slopes of Mount Hermon, salt is the only way of preserving meat or the fish you catch in the nearby Sea of Galilee. Jesus is telling his followers that the world needs them to be that preservative, slowing or preventing decay, keeping society more wholesome. That image, of course, implies certain assumptions. For a start, it assumes that the earth (the words 'earth' and 'world' are used interchangeably here) is a place of festering decay. To put it bluntly, it has a tendency to go bad. Jesus permits no illusions about the ability of humanity to create a better world unaided: the reverse is the case. Without the activity of the kingdom, human society – including the little corner of it that we are familiar with – is like a rotting corpse. The second assumption is that it *can* be preserved; it can be protected against decay and moral collapse. If that were not possible, Jesus would not have used this illustration.

So how do kingdom people function as salt? Clearly, the first requirement is that the salt must be in contact with the meat. In fact, it has to be in *very close* contact with the meat. We don't want to push this image too far, but all cooks know that when salt is rubbed into meat, the salt itself soon disappears. It does its work *invisibly*. (Modern cooks, of course, generally use salt for flavouring, not as a preservative, but the point still stands. It's unlikely that Jesus had flavouring in mind and it's probably not what his hearers would have thought of!) The picture that comes to mind, then, is of Christians dispersing into our communities and quietly, unobtrusively, even invisibly, doing the work of preserving society from rot and decay.

This might mean many things in practice. It begins with the attitude of seeking opportunities to do good in every situation. The most trivial action, done for the good of others and for the glory of God, contributes to our salty work. We can summarise it best by saying that being the salt of the earth means living out the character of the Beatitudes in close contact with the non-Christian world. Jesus says we are people who long for righteousness (5:6) – in society as well as within ourselves – so we will naturally get involved with issues of justice and integrity. That might mean being an activist for Fairtrade, or becoming a school governor, with all its opportunities for promoting God-pleasing curriculum content and ensuring good employment practices. Jesus says we are peacemakers (5:9) – so we will naturally become agents of reconciliation, whether among neighbours, in our work-places, at the school gate, or even in official mediation services. Jesus says we are merciful (5:7) – so we will naturally look out for those in difficulties and serve those who are weak.

In all these ways (and in countless smaller acts of daily goodness), we will be fulfilling our commission to preserve and enhance the health that remains in society. Many of these ideas require initiative and thought. They all require giving priority to the needs of others and a willingness to get our hands dirty. We are absolutely not to retreat from contact with the world we live in. The point is that acting as salt is an inescapable part of belonging to the kingdom of heaven.

So much for our responsibility: still in verse 13, Jesus now adds a warning. To understand this, we need to know that in Jesus' day, salt is obtained from the Dead Sea by evaporation. This is still done in our own time, but the difference is that in those days, the impurities cannot easily be removed from the salt. They are still mixed together when the salt reaches the consumer. Consequently, if the salt gets wet, the sodium chloride (the actual salt!) can be leached out, leaving the impurities behind. This residue might still *look* like salt, but it certainly isn't; and it certainly can't be restored to its original condition. It might be useful for filling in potholes for people to walk over, but it's useless for anything else[14].

That's the danger Jesus is warning of: that we might lose our kingdom distinctiveness and thereby become useless. Taken out of context, it might sound like a threat of losing our salvation. In the context of the Sermon on the Mount, however, it's clear that Jesus is simply pursuing the image of salt to press home to us the vital importance of retaining our kingdom distinctiveness. The rest of the Sermon will give a number of examples of how that might happen: we might be hypocritical in our giving or our prayer life or our fasting (6:1-18); we might be seduced by the attractions of this world and lose our focus on heavenly treasures (6:19-24); we might worry and fret just like the people around us (6:25-34). We are warned against all those things in turn: here in verse 13, Jesus is simply telling us, in summary, to make sure we remain *different*. The original meaning of the word translated 'loses its saltiness' (the verb *moraino*) is 'to be foolish'. Perhaps there is a suggestion that, as Don Carson puts it in his commentary on this verse, 'disciples who lose their savour are in fact making fools of themselves'. Un-salty Christians are useless, disobedient and foolish.

Note: Although most interpreters agree that Jesus is using the image of preservation here, it has also been suggested that he is really talking about *judgment*: that Christians, through their distinctive lives and uncompromising witness, are declaring judgment on the world that rejects both them and the gospel. 'Salt' is used in Scripture to represent a number of different things. Salt might be spread on land to curse it or to destroy its fertility (Judges 9:45). In Leviticus 2:13, God commands that salt be added to all the grain offerings. Salt is a reminder of the covenant God has made with his people (Numbers 18:19, 2 Chronicles 13:5). It seems to be the idea of salt making offerings acceptable that lies behind Mark 9:49 – 'everyone will be salted with fire', referring to the persecution that Christians (especially Mark's readers) can expect to undergo. But in the next verse, Jesus echoes Matthew 5:13 and then tells the disciples, 'Have salt in yourselves, and be at peace with each other', which in its context seems to refer to a special, distinctive quality they have as people of the kingdom, and which they must never lose. This understanding of Mark 9 supports the most natural reading of Matthew 5, which is the one that I have followed here.

Light of the world
Look now at verses 14-16. The image of light is both similar to and different from that of salt. Again, a little background will help us. Most of us live in cities or towns where it never gets properly dark. We are used to being able to find our way easily through the streets, even in the middle of the night. The situation in Jesus' day is very different. At night, deep darkness is everywhere: where light is available, it is both precious and very obvious. It has been suggested that the 'city on a hill' mentioned in verse 14 is a direct reference to the nearby Galilean town of Safed, which stood on a hilltop, three thousand feet above the lake. Perhaps as Jesus is speaking at this point, evening is drawing on and the first lights can be seen twinkling in the distance! Certainly, the lights of such a town would be visible at night from a great distance.

The illustration in verse 15 is of a more domestic variety. The point of a lamp, Jesus says, is to give light. There would obviously be no point in lighting an oil-lamp and then hiding it under a bowl (the word refers to a large grain container with a volume of around nine litres). The suggestion is absurd: lights are for lighting things up! Again, Jesus' use of this illustration – 'You are the light of the world' (5:14) – makes some important assumptions. The world is a place of darkness, he is saying. Remember, this is real darkness: in such darkness, people get lost, or they stumble and fall. That is how people are in their natural state: lost, spiritually in darkness, in desperate need of light. And this dark world cannot solve its own problem: just as it could not prevent its own decay, so it cannot illuminate itself.

So the image of light is similar to that of salt, in that both represent the benefit that kingdom people will bring to the world they live in. But there are significant differences too. Whereas salt does its work invisibly, the opposite is true (by definition) of light. And while the action of salt requires close contact, a certain separation is necessary for light to do its illuminating work. This means that the people of the kingdom must be recognisably *separate* from the world. The fact that Jesus uses two images of light, on very different scales, suggests that the city represents the *corporate* witness of believers and the household lamp stands for the witness of the *individual*.

What is really striking about Jesus' statement is that it's exactly what he says about himself in John 8:12. The promise is that whoever follows him will no longer be in darkness but will have the light that is life. Yet verse 14 says, in effect, '*only* you' are the light of the world. That clearly implies that the light of Jesus, after the conclusion of his earthly ministry, is to be seen only through his people. We are to be little Christs (which is what 'Christian' means). Without us, the saving light of Christ is extinguished. A similar connection is made in Ephesians 5:8-14. We have been illuminated by his light; we are now 'light in the Lord' (5:8); by means of this light, we are to expose the deeds of darkness (5:11), which amounts to convicting people of their sin. More than that, there is no other such light for the world: no light in other religions, no light in philosophy, no light in intellectual achievements, no light in scientific progress. The claims of Christ are absolutely exclusive – and, Jesus says, they can be seen and heard only through us.

Jesus gives a specific reason for this clear witness in verse 16. We don't visibly maintain our Christian identity and declare its message just for its own sake; we do it so that as people see the good deeds that we do[15] – the Greek word (*kalos*) specifically suggests attractive or beautiful rather than morally good – they will respond by praising our heavenly Father. Now what does that suggest? Jesus has just been talking about persecution as the characteristic response of the unbelieving world. Yet here he is talking about the world praising God for us! That surely implies a response of faith – that the people who see our attractive works may go on to understand who we are and will respond by trusting in Christ for themselves. This connection is made absolutely explicit in John 15:8 and 1 Peter 2:12. In other words, our objective as lights for the world is to win people for the kingdom! Deeds alone are not enough for that. The slogan popular in some Christian circles – 'Preach the gospel: if necessary use words' (often attributed to Francis of Assisi, but probably wrongly) is seriously misleading. Gospel deeds require gospel words to interpret them; and no-one will ever come to praise our Father, to know him for themselves, without the words of life which point directly to Christ.

Now, if we are to be lights of the world, two things are necessary. The light must be *shining*, and the light must be *visible*. The first requires us to hold to the gospel accurately and declare it faithfully, whether in our churches or individually. Holding out a flawed or deficient version of the gospel – one that denies the uniqueness of Christ as Saviour, ignores the reality of judgment or omits the call for repentance, for example – is the equivalent of turning out the lights[16]. The second requires that we let people see the light. If our gospel activity is confined to meetings within the walls of our buildings, using obsolete language and doing nothing to welcome the unchurched outsider, let us not fool ourselves: we are not the light of the world. We are fulfilling the Lord's mandate only to the extent that the world can *see* the light.

Two pictures – one discipleship
The pictures of salt and light are not alternatives: they are complementary. As faithful followers of Christ, we need to be mixing directly with the world (salt) while also remaining holy (light). Christians have often got the balance wrong. If we emphasise 'mixing with the world' too strongly, we are likely to forget about holiness. In terms of Jesus' imagery, actually, that amounts to losing our saltiness. It is useless to be engaged in social action if we abandon the distinctiveness that is our identity as kingdom people. On the other hand, if we emphasise holiness to the exclusion of mixing with the world (and let's be honest, that is sometimes out of

cowardice or indifference, not for any theological reason!), the light we think we are shining will actually be invisible and do no-one any good.

We need to be both salt and light. In our churches, that means active social engagement, becoming directly involved with the suffering and needy in the communities we serve. As churches, we can use our louder corporate voice to agitate for just and righteous laws and practices; we can run projects where the love of Christ is demonstrated; we can support similar activities across the world. But let us also make sure that the light of the gospel is clearly visible in those projects of mercy; and let us also ensure that our gospel proclamation from pulpit and on the street corners is pure and clear. As individuals or smaller groups, we can serve our neighbourhoods, our schools, our offices. Such action will often be completely invisible outside our immediate circle, but still we are obeying the Lord's call upon us. And as the opportunity arises, may we always be ready to point people to the Saviour who has called us.

Questions to reflect on or discuss

1. Have you ever experienced persecution for the name of Jesus (rather than for being awkward, strange or difficult!)? If you have, what form did it take – and do Jesus' words in 5:10-12 ring true for you? If you have not, why do you think that is?

2. Have you faced up to the fact that Jesus did not save you in order to give you an easy life? And that trouble and persecution are perfectly normal for Christians?

3. Are you convinced that the benefits associated with persecution are enough to make it a 'blessing'?

4. What can you do to support Christians who are being severely persecuted, perhaps in a different part of the world from you?

5. In what areas do you act as effective 'salt of the earth', and how could you be more effective?

6. In what ways do you (and your church) act as 'the light of the world'? Is the light clearly visible, or is it hidden by some obstruction?

Chapter 5
Jesus and the law
Matthew 5:17-20

A good friend of mine is a civil servant in the Department for Transport in London. He works in finance, which never sounds very exciting to me, but he seems to enjoy it! When David and his family came to visit us recently, one issue was looming large in his mind. The 2010 general election was approaching; the economic outlook was not good; and it seemed certain that serious cuts to his department were inevitable. I remember discussing his future as we walked our dog across the fields. At this point David was not sure how all this would work out. He didn't know how his own position would be affected: whether he would still have a job after the election or whether he would lose it. He didn't know how much would change and how much would remain the same. But he *did* know that the election was the crucial event on which his future career would turn.

That May, election day arrived. The new government took office and the situation became a little clearer. We had known what they had been promising. Now we knew what they were actually going to do. Not everything would change: we would still need a Department for Transport; we would still need some people to run it. But everything else seemed to be up for grabs. After a few months it became clear exactly how those plans would be fulfilled. I had an email from David. He was being interviewed for his own post. A number of managers at his level would lose their jobs and the finance area was to be hit particularly hard. More months passed, and I had another email. David had kept his job, but many others had indeed lost theirs. For better or worse, the promises and the plans were being fulfilled.

The Kingdom Manifesto

Now this story is a little bit like what Jesus is talking about in Matthew 5:17-20. He speaks of a past time, a time of promises made and plans laid out. It was a time when people looked ahead, wondering exactly how those plans would work out. Jesus speaks also of a day on which the story of the whole world depended, a day when everything would change and yet some landmarks would remain. And he speaks of the way in which those promises and plans are being fulfilled *now*. Jesus, of course, is not talking about politics but about the plans and purposes of God. He is talking about the greatest story of all – the story of God's salvation plan. Above all, he is talking about himself.

By common consent these are regarded as some of the most difficult verses in the whole New Testament. There is plenty in the Sermon on the Mount that is difficult for us to *do*; these verses are difficult for us to *understand* as well, but we are going to do our best. Jesus is talking about the Law that God gave his people through Moses, and what that Law means for us today. We have to admit at the outset that Christians have very often been confused about this subject. Today, even among evangelicals, there are widely differing views about the place of the Law for Christians. We will deal with some of those differences in this chapter, though we will only be able to scratch the surface of what is a massive subject.

The New Testament makes many statements about the Law, and at first glance they don't all seem to agree. Yet what we say about Matthew 5:17-20 – and that of course is my main business here – has to take all those other references into account as well, and that is not easy. Christians have found themselves asking all kinds of questions about the Law of Moses. Do we still have to obey it, or does it have nothing to do with us? How is it that we still quote the Ten Commandments, which are part of the Law, but we don't stick to kosher food, which is also part of the Law? God *said* it, so why don't we *do* it? Why do we eat pork when the Law forbids it? For that matter, why don't we make animal sacrifices? It's confusing – and some would say, this passage doesn't help very much. We shall see!

So far, in 5:1-16, we have really only looked at the introduction to the Sermon on the Mount. That first section has introduced us to who we are as God's people and what our lives should look like. Now we are entering the main body of the Sermon on the Mount, which runs through to 7:12.

Jesus and the law

It is bracketed by the two references to the Law and the Prophets, which were so vitally important for the Jews – a structure known as an inclusion (or *inclusio*). The very fact that the Sermon on the Mount – the manifesto of Christ's kingdom – is structured in this way signals that the Law's significance is by no means confined to the Jews. More immediately, verses 17-20 lead into a series of six specific cases which Jesus goes on to talk about in the rest of chapter 5 – murder, adultery, divorce, taking oaths, justice, and love for enemies. When we come to those six case studies, we will find that Jesus is applying and working out in practice the principles which he has first given us in 5:17-20.

We will begin by summarising what Jesus is saying in these verses, then we will work through it and unpack exactly what he is getting at. As we do that, we will touch on some of the disagreements about how Christians should understand the New Testament's teaching on the Law. Finally we will ask what difference this ought to make to our lives. So to begin with, to help us get the basic message into our minds, let me give you this summary. By doing this, I'm assuming the answers to some of the questions we will be asking, but I think it is helpful to have a concise summary at the outset. Here it is:

"Jesus has come to fulfil the Old Testament, not to abolish it – in fact the Law will endure in every detail as long as the present universe. *Therefore* we must keep (and teach) every element of the Law as fulfilled by Jesus. *Because*, if we don't, we won't enter the kingdom."

Those are the essentials of what Jesus says here. Now with that in mind, let's work through the passage in more detail.

Jesus has come to fulfil the Old Testament

Look at verses 17-18. Why does Jesus choose to say this now? Why might people suppose his aim *was* to abolish the Law? The reason is that Jesus' teaching is so different from what they are used to. The Jewish religious teachers talk endlessly and obsessively about the details of the Law and precisely how to interpret it. They spend their time quoting one authority after another and issuing rulings about how this or that aspect of the Law should be obeyed. As we will see, that is not Jesus' style! And more than that, it is likely that there is already some official suspicion of

Jesus' attitude to the Law. Very early in his ministry he begins to tangle with the official line, especially on the Sabbath rules.

So it's quite natural that both officials and the ordinary people are thinking that Jesus is indeed setting out to abolish the Law. In fact, 'the Law and the Prophets' is a standard way of describing the whole of the Jewish Scriptures, what we know as the Old Testament (for other uses of this expression, see for instance Matthew 11:13 or Romans 3:21). People are suspecting that Jesus is making a clean break from the Old Testament. Actually, that is exactly what a lot of Christians think today – that because we have Jesus, we don't need the Old Testament any more – it's obsolete, it's finished! Most would not say so outright, but they still struggle to see the point of the Old Testament. If they read it at all, they don't know what to do with it.

But Jesus says, Not at all. 'I have not come to abolish them but to *fulfil* them'. The key word here is 'fulfil'. It means to bring something to its intended outcome, its full fruition. When a government gets elected and carries out its promises – which sometimes happens! – we say those promises have been *fulfilled*. They have been put into effect as intended by those who made them. In the same way, says Jesus, the Old Testament plans and promises have all been put into effect in *him* (2 Corinthians 1:20).

Now what does that mean? Actually, Jesus fulfilling the Law and the Prophets means many things. It means, for instance, that the *prophecies* that were made about him have come true. Think of some of the passages in Isaiah, for instance: 'for to us a child is born' (Isaiah 9:2-7), 'a shoot will come up from the stump of Jesse' (Isaiah 11:1-5), 'he was pierced for our transgressions' (Isaiah 52:13-53:12) – along with many others: direct prophecies about Jesus, the coming Saviour, the suffering Servant, the conquering King – they are all wonderfully *fulfilled* in him.

But this idea of 'fulfilling' goes much wider than those *direct* prophecies. The Old Testament is full of pictures, what we call *types* (from the Greek word tupos, meaning 'form' or 'pattern'), that illustrate various aspects of Christ's ministry and point forward to him. The sacrificed lambs of Passover; the High Priest who ministers at the altar; David the great king, were all real, they all happened; but they are all pictures that prepare the way for Christ. And he fulfils all of those as well, because he is the true Passover lamb; he is the everlasting High Priest; and he is the perfect and righteous King of his people. The technical term for this is that Christ is the *antitype* to all those Old Testament *types*.

There are many other aspects to Christ's fulfilling the Law and the Prophets, not least the fact that in his own life he obeyed the Law perfectly. Clearly, however, what Jesus is mainly talking about here is the way that his *teaching* fulfils the Law. And in the rest of this passage (5:18-20) it is the Law and its commands that he focuses on. The whole Sermon on the Mount is Jesus *teaching* us the ways of the kingdom. So when Jesus says he is fulfilling the Law, what he means is this. He is giving us his own new interpretation of the Law. It is *absolutely* true to the Law's original intention, but it takes account of his own unique role in God's plans. With Jesus, the Law of Moses is not abolished. It is brought to its intended outcome. It is fulfilled.

Jesus hammers home this point in verse 18. Do you want to know how long the Law will remain, he asks. The Law – the *entire* Law – will endure as long as this present universe continues to exist. After that's finished, the Law won't be needed because in the new heavens and earth there will be no sin! It is God's Word and it's as permanent as that. Not the smallest letter – that would refer to the Hebrew letter *yodh*, which is written as a little comma in mid-air; not the smallest stroke of a pen – that would refer to a little tail which distinguishes some Hebrew letters from one another so you can tell them apart – in other words, not the minutest element of the Law will be lost. It's an unmistakable message. The Law of Moses *stands*.

Therefore we must keep the Law

So now we move on to the second stage of what Jesus says. Look at verse 19. Some of the commandments may be more vital, carry greater weight, than others; but, Jesus says, if you neglect even the *least* of them, you will be counted as *least* in the kingdom. If you encourage others to neglect the least commandment, you will be counted as least yourself. But on the other hand, if you do them all faithfully, and you encourage others to do the same, you will be counted as great in the kingdom. It all follows on quite logically from what Jesus has said just now. The Law still stands, it has not been abolished – therefore we must keep the Law.

The Kingdom Manifesto

This at once rules out the view known as antinomianism, the idea that picks up on the more negative comments about the Law elsewhere in the New Testament, especially in Galatians (such as 3:2-3, 10-13, 23-25, 4:21ff, 5:6-18) and concludes that Christians should have nothing to do with the Law. We have been set free from the ways of the Law and are led purely and simply by the Spirit. There is no Law that is binding on Christians. Very few Bible-believing Christians would go that far, but the idea is widespread that apart from the Ten Commandments, the Law of Moses has little relevance to Christians. Galatians itself, of course, does not say that. Paul wrote the letter to persuade the Galatian churches to resist the false teaching which told them that *salvation itself* comes through obedience to the Law (the specific issue being over circumcision). Paul insists that the gift of salvation is received only through faith in Christ, not by complying with the Law. That is very different from saying that the Law has nothing to say to us once we are trusting in Christ for salvation. The Law remains what it has always been – an expression of God's glorious character. It should therefore be inconceivable for Christians to regard it as obsolete.

Antinomianism is also widely found in a softer form, which says that the Law has only an advisory capacity for us today. According to one description I read, the Law is 'like a retired professor – useful to consult for advice, but he no longer sets the exams'. We have to say that such a view cannot be squared with Jesus' words in Matthew 5:19. Jesus is clearly speaking of obedience to the Law, not merely asking it politely for advice!

But hang on a minute, you might be thinking! We must keep the Law? What are you talking about? Do you realise what's in the Law? It's not just the food laws – no pork (Leviticus 11:7), no shellfish (Leviticus 11:9-12) and all the rest of it. If I have a bit of eczema, or dermatitis, do I have to go and live alone in the countryside (Leviticus 13:45-46, Numbers 5:1-4)? Not to mention all the other embarrassing ways the Law said you could become unclean (Leviticus 15)! Are we clamouring for the death penalty for adultery (Leviticus 20:10) or for gay sex (Leviticus 20:13) or for blasphemy (Leviticus 24:15-16)? It's in the Law! What about this shirt I'm wearing? Are there any mixed fabrics? It'll have to go (Leviticus 19:19). And by the way, I don't see any blood-spattered altar in my church! How can we possibly say – how can Jesus possibly mean – that we must keep the Law?

Jesus and the law

Let's try and find some answers to these difficult questions. Jesus has *fulfilled* the Law. That does *not* mean he has left it untouched. Look at verse 19 again. When Jesus says *'these* commandments', he is probably referring in the first place to his own teachings in the Sermon on the Mount and elsewhere, starting with the six case studies which follow on from this passage. In those cases, Jesus doesn't leave the commands of the Law untouched, as we will see when we look at them in detail. Instead, he tells us exactly how they will now apply to us. So in those six cases at least, it is clear that Jesus is not demanding that we obey every detail of the Law in its original form. But by extension, it would seem that 'these commandments' covers the *entire* Mosaic Law. There is no reason in this passage why this should not be the case. So let's look at how kingdom people – Christians – are to keep the Law, according to the New Testament.

Think first about those sacrifices – the sin offerings, the burnt offerings, which the Law prescribes and which the Jews observed for all those centuries. We don't still keep those, do we? Yes we do – we keep the sacrifices *as Jesus has fulfilled them*. Jesus is THE sacrifice for sin – and so as we put our trust in him, the one who takes away our sin; as we look to him on the cross, slaughtered in our place, we are *keeping* the Laws of sacrifice. Hebrews 7 to 10 has a great deal to say about Christ fulfilling the sacrificial types. We keep the *Passover* laws as Christ fulfilled them, no longer with the blood of a lamb but with the blood of Jesus[17]. The Law is not abolished, it is *fulfilled.*

But what about those food laws? Surely we don't keep those? Yes we do – as Jesus has fulfilled them. The food laws were given mainly to teach lessons about purity and holiness, and they have done their job[18]. Jesus explicitly declared all foods clean – Mark 7:19. We can eat *whatever* we like – it's part of a Christian's freedom – oysters, black pudding, ham sandwiches and a glass of chardonnay. In that sense, the rules about food do not apply any more. But that doesn't mean the food laws are abolished: in fact we keep them in the *fulfilled* sense of living pure and holy lives, clean lives – which is exactly what Jesus is talking about in Mark 7.

What about those civil laws, as they are called – the laws about legal penalties, crime and punishment? Those laws were originally given to a unique nation, the people of Israel. And today, after Christ, God's people are no longer a political entity here on earth. The church – made up of believing Jews alongside believing Gentiles – is the new Israel (Galatians 6:16); and as you might guess from that, the civil laws of Israel are fulfilled in the church. This is not explained in the Sermon on the Mount, but it is made clear in a number of passages in Paul's letters. A good example is 1 Corinthians 5, where Paul talks about church discipline. The problem is being caused by an illicit sexual relationship within the church in Corinth. Under the Law, such a relationship would be punishable by death. Paul instructs the Corinthians not to execute the offender, but to put him out of the church. Yet the text he quotes in support (1 Corinthians 5:13) is the one repeatedly used in the Law to command the Israelites to execute law-breakers (Deuteronomy 17:7, 19:19, 21:21, 22:21,24, 24:7). Exclusion from God's people by execution has become exclusion from God's people by excommunication. The Law still applies[19]. Further examples are found in 1 Corinthians 9:9 and 1 Timothy 5:18 where Paul talks about not muzzling an ox. That command is in the Law (Deuteronomy 25:4) – but he deliberately applies it to ministers in the church!

We keep the Law, the *whole* Law, in its fulfilled sense. Some Christians would say that the Ten Commandments remain untouched by the ministry of Jesus and remain exactly as before, but it is evident that even the Ten Commandments are fulfilled by Christ. Later in chapter 5 we will see that two of them – about murder and adultery – are expanded by Jesus right here; they are raised to new heights. Moreover, Jesus gives the Sabbath command new clarity (Matthew 12:1-14), and later on the New Testament gives it a new dimension – that's in Hebrews 4.

At this point it is worth saying a little more about what many Christians understand as the 'three-fold division' of the Law. This means that the Law of Moses falls into three categories: there is the moral law (mainly the Ten Commandments); the ceremonial law (mainly the sacrificial system) and the civil law. It has often been taught, and in some branches of the church it still is (especially among Presbyterians), that Scripture itself recognises this three-fold division and clearly teaches that the moral law still stands, that the ceremonial law is abolished and that the relevance of the civil law essentially finished with the end of the theocracy of Israel.

Although there is a great deal of this truth in this view, and it has behind it the immense weight of the Westminster Confession, I think it is important to add a caveat. Throughout Scripture, when the Law of

Moses is referred to, it always appears to refer to the whole Law. There is no clear sense of a division. True, the Ten Commandments have primacy of place and only they were placed in the Ark of the Covenant; but that does not amount to support for a three-fold division. Later, the prophets summon the people to obey the entire Law, emphasising one aspect or another according to the besetting sins of the time. Amos, for example, lays special stress on the sin of injustice, which is not explicitly addressed in the Ten Commandments. And in Matthew 5, among Jesus' six examples of applying the Law for us, two relate to the Ten Commandments and the other four do not – or at least, not directly. He deals with them all in the same way. As we have already seen, even the moral law does not continue untouched; it, too, finds fulfilment and fresh application in Christ. I would therefore want to say that the three-fold division of the Law can be seen only with hindsight; and also that the three divisions are not really as distinct as is often claimed[20].

The key point to grasp in this discussion is this: *the Law still stands.* Jesus makes it crystal clear that we are to obey the Law; but it's the Law as fulfilled by his ministry. Now on to the third point of Jesus' message.

If we fail to keep the Law, we are out of the kingdom

Look at verse 20. If verse19 was a shock to *us*, verse 20 would have blown Jesus' first hearers right out of the water! The Pharisees and teachers of the law, or scribes, are the pace-setters as far as the Law was concerned. As the common people see it, the Pharisees are the standard-bearers of righteousness and the teachers of the law are the authorities who tell you how it is done.

The Pharisees have done a very thorough job on the Law of Moses, as you may know. They have carefully worked out that the Law contains 613 commands, and 365 of those are negative – which would mean one prohibition for every day of the year. I don't know what happens in leap years! Then they have added double protection by surrounding those genuine commands with lots of additional rules to make sure that you cannot inadvertently break any of the original ones. In a way, that's a great idea. It is good to be concerned about doing God's will! The real problem is that this passion for the Law has taken them in completely the wrong direction. By focusing on a great compendium of regulations, they have ended up measuring their righteousness by ticking off the rules. They have completely forgotten that obedience to God is supposed to come from the heart.

As far as Jesus is concerned, the religion of the Pharisees has gone disastrously wrong. Instead of seeking a pure heart, they are concerned about external appearances. Their priority is to have everything looking right on the outside, to *look* right, to *look* good. For that reason they are often proud and self-satisfied. That's why Jesus spends so much time and energy criticising them for their hypocritical emptiness. We have to say that the Pharisees represent so many people and so many religions, even today, who believe that pleasing God is about counting up your good deeds and hoping that he will accept you. If you are not a Christian, then that is probably what you are doing right now. But that's not the way! You can't please God by a good performance. You don't get into heaven on the basis of your track record.

So these people who were thought of as a byword for righteousness were in reality not righteous at all. That's how we need to understand this verse. Jesus is *not* saying, You see those guys: they are great, they're terrific, now you have to go and do even better! No, what he is saying is: you see those guys – they've got it all wrong – you have to go away and be completely *different*! The Pharisees are not in the kingdom, because they are not really keeping the Law at all. They are a terrible warning to us for any time when we start to measure our own goodness against a checklist of rules. The righteousness we are called to have 'surpasses' theirs not by being similar but better, but by being completely different. It's the righteousness that we have already seen in the Beatitudes[21]. We saw there that righteousness means being like Jesus, complete with his mercy, his purity, his peacemaking. This righteousness is not something we can conjure up for ourselves. In fact, as Christians we know very well that we can't live the life God calls us to through our own efforts. That was exactly the message of the Beatitudes. Blessed are the poor in spirit, the people who know they have nothing to offer to God – because *they* are the kingdom people!

It is vital that we understand this difference between the righteousness of the Pharisees and the righteousness we are called to in Christ. The former is legalism. Legalism means obeying a system of laws in order to win merit – to earn points with God. But obeying God's laws joyfully, out of a renewed heart, is not legalism. That's a common misunderstanding among Christians today. It is simply the Christian life as it is meant to be lived.

That, then, is the essential message of these four verses – so let's return to that summary just to remind us again: "Jesus has come to fulfil the Old Testament, not to abolish it – in fact the Law will endure in every detail as long as the present universe. *Therefore* we must keep (and teach) every element of the Law as fulfilled by Jesus. *Because*, if we don't, we won't enter the kingdom."

What does this mean for us?

What does all this mean for us? In short, what it means is that Jesus is the key to everything! Let's unpack that in three ways.

Jesus is the key to God's purposes
Do you see what an incredible claim Jesus makes here? The 'Law and the Prophets' is God's Word! For Jesus to say that he is the one who *fulfils* them, the one they all point to, is absolutely staggering. As Christians, we tend to take this for granted. But think what the Jews must have felt when they heard him say it! The Law meant everything to them. Children learned to read and write by copying it out and studying it. Written sayings from the Law were tied to people's hands and foreheads and inscribed on their gates and doors. The highest calling a man could have was to learn and to teach God's Law. It was handled with the utmost reverence and when the scrolls it was written on eventually wore out they were not burned but laid respectfully to rest. Now Jesus comes along and says, *It's all about me.*

Still today, that is the message for us. Throughout past history, everything looked *forward* to the coming Christ. Since he came, everything looks *back* to him. He is the key to God's purposes – totally unique, God's final word. He is not one more prophet in a long line of prophets. He is not one more guru or wise teacher. As he speaks, he does not say, as the prophets did, 'Thus says the Lord'. He says, '*I* tell you'. '*I* tell you', with all the authority of one who is himself very God. When Jesus speaks, we don't just stop and listen. When Jesus speaks, we are in the presence of God. And with his coming, the focal point of human history has come,

The Kingdom Manifesto

God's purposes are unlocked, salvation has arrived, God's new humanity is created and heaven is secured. Jesus is the key to God's purposes. Do you know him?

Jesus is the key to the Bible
This follows on from the previous point. The Law and the Prophets all find their fulfilment in Jesus. That makes Jesus the key to the Old Testament and it makes the Old Testament absolutely essential for us. How many of us have tried to read the Old Testament and got stuck somewhere in Leviticus, confused and frankly bored by the endless descriptions of sacrifices? But read Leviticus with *Jesus* in mind, thinking of how *he* is the perfect and final sacrifice, and it will seem completely different. Think of him as the one who fulfils them all, and it all makes sense.

Read the story of the Day of Atonement in Leviticus 16, that one day a year when the High Priest entered the Most Holy Place in the Tabernacle carrying the blood, while all the people watch and wonder whether he will come out again alive. Read those perhaps puzzling details about the goat sent out into the wilderness on that day – and then read it again thinking of *Christ*, who came into the world to carry our sins far away. And as you think of the Israelites coming back to that ceremony year after year, and knowing as they did so that next year they would all be back again, repeating the same process yet again, give thanks to God for the one who came, who has presented the perfect sacrifice in his own blood, that needs *never* be repeated. The whole Old Testament is full of Christ; and knowing that brings the whole Old Testament to life.

More than that, if we understand the Old Testament through Christ, it will give us a whole new experience of reading the *New* Testament. Whole swathes of the New Testament only really make sense when we know the back story from the Old; and it is Christ who holds old and new together. He is the key to the Bible.

Jesus is the key to obedience
You might be thinking, I still don't get this. Surely the New Testament says – Paul says – we are not under law, we are under grace (Romans 6:14)? Yes, he does say that. Yes, as Christians, as the people of Jesus, we are free from the law's *judgment*, free from its *condemnation*, free from its *penalty*. If we are trusting in Christ, we are safe and secure in him because of the cross. Jesus took the Law's condemnation, with the complete list of all our horrible sins and offences, and nailed it all to the

cross (Colossians 2:13-14). It has no power to condemn us any more. The guilt is all gone. That is wonderful and true: that is the grace of God in Christ.

So we are not 'under law'. We are free people. But the Law, as fulfilled by Christ, still stands as God's will for his people to obey. We could never do that by ourselves – our inability is what Paul laments in Romans 7. But Christ has bought us the power to keep the Law. We are set free by Christ, not to *ignore* the Law, not to *abolish* the Law, but to obey it in a way that pleases him. In the remainder of chapter 5, we will find a series of examples to show how this works out in practice. Keeping the Law means living like Jesus. And because of Jesus, because we are now a new creation in him, because we have the Spirit within us, we now *want* to obey him from our hearts – and thanks to him, we can!

Questions to reflect on or discuss

1. Have you come across the idea that the Law of Moses has nothing to do with us today, or that we only need it as a helpful advisor? Does Matthew 5:17-20 give an effective answer to that teaching and if so, how?

2. Is the idea of reading the Old Testament (especially the Law) with Christ in mind a new one to you? How important do you think this is for bringing the Old and New Testaments together?

3. How do you respond to the thought that because of the Holy Spirit within us, we now have the power to obey God's Law in a way that was never possible before the ministry of Christ?

Chapter 6
You have heard it said... Part 1
Matthew 5:21-32

You have heard it said... Murder

It's the day you have been dreading, the day of your trial. You are sitting in a heavily-protected prison van, arriving at the Crown Court, under the archway, out of the van and into the building. They escort you along the corridor, inside the courtroom and finally into the dock to face your trial. All eyes turn as you take your place. The evidence is read out. The witnesses are called. Your barrister does his best in your defence, but really there is not much he can say. It is an open and shut case. The jury retire to consider their verdict; it doesn't take them long. Finally, the judge turns to you and declares the sentence. 'This court has found you guilty as charged, that on 7th January you had angry thoughts against your next-door neighbour and wished him harm. Anger is a serious crime; and none of the circumstances you have quoted provides any mitigation. I have no alternative but to sentence you to life imprisonment.' And they take you away to face the consequences of your crime. It sounds like a nightmare. How could *anger* be considered a crime? How could a court possibly put you on trial for being angry? The answer, of course, is that it couldn't; and anger is not a criminal offence – at least, not according to English law. But according to Jesus, the picture is very different. According to Jesus, in the sight of God anger is as much of a sin as murder, and the consequences for the offender are just as serious.

In the previous chapter we looked at that difficult passage in 5:17-20 about Jesus and the Law of Moses. We saw that the Law is not abolished by Jesus, it is fulfilled – which means that Jesus brings the Law to its intended outcome. Jesus gives the Law his own fresh interpretation. He has the authority to do that. It is absolutely true to the Law's original intention, but it takes account of his own unique role in God's plans. Now: that's all very well, but what does it mean in practice? Well, verses 17-20 are just the beginning. Those verses introduce six specific cases which fill the rest of chapter 5. In the rest of the chapter, Jesus is setting out the realities of living as kingdom people, *his* people. Six specific examples – about murder, adultery, divorce, oaths, retribution and enemies.

As we look at those one at a time – three in this chapter, three in the next, just to keep the chapters to a digestible length – we will see that each one of them impacts a huge area of life. They sound quite narrow, when you just list them like that, but it's not so. In each case, Jesus follows a very similar pattern. 'You have heard that it was said... but *I* say to you.' In verses 21-26, we are looking at the first of these: murder. It will sound shocking. We'll break the passage down into three little sections.

Anger is as bad as murder
Look at verse 21. Jesus is restating the sixth commandment, directly from Exodus 20:13. This is what the Israelites heard at Mount Sinai, 1500 years before. Then he summarises the provisions that were made for bringing people to justice, such as Exodus 21:12-14. That is what they have heard from long ago; and it's true. So Jesus reminds them; and no doubt there is much nodding of heads. This is familiar ground. But now comes the shock: 'But *I* tell you'. In the Greek, the 'I' in this six times repeated formula is very emphatic. That's what you have heard – but this is what *I* tell you. Immediately we are confronted with Jesus' towering authority. No rabbi would dream of speaking like this. Those opening four words in themselves are enough to demand a response. Everyone who hears Jesus speak has to decide: does he have any *right* to speak like this? If he does, then we have to submit to his authority. Now what is he going to say? Here comes our first example of 'fulfilling the Law'. Jesus *doesn't* contradict the Law. He *doesn't* contradict what the Old Testament says. Instead he makes the demand of the Law higher, deeper, broader – verse 22.

There are three elements to what Jesus says in this verse. The second one needs a bit of explanation. This word 'Raca' is a bit of a mystery.

You have heard it said ... Part 1

It is probably an Aramaic word (Aramaic being the language Jesus was actually speaking) meaning something like 'empty-headed' or, as Morris suggests, 'numbskull'. It's a contemptuous insult of some sort. The 'Sanhedrin' is the highest court in the land: it is the assembly of Jewish leaders. In Israel, which was a theocracy, to be condemned by the Sanhedrin meant that you were condemned by God himself; so invoking the Sanhedrin is Jesus' way of underlining the seriousness of the insult.

Some commentators have looked at these three sayings and tried to distinguish between them, as if Jesus is describing an ascending scale of seriousness or laying down different penalties for different kinds of anger. They have tried to work out whether the word 'Raca' is more or less serious than 'fool'. I don't think that makes sense; and in any case we can't really imagine Jesus, from all we know of him, nit-picking over different penalties for different insults. 'If you say 'Raca', this will happen; if you say 'fool', that will happen.' We can imagine the Pharisees arguing like that, but not Jesus! No: what Jesus is doing, like any good preacher, is hammering home his point by stating it in three different ways. If you're angry with your brother – you're in trouble. If you call him an *idiot* – and you really mean it – you're in trouble. If you call him a *fool* – you're in trouble. Eternal trouble, in danger of hell fire[22]. Why does he talk about 'a brother'? Remember Jesus is speaking to *disciples*. This is ethics for believers, not for the world in general. So his main concern is about relationships within the kingdom, relationships between spiritual brothers and sisters. But if it is a sin to be angry with a brother, it follows that the same must be true of our attitude to those outside the kingdom as well.

What is really striking here is the parallel between judgment for *murder*, in verse 21, and judgment for *anger*, in verse 22. Jesus deliberately uses exactly the same words. That tells us unmistakably that God views anger in the same light as murder. Anger is as bad as murder: that's the shock. Jesus is speaking to people who know God's commands. Of course they know the command 'Do not murder'. But according to the leading authorities of the day, as long as you haven't actually killed someone you have kept that command. You could hate someone for life, you could wish they were dead, but as long as you haven't actually lifted your hand against them, you are in the clear. Jesus is saying, Look, this is what God really intends. It's not enough not to kill someone. If you are angry, if you hate them, it's just as bad.

We need to sense the full force of what Jesus is saying. He is talking about the anger in our hearts that wants to strike out and hurt or destroy, but thinks it's OK because no-one ever sees it. He is telling us that God sees it, and God condemns it – even down to the cross words and fits of irritation that we think are perfectly normal. But straight away we are probably thinking, Hold on, surely not all anger is wrong? Surely Jesus *himself* was angry at times? Yes, that is true. On several occasions in the gospels we read about Jesus being angry. He is angry with the people who are selling in the temple courts (John 2:15-16), angry with the stubborn blindness he meets among the religious leaders (Mark 3:5a), angry with their hypocrisy (Matthew 23:17). Jesus gets angry, but what kind of anger is this? Is he ever angry on his own account, for his own sake? When he is insulted, scorned, mocked – crucified? Luke 23:33-34 tells us. He suffers the world's greatest ever injustice, the only innocent man the world has ever seen is condemned to torture and death – and he is not angry. He loves and forgives. But is Jesus angry about sin and its poisonous effects in people's lives? Yes, absolutely. And that's the key. What Jesus is speaking of here in Matthew 5 is the kind of anger that takes offence, the anger that leads to hatred, the anger that is ultimately the seed of murder (1 John 3:15)[2]. Next we can see how that kind of anger works out, as Jesus goes on to apply it in two specific ways. You see he changes at this point from 'anyone' to '*you*', making the message more direct and personal.

Anger is as bad as murder – so, make peace before worship
Look at verses 23-24. Here's the scenario. You have gone up to the temple to worship and to make one of the offerings which the Law prescribes. You're in the middle of doing that, and suddenly you remember that there's a problem. You've offended one of your friends. What do you do? Jesus says, everything stops until you sort that problem out. You leave your gift – which might actually be a live animal! – standing in front of the altar while you scuttle off to put things right with your brother. Notice that in this case, Jesus says, *he* is angry with *you* – the assumption is that *you've* provoked *him*. So it's not just our own anger that's a problem, it's also that we infuriate other people. Then, once you have put things right, you can return to worship God. Hopefully your gift hasn't wandered off somewhere in the meantime!

Now do you see how strong this is? Jesus is speaking in Galilee. For his hearers, the trip up to the temple in Jerusalem is the highlight of their year. This is not some casual event where you wander in and out as you please. The temple is the very heart of Jewish life – to interrupt that rare opportunity of worship, sacrifice and offering is almost unthinkable. But that's what Jesus is saying. You have to be at peace with your brother before you can worship God.

Anger is as bad as murder – so, make peace or be judged
Look at verses 25-26. This time, someone is taking you to court. He's going to sue you – you're about to lose everything. Jesus pictures the sequence of events as you are sentenced by the judge, handed over to the court officer and hauled away to prison. In fact the picture is a debtor's prison – we used to have them in Britain until fairly recently – where you would be locked away until somehow you could pay everything you owed. On one level, this is simply common sense for everyday life. Stay out of trouble. If you've got a problem with your next-door neighbour, be reconciled if you can. Don't let it escalate to the point where the courts get involved. But in the context of this passage, the saying has far more serious overtones. Jesus has just been speaking about eternal judgment, where we will face a judge with power to condemn us, not just to prison, but to hell, where there is no escape. All our sins of anger, and all our other offences as well, are clearly on the record. No earthly court will try you for anger, but God will. He will hold you to account for every word you have spoken and every thought that has passed through your head. And we need to make peace with him before judgment comes. We need to make peace with the One who is both adversary and judge, to make him our friend and our Saviour. Anger is as bad as murder: so make peace before worship, and make peace or be judged. Now let's apply these powerful words to ourselves.

We need to repent of our anger
This sinful, destructive anger takes many forms. Sometimes it seems quite trivial. It's the anger we feel when we have made our plans, and things don't work out. The anger we feel when we're driving and someone cuts us up – road rage, as we jokingly call it. The anger I feel because someone has offended me – the work colleague, the teacher, who has been a little unfair. They didn't take me seriously, they didn't give me respect. We are all guilty of this kind of anger: it's a sin. I am guilty of this. We need to stop making excuses for ourselves and recognise that this anger is sin. Call it what it is. Repent of it – however trivial it might seem.

Sometimes it is bigger than that. It's the anger we feel towards God because he hasn't given us what we think we deserve, or something we desperately want. That job – that success – that marriage – and we are angry. It is the anger we nurse in our hearts because of some ancient grudge. It may be very hard, but we need to repent of our anger. For some people, that is asking a lot. Perhaps you have suffered terribly in the past, even been abused as a child or in later life, maybe had to flee your own country or your own family because of some dreadful injustice. The pain of it may be buried, but it still devours you. You know who has done those things to you and maybe you know what you would like to do to them. But the Lord is calling even you to let go of that anger. You may well need to talk that through with someone and it will probably take time and a lot of prayer. It's unlikely to be quick or easy, but if you want to follow Christ, it has to happen. If you want to follow Christ, you want to be like him. And the Lord doesn't give us commands which are impossible. What he *wants* us to do, he will *help* us to do. He calls us to repent of our sinful anger – so he will give us the grace to do it.

We need to seek reconciliation
Is there someone in your church that you always avoid – someone you had words with, years ago, and you've steered clear ever since – and you let that old grudge sit in your heart? It's time to seek reconciliation. You take the first step. Don't wait for the other person – they may have forgotten the incident years ago! But let's be serious about this. 1 John 4:20 is very clear. We cannot pretend to be worshipping God if our heart is nursing a grudge. Quite apart from the fact that that grudge will poison you, it's a sin. How dare you pretend to worship and praise the Lord, above all how dare you share Communion, when all the time your own attitudes deny his love and destroy the very unity it celebrates? So at the next opportunity, find a quiet corner and make some peace.

The same applies in our own families as well – relationships that are broken by anger and resentment. It may be someone who lives with you or someone you haven't spoken to for years – well, you take the first step. Ask the Lord for courage and wisdom, and take the first step. Remember that Beatitude? 'Blessed are the peacemakers, for they will be called sons of God' (5:9). Who was the supreme peacemaker? The Lord Jesus, of course. Do you want to be like him? Well then, go and make some peace!

You have heard it said ... Part 1

We need to pray for the right kind of anger
We are ever so good at being angry when our feelings are hurt; but, strangely, when other people are suffering we're not so quickly moved. Again we need to look at the Lord Jesus, who was angry when he saw the horrible damage that sin had done. Anger at the injustice that makes the innocent suffer – where Christians are attacked with bombs in the Middle East or in Africa, or through the courts in Pakistan. Anger at what sin and Satan have done to destroy people's lives – whether on the streets of our inner cities or behind the comfortable walls of suburbia or rural villages. Anger at the way that sin has blinded people to the truth and life of Jesus, through religious hypocrisy or simply through religions that are false. This is not the kind of anger that leads to hatred and murder, that will devour you or lead you to hopeless despair. It's the kind of anger that will lead us to pray, seek God's mercy, and work for justice. If we don't feel any of this kind of anger, let's pray that we will.

We need a new heart
Over and over again, the Sermon on the Mount shows us that we simply cannot meet these standards by ourselves. We are all guilty of failure, every one of us. How can *any* of us say that we have never been angry like this? How could we claim to live according to this Law of Christ? We can't, not in ourselves. We need a new heart. We need a new beginning. That is exactly what Jesus came to give us. Because Jesus died on the cross for our sins, he is able to forgive us everything we have done. He can forgive us for what we might think of as the big sins, the ones people see, that really do get you into court; *and* the sins that we are all guilty of, what we like to think of as little sins, like our anger, which really aren't little at all. He can forgive us for them all. He gives us a new heart to love him, a new ability to follow him, a new power to do what he asks of us, through the Holy Spirit who will live in us. When we still fail, as we do, he will still forgive us, pick us up and get us going again. Do you have this new heart?

You have heard it said... Adultery

In 2012, London hosts the Olympics. As I write, I have been applying for tickets, so far entirely without success! British hopes are running high for an impressive haul of medals in these Games – none more so than the swimmers. Now what really scares me about these swimmers is their training regime, the frightening demands they have to endure. The man credited with transforming British fortunes at the previous Olympics in 2008 was national performance director Bill Sweetenham, and he is clearly a scary guy. Under his leadership, the team for Beijing were even made to sleep on the floor to prepare for uncomfortable conditions in the Olympic village. But his regime wasn't confined to the Olympic squad. In the national squad system, at the age of 14, you would be required to spend up to 27 hours per week in the pool, along with work in the gym and a full day at school. Even when you get to the top, it doesn't get any easier. Typically, they are up at 5 a.m., six mornings a week, and train for four hours every day, with physiotherapy, massage and strength training on top.

For the sake of being a champion swimmer, these athletes give up many good things that the rest of us take for granted. They give up sleep because they need to get to the pool at the crack of dawn. They give up interesting food, mainly eating vast quantities of carbohydrate, because that's the only way to get the energy their body needs for training. They give up holidays, because if they take holidays their bodies will lose their competitive edge. And they give up their social life, because they're in bed early every night and also, I can't help thinking, because they can never quite banish that faint smell of chlorine! But in spite of all that, in spite of all those demands and all the normal privileges they have to cut out, they do not give up. As Rebecca Adlington put it recently, 'It has never crossed my mind to give up swimming as I love the sport so much. I just love swimming.'

Now, I don't know if you can identify with that. But if you are a Christian, you need to have just that kind of passion, just that kind of motivated commitment – because according to Jesus, that is exactly what following him demands. In verses 27-30, Jesus tells his people that if we want to follow him, we have to be serious – so serious that anything that gets in the way simply has to go. We need to be just as ruthless about our own lives and lifestyles as the Olympic swimmers are with theirs, and for an even greater goal.

We now come to the second of Jesus' six examples of obeying the Law as he has fulfilled it. It's a message perhaps even less comfortable than the first, as we hear what Jesus has to say about adultery and the lust that lies behind it. Looking at the passage, you can see that in outline it is closely parallel to the previous one about murder. We will take the same approach too, beginning with the core message that Jesus gives.

Lust is as bad as adultery
Once again, Jesus starts by reiterating the words they are so familiar with (5:27). It's a direct quotation of the seventh commandment – murder was the sixth of the Ten Commandments, this one is the seventh – found in Exodus 20:14. His hearers all know that; it's taken for granted, adultery is outlawed by God. Again, at face value the meaning is very simple. If you are married, you must not have sex with anyone except your wife or husband. That's the basic definition of adultery. But now here comes Jesus' fresh take on that command (5:28). Again we are struck by the way Jesus simply assumes the right to interpret and redefine the Law of God. Words that have stood unchallenged for 1500 years are being taken in a fresh direction: the crowd must have gasped at the authority Jesus is claiming here.

Now what is Jesus saying? Just as he took the command 'do not murder' and broadened it to encompass anger and insults, so now he takes the command 'do not commit adultery' and broadens it to encompass the lustful look. A literal translation would be, Everyone who looks at a woman *with the purpose of desiring her'*. That is what sexual lust means; and whether the woman in question is standing in front of you, or whether she is in a picture or an image on a screen, doesn't make any difference. It amounts to the same thing: Jesus says, unless she's your wife, it's adultery. Thinking about the act, desiring the woman sexually, is on a level with the action itself. Obviously it's not the *same* as the action; it certainly doesn't have the same impact on the target of your feelings; but as far as you and your heart are concerned, as far as God's view of sin is concerned, it's *exactly* the same. There is adultery in your heart, which means in the core of your being.

You may be thinking, This can't apply to me. Jesus is clearly addressing this to men, and I'm not a man, so I'm in the clear; or else, I'm not married, so by definition I can't commit adultery. Well, if you're thinking that, I'm afraid I have to say, 'Welcome to the world of the Pharisees'; because that's just how they would have weaselled their way out of it! Clearly, Jesus is laying down a principle here. He addresses it initially to men, probably for two reasons. One is that sexual lust is *generally* more of a male problem, though not exclusively, as we shall see. But the other reason is that in those days adultery was often seen as something that only men could do. It was widely thought that it was fine for married men to sleep around, as long as the women involved were not married – whereas women were expected to keep themselves for a husband and then be 100% faithful after marriage. That view, of course, is gross hypocrisy on the part of men, but it has been a common view in many cultures in history.

So when Jesus addresses the problem of adultery and the lust that inspires it, naturally he directs his attention mainly to married men. But the *principle* Jesus gives clearly applies just as much to any sexual encounter outside marriage – whether it ends in sexual intercourse or only gets as far as a fantasy. Whether we are married or not, whether we are men or women, this applies to us all. In God's court, when we stand accused of adultery, it will not do to say, as an American president once famously said, I did not have sexual relations with that woman – *or* that man – if it was even in our hearts to do so. It makes no difference if no-one else ever knows. God knows our hearts. This word applies to us all.

In fact, this principle is not really anything new. Look at the *tenth* commandment (Exodus 20:17). *Coveting* is what goes on in my heart when I desire something that doesn't belong to me. *Lust* is simply a form of coveting. But part of our sinful downfall is that we love to say, Well, as long as I just thought about it, it's OK. As long as it stayed hidden in my heart and mind, no-one's been hurt, no damage has been done, so it's not really a sin. Wrong: it's a sin. Lust is as bad as adultery.

When we looked at murder, and Jesus' statement that God will judge anger in just the same way, the shock was unmistakable because no-one doubts today that murder is wrong. But in this case, with adultery, perhaps the shock value is less. We live (in the West, at least) in a society that's become accustomed to adultery. In fact, even the word seems to be passing out of use. We prefer to speak of 'an affair' or 'a fling' or some such neutral word which sounds less blunt and uncompromising than 'adultery'. Our society has become so intensely sexualised that anyone who is not sexually active is seen as abnormal. The world is no longer shocked by adultery. Even as Christians, perhaps we find ourselves thinking the same way – forgetting that the only truly normal man who's ever lived was never sexually active. Jesus never married; and therefore he lived the whole of his perfect life in celibacy. Jesus died as a virgin; and yet he was complete and perfectly well-adjusted.

In a world like ours, to say that even fantasising about sex outside marriage is wrong sounds weird, repressive and unhealthy, but that's what Jesus says. God has given us minds and imagination, and that's a great gift. Lust is the twisting and pollution of that good gift just as adultery is the twisting and pollution of the good gift of sex. And we need to say that the Bible is constantly outraged by adultery. The ultimate proof is that the Bible uses adultery to picture the breach of faith of God's people against God (read Hosea 1 to 3 or Ezekiel 16 – though the language may shock you). We need to say that now, as always, adultery destroys people, it breaks relationships, it steals the security of children. Sexual activity before marriage sets the tone for adulterous behaviour within marriage. Sexual lust is the root of it. The shock is that lust is tantamount to this terrible sin called adultery. That's the core message: now Jesus proceeds to explain what must follow.

Lust is as bad as adultery – so, be ruthless with sin
Look at verses 29-30. Striking words! In view of what Jesus has just said, these verses tell us what we should do about it. Verse 29 applies specially to the issue of lust; verse 30 is more general. The word behind 'causing you to sin' has the idea of trapping you in a snare, as a hunter would do with an animal.

We'll look at verse 29 first – *be ruthless with lust*. Lust begins – at least for many of us – with our eyes. Jesus says, If your right eye causes you to sin, get rid of it. The right eye was thought to be more important, probably because of the way soldiers would face in battle. So is he speaking literally? Some people have taken it that way. There is a famous story about the early church leader Origen, in Egypt. It was said that he was so concerned about the problem of sexual lust that he actually castrated himself. Origen was well-known for his eccentricities and the story has been circulating ever since. The evidence suggests it's not actually true, and it was a rumour put out by his enemies to show how crazy he was[24] – but even so, people have been known to take these words, and other similar words in the gospels, at face value. So is that what we have to do? Does Jesus *literally* mean we should gouge out our eyes, and does he *literally* mean we will go to hell if we fail just once? The answer on both counts is no. Jesus has already made it clear where the roots of our problem lie – they lie in our sinful hearts, the sin that lurks there like a monster waiting to strike. That's what we are dealing with. Gouging out one eye, or even both, won't deal with the fundamental problem.

No, what he is telling us here, using the most extreme language, is that the stakes are incredibly high. He is forcing us to take notice. Sin is what takes you to hell. It will destroy you for eternity, so you must be willing to take the most extreme measures to fight it ruthlessly. If gouging out an eye and throwing it away *could* stop you from lusting, in fact, it would be worth it. Your right eye for your eternal soul? It's a good exchange.

In verse 30 he repeats the message in broader terms. *Be ruthless with any sin.* If 'lust' relates naturally to the eyes, your hands are what you use for a vast range of daily activities, both good and bad. The right hand is the more important one, for most people – though not for me, I'm left-handed! – but the point is plain: it would be worth sacrificing *any* part of your body, even the most valuable of them all, if it would keep you clear of sin. So be ruthless with sin. Like those Olympic swimmers, we must be willing to cut out anything that will cause us to fail. They have their reasons – the joy of the race, the glory of victory – we have our reasons too. And they are *better* reasons. If as Christians we persist in sin, we will destroy our joy, we will compromise our witness and above all we will grieve our Lord. So now let's be very specific, and very straightforward, as we ask exactly what Jesus' words mean for us. Focusing on the issue of lust, what do we need to do?

We need to stop pretending
This is an issue for us all. Sometimes we give the impression that lust and sexual fantasies are a problem confined to men. That's not true. A number of recent surveys, for instance, agree that around one in five Christian women use internet pornography. For men – including church leaders – that figure is much higher. That's not good, but it does seem that this is one area, perhaps the only area, where women are less willing to talk about and admit the problem than men! For most women, lust takes a different form than it does for men. Female sexual fantasies are likely to be provoked differently, usually less connected with what they see, and may focus on different objectives – but it is still lust. The

evidence shows that women are more likely to act out their on-line fantasies in real life. It's worth saying that this highly sexualised culture of ours is pushing women into patterns of sinful thinking and behaviour that were previously reserved for men. It's getting tougher than ever for women to remain sexually pure. Christian women need to talk about this.

As for men – well, if there is a Christian man reading this who doesn't have a problem with lust, I'd like to hear from you – that's if you're still breathing, which I would find hard to believe! Don't pretend there is no problem. Don't pretend the problem disappears with age – it doesn't. Don't think the problem will vanish if you get married – it won't.

We need to get serious
Jesus tells us in verses 29-30 that if anything – any body part, or anything else – leads us into sin, we must cut it out! We need to get serious about fighting lust. So, if watching late-night TV causes you to sin, cut out late-night TV. If spending time with particular people causes you to sin – if you fantasise about the guy in the office or the girl in your hall of residence – keep clear of them, or at least only see them when other people are around. If internet access causes you to sin, cut it out. There are all kinds of ways of making your internet viewing accountable, keeping yourself out of temptation. There will be people reading this, mainly men, who are addicted to internet porn. You sit there night after night, and it rules your life. You find it impossible to see women as anything but sex objects. It's just as serious as any other addiction, because you are its slave – only the symptoms are less visible. If that's you, then ask for help. It's not hopeless, but you must face up to it.

The same applies to internet chat-rooms and even to using Facebook. If you doubt the power of Facebook, let me refer you to the case of the sex offender Colin Blanchard, who was recently sentenced in Bristol. Three of the four women in his circle of paedophiles were induced into sexually abusing children just by internet conversations, starting with Facebook. At least one pastor in America has banned his congregation from using Facebook because it is destroying so many marriages. If internet access causes you to sin, cut it out and throw it away. If reading romantic stories causes you to sin, or watching weepy films causes you to sin, and you know it – cut them out as well.

As we relate to one another in the kingdom, as a Christian family, there are also steps we can take to help the opposite sex, so that sisters

113

can support brothers and brothers can support sisters. Men, don't give false signals to women, relational signals that are conveyed through touch or by opening yourself up emotionally. That is how countless episodes of adultery have begun. Women, don't dress to seduce, even if contemporary fashion tells you that you must. Do you really want to lead your brothers astray?

Now if we stopped at this point, it would all have been true; and yet we would have given a false picture, that this is all very negative, and rather heavy, and that the best answer we could give to sin and temptation is to walk around with a bag over our head or go and live as a monk! But thankfully, there is more.

We need to love Jesus
It's not enough to root out the sources of temptation. So many Christians have battled with this sin and fallen, over and over and over again, to the point of absolute desperation. You may well have been to that point yourself, thinking that this sin above all others has you helpless in its grip. Well, if we are going to defeat the power of lust, we need a greater power. We need to love something else *more*. Let me quote from Tim Chester's book *You can change*. This is what he says about the reason why we sin: 'We sin because we believe the lie that we are better off without God, that his rule is oppressive, that we will be free without him, that sin offers more than God'[25]. Let's pick up the last part of that sentence.

The deepest answer to sin is simply to love the Lord more than we love the sin. We need to get it firmly fixed in our minds that though sin may be fun while it lasts (and it usually is), there is *nothing* worth more than knowing Jesus Christ. We will never defeat temptation *only* by telling ourselves, This is wrong and I mustn't do it (though that is true). We will never defeat temptation *only* by avoiding the trouble spots, though we must certainly do that. We defeat the most powerful and enticing temptations by telling ourselves this truth, by preaching the gospel to our own hearts, that the Lord Jesus has died on the cross for me, he has made me a new person, he has set me on the road to eternal glory, I love him, and he means more to me than any cheap and easy thrill that is on offer to me right now. And I am not going to cloud my relationship with him, I am not going to grieve his Holy Spirit, and I am not going to live a life of compromise, because I love him and I want to please him.

The more we love Jesus, the less we will want to sin. The more we love Jesus, the more we will detest anything that gets in the way. The more clearly we can see eternity, the less we will hesitate to make sacrifices here and now, because we will know that it's all worth it for him and for our future.

You have heard it said... Divorce

There are a number of ways for a Church of England bishop to get himself into trouble; and not long ago, Bishop Pete Broadbent found a new one. Pete Broadbent was Bishop of Willesden in London; and the trouble he got into related to his comments about the royal wedding which was then on the horizon. First he criticised the 'nauseating tosh' surrounding the announcement of William and Kate's engagement. He disapproved of the fact that the wedding would cost the public 'an arm and a leg'. But what really got Bishop Broadbent into hot water was his parting shot. 'I give the marriage seven years.' That certainly caused a stir! He was suspended from public duty and had to issue a fulsome apology to those he had offended. Still, it's that statement that the marriage can't be expected to last that really sticks in the mind. Perhaps the bishop is right. After all, as he pointed out in his own, rather colourful language, recent royal marriages don't have a great track record of success. Most of them have ended in divorce. It might not be very kind to say so, but perhaps seven years was a reasonable guess.

So what are we to think about divorce today? We are no longer surprised to hear about celebrity divorces. We hear the news of a high profile divorce; and people might think it's a bit sad, it's a shame they didn't make it, but it's nothing unusual. Often attention focuses not on the tragedy of the break-up but on who's getting what, and who will they go on to marry or live with next? Divorce, at least for the onlookers, is almost routine; all that matters is that it should happen as tidily as possible so that both parties can happily move on to pastures new. And there is a strange kind of parallel between that view today, and the world that Jesus knew. The people Jesus dealt with were obsessed with the detailed *process* of divorce, how you did it and what you were entitled to do afterwards. They had largely lost sight of the deep meaning of marriage and the tragedy of divorce. In verses 31-32 we are looking at Jesus' radical response to that outlook and how his response still speaks to us today. This is the third of Jesus' six case studies; and after speaking about adultery, it's not really a surprise that his next topic, in a section of just two verses, is divorce. Divorce is so often the outcome of adultery; adultery so often leads to divorce. Once again, Jesus' statement about divorce is radical and cuts deep and goes far beyond the letter of the Law.

Look at verses 31-32. You see that compared with the other five cases, the opening formula is a little shorter here, perhaps because these two verses are so closely connected with Jesus' words about adultery. Otherwise the structure is the same: 'It has been said' and 'But *I* tell you', with that recurring note of authority that Jesus is asserting for himself. So we'll begin by looking at the principles Jesus sets out, and then we'll see exactly what this means for us.

First of all, we need to do some digging into the background. What's this about a 'certificate of divorce' (5:31)? The reference is to Deuteronomy 24:1-4. This is not part of the Ten Commandments – it's part of Israel's civil law. It's a little complicated, but the basic meaning is this. If a man divorces his wife and gives her a certificate to say so, and *if* she then marries again and the second husband divorces her as well (or he dies), the first husband can't marry her again. At first hearing that probably sounds very odd, but the point of the divorce certificate was actually to give the woman involved some degree of protection. In that society, men had all the power; and it was quite possible for a man to kick his wife out whenever he pleased, and then to change his mind again and summon her back. But under the Law of Moses, he would have to provide this certificate, which would state that the marriage was over, the man renounced all his claims on the wife and, crucially, she was free to go and marry again – which in most cases she would have to do, in order to survive. So the Law provided this somewhat minimal, but still very useful, protection for divorced wives. The certificate was simply a way of regulating a chaotic situation. Thus the Law did not encourage divorce; it did not commend it in any way; it simply recognised that divorce would sometimes happen and placed limits on the abuses that might follow.

Now: fast forward 1500 years to the time of Jesus; and let's see what has happened to that system. Verse 31 is Jesus' brief summary of the way that ancient law was now understood. 'If you divorce your wife, give her a certificate.' All that's left is this focus on the *mechanism* of divorce. We know from other passages in the gospels that the Pharisees are very interested in divorce. Another time, they tackle Jesus' views about the legitimate *grounds* for divorce (Matthew 19:3); and we know they are also very concerned about *doing* divorce properly. Around the time of Jesus there was a vigorous dispute about the reasons a man could divorce his wife. It was a dispute between the followers of two great Rabbis, Shammai and Hillel. We know this because in the second century, it was all written up in the Talmud, which is a huge multi-volume compendium of the teaching of the rabbis, drawn up by the Jewish leaders after the temple was destroyed. It is interesting to see the actual words in which this dispute was recorded. Just to explain, when it says 'Beth Shammai' and 'Beth Hillel', Beth means 'the house of' Shammai or Hillel. Another point: the Talmud consists of two parts, the Mishnah, which means 'instruction', and the Gemara, which means 'completion'. So here's the dispute over divorce, straight from the horse's mouth.

> **Mishnah.** Beth Shammai say: a man should not divorce his wife unless he has found her guilty of some unseemly conduct, as it says, Because he hath found some unseemly thing in her[26]. Beth Hillel, however, say [that he may divorce her] even if she has merely spoilt his food, since it says, Because he hath found some unseemly thing in her. R. Akiba says, [he may divorce her] even if he finds another woman more beautiful than she is, as it says, It cometh to pass, if she find no favour in his eyes.

So as you can see, the followers of Hillel believed a man could divorce his wife for the most trivial of reasons – even if her cooking had an off-day or her looks had started to fade. Shammai's followers took a much stricter line. Just to give an insight into the way these people argued, listen to the other section at this point, the Gemara:

> **Gemara.** It has been taught: Beth Hillel said to Beth Shammai: Does not the text distinctly say 'thing'? Beth Shammai rejoined: And does it not distinctly say 'unseemliness'? Beth Hillel replied: Had it said only 'unseemliness' without 'thing', I should have concluded that she should be sent away on account of unseemliness, but not of any [lesser] 'thing'. Therefore 'thing' is specified. Again, had it said only 'thing' without 'unseemliness', I should have concluded that [if divorced] on account of a 'thing'

she should be permitted to marry again, but if on account of 'unseemliness', she should not be permitted to remarry. Therefore 'unseemliness' is also specified. And what do Beth Shammai make of this word 'thing'?

And you thought our lawyers talked gobbledegook! And so it goes on. Unbelievably, the whole of this volume of the Talmud (tractate *Gittin*, as it is known) is concerned with the right way to serve notice of divorce. That is how obsessed the religion had become with the pedantic detail of dissolving a marriage. I have gone into the detail here in order to show what man-made religion is like. Human religion starts with a principle – and it may be an excellent principle, like the Law of Moses – and turns it into a detailed rule-book. The Pharisees were not the last people to produce something like that. In Islam, the method of arguing is very similar to the Talmud, with the debates recorded in the Hadiths and their appeals to the *sunna*, the practices of Mohammed and his first followers.

It's very appealing to our sinful human hearts, for two simple reasons. One: if you have everything written down in a rule-book, so you know exactly what you should do in every situation, it becomes very easy to measure how well you are doing, and very easy to claim you are doing rather well. Life becomes a series of tick-boxes. People like that, because it spares us doing what we hate to do. It spares us having to look into the rotten depths of our own hearts. If you have a detailed rule-book, you don't have to think about your motives or attitudes, you have only to look at the checklist. This is part of the great appeal of Islam today – that in a world of moral chaos, Islam lays down exactly what to do in every situation. Just what the Pharisees would have claimed for their own religion.

The second reason this is so appealing is that complex lists of rules like this inevitably provide loopholes which clever people can use to escape from what God's Law actually says. The gospels contain various examples of this; so for instance, Jesus accuses the Pharisees of evading the true command to honour their parents by throwing up a smokescreen of detailed regulations (Matthew 15:3-9). That is human religion at work – totally different from the message of Jesus, who begins by giving us a new heart, transforming us from the inside outwards. And that is just what is happening with this discussion of divorce. The real tragedy of divorce, and the true status of marriage, is being lost in pedantic regulations. And in the light of that, we can see how radical Jesus is in verse 32.

Now this isn't all that Jesus has to say about divorce. He says much more about it in Matthew 19. But here we are focusing on this one verse, and although the words are about divorce, the main effect of them is to declare the importance of *marriage*. In order to make sense of verse 32, we need to understand that a divorced woman would need to re-marry. That was simply how it was in those days: economic survival dictated that she would need a new husband. So Jesus is saying that if you divorce your wife, then when she re-marries you have made her an adulteress – she's been forced into a new marriage that amounts to adultery, and *you* will be responsible. In other words, Jesus says, though you may have divorced her, in the sight of God *she is still married to you*. The message is that marriage is not so easily dissolved as his hearers seem to think, or as many people believe today.

There is just one exception, Jesus says, and that's what the NIV translates as 'marital unfaithfulness'. It's a tricky word: the Greek word is *porneia*, and there is some dispute about its meaning. It's certainly something sexual; the most likely meaning is that it's a general term for a sexual relationship outside the bond of marriage. In that case, Jesus is saying that if there has been adultery, the marriage bond has been compromised and you are free to divorce *and* to re-marry. In the case of adultery, you certainly don't have to divorce[27]; Jesus does not command us to do so; but it is an option. If you do, and then the victim remarries, the new marriage will not be adulterous. It will be entirely legitimate.

We have to admit that evangelical Christians do not all agree on this issue of remarriage. There is a wide variety of views. One extreme is represented today by David Instone-Brewer[28]. His view is that the Bible permits divorce and remarriage for a variety of reasons, including not just adultery, mentioned here, but even a failure to *honour* your wife or husband sufficiently. You'd have to read his book for a full explanation, but it relies on a technical analysis of early Jewish writings. That view really does not seem to do justice to the New Testament's very strong emphasis on the permanence and holiness of marriage. And let's be honest, almost any spouse could complain at some time or another that his or her partner hasn't given them sufficient honour. We could all divorce on that basis!

At the other extreme, John Piper believes that this *porneia* refers to sins committed before marriage and that Jesus is permitting divorce *only* during the period of betrothal that preceded the full marriage. Piper would say that the Bible forbids divorce even on the grounds of adultery, that therefore *no* Christian should divorce and you certainly cannot remarry if your original spouse is still alive. That's a hard line, and in fact Piper's own church has not taken that line as its official policy. Most evangelicals occupy a position between these extremes; but what this implies is that we will encounter Bible-believing Christians who sincerely hold different views and who have heard different teaching about divorce; and that's another reason for being very humble and sensitive with one another on this issue. As for my own view: in our church we believe there are two biblical grounds for divorce and remarriage: one is adultery and the other, working from what Paul says in 1 Corinthians 7:12-16, is deliberate and wilful desertion. These are ways in which the marriage bond can be broken: we recognise that and we try to deal with people on that basis. So much for the principles. Now how does all this affect us?

Divorce is always an evil
The bluntest statement in the Bible about divorce comes in Malachi 2:16a. That is pretty explicit[29]. God hates divorce because it destroys the unique and special bond that he has created. So in Matthew 5 Jesus is saying that what matters about divorce is not how you *arrange* it but how you can *avoid* it. In Matthew 19:4-6, Jesus explains that marriage goes right back to the time of Creation. He is quoting from the very first chapters of the Bible. God introduced marriage before sin came into the world. Marriage pre-dates the Fall. Sin has corrupted it, like everything else, but it is still God's wonderful gift to us and it is still his purpose that the marriage relationship stands at the heart of human society.

We need to be very wary of the notion that gets bandied around today, that marriage is just some kind of cultural idea, a convention that has evolved as one possible way of arranging relationships. No: the Bible is absolutely clear on this. Marriage – between one *man* and one *woman* – for life, is what God always had in mind. So don't focus on how to end it. Focus on how to sustain it! This is so different from the views of today's world. A world in which pre-nuptial agreements – 'pre-nups' – are becoming a routine preparation for marriage, because people's expectations are so low. They go into marriage with an exit strategy already mapped out. Isn't it obvious that that's a recipe for disaster, that if you get married already thinking it's likely to be over in a few years, then it almost certainly will be? It's a world where people get divorced even for what they call 'incompatibility'. The Bible says that even if you find yourself as a Christian married to an unbeliever, you are not to press for divorce. As Martyn Lloyd-Jones points out, that is the ultimate 'incompatibility'.

Divorce is always an evil. There will be times when it's a *lesser* evil – when that bond of marriage has been broken by the sin of one partner, or both, and reconciliation is impossible, Divorce then simply recognises the fact. Divorce can be a lesser evil; but it is always an evil. There is always sin involved, and there is always pain. That raises the question, What hope do we have – what hope of avoiding divorce, what hope of protecting our marriages, what hope of recovery and healing if we have been through a divorce – and even, as Jesus' own disciples ask him in reply to this same statement in Matthew 19:10, If this is how it is, isn't it better not to get married in the first place? The Bible's message is that there *is* hope – there is plenty of hope. Now we'll see why.

Our God is always faithful
The Lord does not only give us commands, difficult and demanding commands like this one – he also gives us the hope and the strength to keep them. Look at Jeremiah 3. This is where God uses exactly this picture of marriage and divorce to show us what he is like. He is speaking of Israel, his covenant people, and his relationship of love. It's a close relationship which the Old Testament often pictures as a marriage. Look closely at Jeremiah 3:1-2, 6-8, 14. You see the picture? God's people have been so unfaithful to him. Spiritually, they have committed adultery by following all sorts of other gods, not once but many times. How will God respond? With sorrow, yes. With righteous anger, yes. He even speaks in terms of that 'certificate of divorce'. He certainly has every right to divorce her – and yet he calls her back (Jeremiah 3:14). It's the story of the Old Testament, actually: endless sin matched by endless grace. The story of the prophet Hosea tells the same story – Hosea himself is instructed to go and love his adulterous wife once more – it's a picture of the faithful, enduring love of the Lord for his wayward, rebellious people.

God's faithfulness is our model and our hope. It's our model *for forgiveness in marriage* – the forgiveness we will need, time and again. If marriage gets tough, we do not simply say, *He* has spoiled my life, *she* has spoiled my life, I must end it. We've received this incredible grace from God – now we need to show that same grace in our marriages. Every marriage has its difficult moments, and most have far more than moments! The most idyllic marriage will need forgiveness. God's faithfulness is our hope of that.

If you are struggling with your marriage now, and divorce is on your mind, don't be thinking about whether you've got reasonable grounds to divorce. Don't think about whether your partner's behaviour – or your own – ticks some particular box in a list of offences. Think about the grace of God, and what you mean to him. Think about the Lord, reaching out to you in love, day after day. Start there, with God's faithfulness.

More than that, God's faithfulness is our model *for grace in all our relationships*. Some of us will never be married, but all of us need grace to build and sustain true relationships. What do you do or say when your friend or family member turns nasty or offends you? Do you just walk away? *No*, we show the grace of God and we stay, we work, and we build. Among Christians, it's this love that is to mark us out, Jesus says – love that is unmistakable because it is so committed, so forgiving. The kind of committed love which the Lord himself showed to us.

Lastly, God's faithfulness is our hope *for when we fail* – however badly. Perhaps you have been through a divorce. You don't need anyone to tell you how painful and complicated it all is, how much guilt is involved. Perhaps you are deep in that pain and guilt at this very moment. Perhaps it feels as though you will never be free of it. But divorce is not the unforgivable sin. If you are in Christ, nothing is unforgivable. Yes, divorce will leave its scars, and the scars will remain. Only when we get to glory will those scars be fully healed – but they *will* be! This is the God we can always depend on. He has proved it in Jesus Christ by sending him into the world to die for us – the ultimate proof of the greatest love that could ever be. That commitment to his people that the Bible talks about over and over again, in Jeremiah and Hosea and in scores of other places, and in the Law itself – but the true measure of that commitment stands in the bloodstained wood of the cross at Calvary.

You have heard it said ... Part 1

Questions to reflect on or discuss

1. How do you respond to the idea that anger is as bad as murder, and lust as bad as adultery? What does your response tell you about the state of your own heart?

2. What kinds of things regularly make you angry? Do you get angry about any of the 'right' things or is it always in defence of yourself? What do you need to do about that?

3. (Not for discussion in mixed company!) Sexual lust takes different forms for different people. In what ways is it a problem for you? Do you take serious measures to prevent it from taking hold in your life? If not, are you willing to?

4. Do you ever, deep down, believe that sin offers you more than God does? If you do, what biblical truths can help you get clear in your mind that Jesus is worth more than the enjoyment of any sin?

5. What can we do to reinforce the status of marriage, and its permanence, among Christians and in churches?

6. If you know people who are going through a divorce, or who have recently been divorced, what can you do to help them – especially if they are Christians?

Chapter 7
You have heard it said... Part 2
Matthew 5:33-48

You have heard it said... Oaths

Do you know the story of the boy who cried Wolf? It's one of those old fables, attributed to Aesop, a Greek story-teller from the sixth century B.C. We don't know if it *really* goes back as far as that, but it's certainly an old, old story; and its message was certainly drummed into me as a child. It goes like this. There's a young shepherd boy who spends his days sitting on the hillside, keeping an eye on the sheep which belong to the people in the nearby village. It's not the most thrilling occupation; and one quiet day, feeling particularly bored, he decides to create some excitement. So he runs down into the village yelling, Wolf! Wolf! The villagers all turn out and rush to the pastures to get rid of the wolf. Of course, there is no wolf; and with some rather dark looks at the shepherd boy, the villagers troop back to their homes. Well, the shepherd boy feels rather pleased with that result, and before very long he tries it again. He runs down into the village yelling, Wolf! Wolf! A shade more reluctantly, this time, the villagers run up to the hillside in search of the wolf. But again, there is no wolf to be seen; and they retreat, muttering to themselves.

I think you know what happens next. Not long afterwards, the shepherd boy is in the field when he spots a sinister grey shape among the trees. The wolf has arrived. As the wolf emerges from the trees and prowls towards the sheep, the boy rushes down once more crying, Wolf! Wolf! But the only sound now is the slamming of doors and windows as the villagers will have nothing to do with him. However much he insists, whatever words he uses to reinforce his plea for help, there is no response. In desperation, the boy returns to the field where the wolf is enjoying his free meal. And – in what I guess is the original version of the story – the wolf then eats the shepherd boy as well. Like most of these fables, this one has been cleaned up a bit for children – in one version I found, the boy is comforted by an old man who assures him the sheep are only straying and they can easily be rounded up tomorrow! But in every version of the story, the moral is the same. *Even when liars tell the truth, they are never believed.*

In Matthew 5:33-37, we come to some words of Jesus that might almost have inspired that story. In one sense, this passage might seem an anti-climax. Jesus is talking about taking oaths, which sounds like rather an obscure subject. We can understand the importance of issues like murder, adultery, or divorce – those are big subjects – but why is Jesus so concerned about taking oaths? Isn't this a bit trivial? But as we look more closely at what Jesus actually says, we will find that yet again these words cut deep. Like the boy who cried Wolf, we will find that the way we speak, the truthfulness of our words, is of life-changing importance. This passage is a summons to be people of real, uncompromising integrity.

Again, it follows the pattern we have become familiar with. First, *You have heard*; and then, *But I tell you.* Jesus takes the way that the Law was understood in his day; and then he clears away the misconceptions and lays down his own demands.

'You have heard'

Look at verse 33. The word translated 'break your oath' can mean either literally breaking an oath you have made, or swearing falsely; that is, swearing something you know is not true. In a law court, that is known as perjury. Now verse 33 is not a direct quotation from the law of Moses, but it's a summary of what the Law had to say. An 'oath' is defined as a solemn statement that someone declares to be true and formally calls God to witness. So it's a way of strengthening or reinforcing an ordinary statement. If it's a promise that is being reinforced in this way, then it is called a vow. An 'oath' is the more general word, and a vow is one kind of oath. Just to clarify: we are not talking here about 'swearing' in the sense of foul language or even blasphemy. Both of those are wrong – all would be agreed that using the name of God casually or lightly is a terrible evil – but that is not primarily what Jesus has in view here.

You have heard it said ... Part 2

So we are looking at oaths and the Old Testament law. The basic sense of the Law regarding oaths can be found in Leviticus 19:12. The context of that verse has to do with deceit and injustice. It's an expansion of the ninth commandment – 'you shall not give false testimony against your neighbour' (Exodus 20:16). That was the concern: you were permitted to take oaths in God's name; but if you did, you had better keep them. Otherwise you would be guilty of blasphemy. But the best summary of the law about oaths comes in Deuteronomy 23:21-23. This is specifically about vows – promises reinforced with an oath. The message of these verses is: if you make a vow, then keep it, and keep it on time; but if you don't make a vow, that's fine. There is no *command* to go around making lots of dramatic vows or oaths. The point of oaths, in fact, was to encourage people to be truthful. The principle is: Keep your word, and *if you like*, reinforce it with an oath. One example is the Nazirite vow, which you can read about in Numbers 6: a very special vow of commitment to the Lord; but it was purely voluntary, it was not commanded.

Now if we come back to Matthew 5:33, although it does represent what the Law said, it does so in a rather slanted way – because it suggests that taking oaths is a routine part of everyday life and that what matters most is regulating them properly. If we put this verse alongside what Jesus says elsewhere in Matthew, we can confirm that that's true. So let's have a look at oaths in the time of Jesus – and some of this will no doubt seem very familiar from the previous section on divorce! Look at Matthew 23:16-22, where Jesus is talking to the Pharisees and teachers of the law. Once again we get the flavour of the debate. Here is the basic principle of the Law – that you keep your word, and if you like, reinforce it with an oath – and the religious authorities have turned it into a complex minefield of interpretation and argument. Again we see what happens when human religion gets to work: the outcome is this ridiculous proliferation of pedantic regulations. And it provides the real expert with plenty of loopholes to escape the true demand of the Law.

Let's imagine one of our Pharisee friends in action. There's a poor man who's in trouble: tomorrow his house is going to be repossessed by the landlord and he's begged the Pharisee to come and help him out. The Pharisee says, Yes, I'll come and help you sort out your problem tomorrow. I swear by the temple, I'll be there! It sounds very grand – here is someone you can really rely on. But tomorrow comes, and the Pharisee doesn't show up. The man says, Where *were* you – I needed your help – you swore you'd be here! Oh no, says the Pharisee, something else came up. Anyway, I only swore by the *temple*, that doesn't count. Now if I'd sworn by the *gold* in the temple, that's another matter! Again, you see, we have these nit-picking attitudes, very similar to the rabbinic debates over divorce. And again, there is a whole volume of the Talmud devoted to oaths – and another one about vows. There is even one rabbi who says that if you swear *by* Jerusalem, the oath is not binding, but if you swear *towards* Jerusalem, then you are bound! Just as the issue of divorce has been confined to a pedantic debate over how to do it, so the issue of swearing oaths has become a licence to cheat and deceive. Far from encouraging truthfulness, it has become the exact opposite. Now let's move on to Jesus' response.

'But I tell you'
Look at verses 34-36. Jesus says, in fact, it is far better if you do not swear at all. He gives four specific examples, all of which are probably in common use at the time. Heaven, earth, Jerusalem and your own head: don't swear by any of them. The first three of these would all make dramatic-sounding oaths: *I swear by heaven*, etc. Yet they would all provide a get-out clause, on the basis that none of them actually mentioned God's name. Other get-out clauses were available, but the point here seems to be that these dramatic oaths avoid the name of God and therefore could easily be ducked out of.

Jesus says, That kind of thinking is blind and stupid. Don't you realise what heaven and earth *are?* Isaiah 66:1 puts it vividly. Do you think you can invoke heaven and earth and leave God out of the picture? As for Jerusalem – that is the holy city, the city of God's King – which *had* meant King David and would *now* mean the Lord Jesus himself. As soon as you mention any of these, you are actually calling on God. What about swearing by your own head? Well, swearing by your head might be another way of saying, I swear by my own life, since if you lose your head, you're dead; but in any case, the thought would be that this is something that you have control over. I'm entitled to swear by my head, because it's *my* head and I can do what I like with it! Jesus again says, No. You think you have control over your head? You can't even stop yourself going grey! The only one with control over anything is God himself!

The detail here is not that important. Jesus is simply cutting through the whole pointless debate about oaths. He is saying, Look what you get into when you start swearing oaths. The best way is simply not to swear at all; hence his conclusion in verse 37. If you are saying something, just say it. That is enough. If you are denying something, just say it. 'Yes' and 'no' are sufficient. Anything beyond those simple, unvarnished statements comes from the devil. That's a very strong statement; and it shows us that Jesus is concerned about far more than the detail of what kind of oaths are acceptable, or binding, or otherwise. What is he really concerned about? Well, in John 8 we find Jesus arguing with the unbelieving Jews, and in the course of that argument he says in verse 44 that the devil, the evil one, is the father of lies. That description sheds the light we need on Matthew 5. Jesus is saying, What really matters, my people, is that you are people of the *truth*. You are not from the devil, the evil one, the great liar. You are people of the truth.

The message of these verses is simple. You don't *need* to swear. You don't *need* an oath. Your word should be enough. It's a message that clearly took hold in the early church, for it is repeated in very similar language in James 5:12. As my followers, says Jesus, you should be known for your total, uncompromising integrity. That is what God's law is driving towards: that is what he demands of you: that is what I say to you.

Before we apply this message to ourselves, there are two possible objections to deal with. Objection number one: Jesus is saying, Don't swear oaths. *But doesn't God swear oaths?* Yes he does, at various points in Scripture. God *does* swear oaths, and Hebrews 6:13-18 explains why. The point of God swearing an oath is not to strengthen what he says – how would it be possible to strengthen the word of God? – but for the sake of our *faith*, so that we might 'be greatly encouraged', so that we weak, wavering human beings might have greater certainty in our feeble minds. So God swearing by his own name is simply a concession to our weakness! By the way, it is also said that Paul swears oaths at various points in his letters. I don't think they are actually formal oaths; but what he does at particularly solemn points, such as Romans 1:9 or the opening verses of Romans 9, is to declare that God knows what Paul is saying is true. He puts it like that for the sake of his readers. Now Paul is an apostle writing Scripture; in that sense he is speaking in the name and authority of God; and I don't think you and I are likely to find ourselves in such situations!

Objection number two is this. Jesus is saying, Don't swear oaths – *but don't we have to swear oaths?* You may know that the Quakers, for example, as well as the Mennonites, have taken Jesus' words here to mean that we should refuse to swear the oath in a court of law. Normally, if you give evidence in court, you do so under oath to tell the truth; but the Quakers say that is clearly wrong, and some of the early Quakers and Mennonites got into a lot of trouble for taking that very brave and honourable stand. But there is a big difference between swearing an oath because you decide you need it to sound more convincing; and swearing an oath when the law of the land and legal process demands it of you. Given the background we have looked at, it is clear that what Jesus is concerned about is our truthfulness; and agreeing to give evidence under oath certainly does not compromise our integrity. The clinching argument here is that Jesus himself, at his own trial, gives evidence under oath (Matthew 26:63-64a). Now we return to the main point.

Integrity in action
We need to follow this message through and let Jesus' words have their full impact on our lives. The question is, *Can people trust you?* What do you think people say when they are discussing you? Do they know you as someone who is absolutely honest, or are you known as someone who is evasive, who will duck a straight question or simply say what you think people want to hear? Someone who tells 'white lies' – and what a ridiculous expression that is! You may come from a cultural background where it is acceptable to tell lies in order to protect yourself – cultures where your honour is more important than the truth. It's in your background – but can I tell you, very simply: according to the Bible, according to Jesus, the truth matters more. If that is your culture, then that is one part of your culture that you must reject. As Christians we all have to look at our own culture and upbringing and say no to the ungodly and unbiblical parts of it. Jesus has called us into his kingdom, and it is a kingdom of truth.

Can people trust you? Let's make it even more specific. Can they trust you at *home?* Your wife or your husband – can they trust you? If you're home late from work, does your spouse need to check out your story or can they trust you unquestioningly – not because they are gullible but because you are a man of your word? With your children – do you say one thing and do another, or do they know that you will keep your promises – at least as far as you are able? Or with your parents – are you straight with them, even when you feel they don't understand you? The foundation of all deep relationships is trust and truth. Jesus calls us to be people of the truth. This doesn't mean, of course, that we always say everything we know about any subject. We keep confidences. We keep quiet when to speak would be unloving or inappropriate; but what we say must be *true*.

Can they trust you at *work*? Integrity in the work-place or at school is an incredibly powerful witness: when you *don't* join in the gossip, or constantly run down your colleagues behind their backs, or join in the constant moaning about the boss or the teacher. What a testimony it is when a Christian is someone the unbelievers will turn to for straight talking and truth! Someone whose yes means yes, whose no means no. Are you that person?

Can they trust you at *church*? The church above all should be a place of truth and reality. It should not be somewhere we go to put on a show, to put up a front of pretence. It's always sad when we hear that someone doesn't come to church because they feel they can't face people, they can't answer the questions they'd be asked. Actually, if you feel like a failure, church is exactly where you *should* be, because that is your real family, the place where you are accepted just as you are. The church should be a place of truth. You can meet people who have been turned off the church because of the hypocrisy they have found there – sometimes that's an excuse, but sometimes it's true. Our churches should be where we are at our most genuine, when we are with the family of God – the place where we can admit our weaknesses and our failings, find someone to share with, to pray with. That is what the church should be – what it *can* be!

It's right to close this section by pointing us to the Lord Jesus. In him we see someone of such beautiful integrity, as witnessed time after time in the Scriptures. We see it in that hymn of the suffering servant, in Isaiah 53:9: no deceit! We see it in John 8:44-46. No-one could ever accuse Jesus of lying or even of slightly bending the truth, not even once. We see it in Revelation 19:11 as the all-conquering King rides out of heaven to claim his own. And if you know you are not like this – if you know you cannot be like this – if you know that the standard of pure integrity which Jesus calls for is far beyond you – then look at him. It is Jesus that you need. Yet again, the Sermon on the Mount brings us to the end of our own powers and abilities. We need Jesus Christ, who laid down his life on the cross for us, to bury our past and raise us to new life. May the Lord Jesus by his Spirit transform us into men and women of pure hearts, people like Jesus, truth-tellers like him.

You have heard it said… Retribution

Leo Tolstoy, who wrote *War and Peace*, was a philosopher as well as an author. He was a man of ideas. In his later life, Tolstoy became fascinated by the Sermon on the Mount; and especially the passage we are coming to now. Tolstoy was a man of huge privilege: living in late nineteenth century Russia, he was a count, who had great estates populated by serfs who were in effect almost his property. Matthew 5:38-42 had a monumental impact on him. He decided that if we take seriously Jesus' words about not resisting evil, it must mean that we are to have no armed forces, no police, no law courts, in fact no government at all. And so after musing and meditating on these words, Tolstoy was converted to pacifism and became an anarchist. He also started to give all his money away. The book which he then wrote, *The Kingdom of God is Within You*, had a major influence, among others, on Mahatma Gandhi and the development of his ideas, first in South Africa and then in India[30].

So was Tolstoy right? If we believe Jesus' words here, should we be trying to throw off all government, laws and armies, and live in a world entirely free of all such restraints? If that is what Jesus is saying, and if we believe the Bible is true and carries God's authority, then we had better do it. There should certainly be no Christian in the police or the armed forces. Is that where Jesus is taking us, or could Tolstoy have been mistaken?

We have now reached case study number five out of six, concerning retribution. It's one of the most famous passages of the whole Sermon on the Mount; in fact it contains three expressions which are still used in everyday speech today. We still talk about 'an eye for an eye', 'turning the other cheek' and 'going the second mile'. As we have seen, it's had an influence on history; but more than that, for us, it's not only one of the most famous passages, it's also among the most piercingly challenging of them all.

You have heard it said ... Part 2

'You have heard'

Once more we find this pattern where Jesus quotes what his hearers know, or think they know, before he goes on to place his own unique stamp on the issue. The words of verse 38 are well-known, even today. Jesus is quoting almost verbatim from the Law of Moses – in fact these words occur three times, once each in Exodus 21:22-25, Leviticus 24:19-20 and Deuteronomy 19:21. This was to be the law of the land, the law of Israel. At first hearing, it sounds rather brutal. But in fact, in its time, this law had two great strengths. First, it meant that everyone was treated the same. Whether you were a great landowner, or the humblest peasant, if you committed this crime, the penalty was the same; you couldn't pull rank; and if you were injured, whoever you were, the penalty for your attacker was exactly the same. Second, it took retribution out of private hands and placed it under the jurisdiction of the courts. If someone injured you, it was no longer acceptable for you to take the law into your own hands and get revenge – perhaps by killing the offender or even wiping out his whole family. In this way the kind of blood feud which still exists in some places today would be avoided. So this 'eye for eye' law, the *lex talionis* as it is sometimes called, was certainly tough but it kept the penalties just and it kept them in the realm of the law courts.

Now, by the time of Jesus, the literal enactment of these penalties has largely been replaced by a system of fines; but the principle is the same. Limited retribution, *fair* retribution; and all in the hands of the courts. Meanwhile, however, a more problematic move is happening as well. This system of retribution is being transferred back from the courts to the realm of personal relationships. People are thinking, If someone attacks me, I have the *right* to get my own back. After all, the Law says 'an eye for an eye', so that's what I've got a right to. So watch out – don't mess around with me! The way Jesus now goes on to speak confirms that this is the idea of the Law that is taking hold. So now let's move on to Jesus' response.

'But I tell you'

Look again at verses 39-42. The first point to make is that in verse 39 the older Bible translations had 'Do not resist *evil*'; that's a bit misleading and it's probably what rather misled people like Tolstoy. A better translation is 'Do not resist the evil person', or '*an* evil person' as the NIV has it[31]. That is more consistent with what follows. Even so, it's a startling enough command; so let's see how Jesus unpacks it as he gives four examples of what he means.

The first of these, still in verse 39, is the famous one about turning the other cheek. Now if you are right-handed, and you slap someone on the right cheek, the chances are you are hitting them with the back of your hand. That back-handed slap is understood to be specially insulting. Jesus says, don't hit back, don't take this 'eye for an eye' approach; offer them your left cheek to slap as well! Then in verse 40 we have the curious case of the tunic and the coat. To explain: the tunic is the inner garment and the coat or cloak is what you wear over the top. For some reason, someone is taking me to court to sue me for my shirt. What is my response? According to Jesus, I simply say, OK my friend, here you are; and please take my coat as well. In fact, the Law of Moses specifically bans taking away someone's cloak because on a cold night it would be the poor man's only hope of keeping warm (Exodus 22:26-27, Deuteronomy 24:12-13). So what Jesus is saying is even more forceful than it first appears!

Next, in verse 41, Jesus tells his people that they are to go the second mile. The background is that Israel is occupied territory. Under military law, the detested Roman army are allowed to exact forced labour from the populace and make them carry loads for a certain distance. It's a bitterly resented practice. So here's the scenario. You're busy working in your field, minding your own business, when a Roman soldier hails you and brusquely commands you to carry his heavy pack as far as the next town. You have no choice in the matter, so off you go. But when you get to the next town, instead of dropping his load and sidling off into the shadows, you turn to him and smile and say: Why don't I carry it on for you a bit further? In each of these first three cases, the response Jesus calls for is to allow the grievance to double! The fourth and last example comes in verse 42. This is a much more general case. Jesus simply says, If someone asks you for something – he doesn't say what, so presumably it could be anything – give it to him; or if he simply wants to borrow something, fine, don't turn your back on him.

How could we summarise Jesus' teaching here? 'Don't demand your rights.' 'Love, not retribution.' 'Don't retaliate.' Now what sort of person will never strike back but will allow himself to be wronged? Someone who isn't concerned about their rights, who is so secure that when they are attacked, though it might certainly hurt them, it doesn't shake them. In other words – someone who is *meek*. Think back to the Beatitudes – it's there in verse 5. And contrary to what we might think, and what the world may say, this is not a picture of weakness. To be truly meek is to be truly strong. The meek person is one who knows he or she is completely secure because completely accepted by God.

It's the meek person who does not strike back: supremely, the Lord Jesus himself. Long before, the prophet predicted just this of him in Isaiah 50:6-8a. When he was attacked, the Lord Jesus quite literally offered his cheeks to his attackers. He was content to be so insulted, brought so low, because he knew that he was utterly secure in God; and he could safely leave it to God to defend and vindicate him. Much later, Peter reflects on Jesus' life and death in 1 Peter 2:21-23. Once again, we see that the reason he could do this was that he trusted completely in God. If anyone truly practised what he preached, it was Jesus Christ! And he calls us, today, to do exactly the same. It doesn't mean we can't defend *others* – love demands that we do that – but it means that we won't spring to the defence of our *own* rights.

Before we think about the difficult question of how exactly this will apply to us, there are a few points we ought to clarify. So let me offer you three vital keys to unlock this passage.

Key number one: this is about personal life, not national life. Jesus is not talking about how law courts should work, or whether we should have an army or a government or any such thing. This passage simply does not address any of these questions. We know that because we have just come from the Beatitudes, which describe *individual* character; and following them Jesus has been talking about issues of the heart, about hatred, lust and integrity, which the law of the land cannot and does not address. It would be very odd indeed if Jesus suddenly jumped out of talking about individual relationships to talking about the life of a nation, and then jumped back in again to personal relationships in verse 43. So this passage is not about how to run the country; and this is where Tolstoy went wrong. 'An eye for an eye' is a perfectly good principle for the legal system. It tells us that the punishment must fit the crime, that everyone's life or injuries are worth the same, and that it's up to the courts to execute justice. The words of verse 39, 'Do not resist the evil person' does not mean that as a nation we should offer no resistance to a hostile invader, like Hitler's Germany – which, by the way, was the message that Gandhi sent to Britain in 1940.

The Bible *does* address the issue of how the State should operate and what it has the right to do. The relevant passage is Romans 13:1-7 which says that God has established the governing authorities, and they have the right to exercise their rule over us, and the right to use violence – 'the sword' – in order to enforce justice. (We should note that this passage immediately follows one where Paul has been dealing with personal relationships and ethics – see Romans 12:19 in particular, which forbids revenge in personal matters and instructs us to leave such matters to God.) I don't know whether Tolstoy read Romans 13, but I do know that he didn't take it to heart. By the way, even Jesus protested at the illegality of his own trial (John 18:22-23).

Key number two: this is about love, not regulations. You see, with a certain mindset we could read this passage and think: OK, if someone slaps me on the cheek, I'll let them have another go. But if they kick me on the shins they'd better watch it! Or we might think: if someone makes me help them out, I'll offer them a bit more of the same – I'll go the second mile, but I won't go an inch beyond that! No! Jesus is not simply replacing one set of rules with another slightly more generous version. The principle he is preaching is *love*. You look at what people need, and you don't respond to that need by looking up the regulations, you respond by opening your heart, whether they are nice to you or not, whether they are deserving or not.

That overriding principle of love will also help us with some difficult decisions. In his book on the Sermon on the Mount, Don Carson tells the story of a research student in Cambridge who was constantly plagued by drunks who knew he was a soft touch. This guy followed verse 42 absolutely to the letter, until he was (a) sustaining the drinking habits of a good proportions of the alcoholics in Cambridge and (b) literally bankrupt[32]. Having been a research student in Cambridge myself, I know that we could be pretty stupid at times. What this guy was doing was not loving. It is not loving to pay for booze for an alcoholic. That is why at my church we have a firm principle that we do not give out money at the church door. But we *will* go and buy food for people. We try to do that without an inquisition about how deserving they are. And although we certainly need to be wise in the way we obey verse 42, that must not become an excuse to wriggle out of Christ's demands on us. This is about love, not regulations.

Key number three, and most important: this is about the kingdom, not the world at large. We've said this before, and we will say it again: So many people read the Sermon on the Mount, and they think, I *like* this, I can *relate* to this, this is how I am going to try to live. If only everyone would live this way, follow non-violence, love your enemy, do to others what you'd like them to do to you – what a wonderful world this would be! They are missing the point. The Sermon on the Mount is not ethics for the world at large. It is not a tract that anyone can pick up and practise. This is the *Kingdom* Manifesto – the charter of the kingdom of heaven. This is the call of Jesus to his own people. People who have come, poor in spirit, knowing their own spiritual bankruptcy, mourning over our sin and the brokenness of our lives – people who have met Jesus, and been forgiven and come into his kingdom, people who are being transformed every day by his grace.

Now we are ready to apply what Jesus says to our own lives. We will do this by asking a few pointed questions about our personal reactions.

How do we react to the needs of others?
What do our hearts say to us when we see news of some distant disaster on the TV? Do we find ourselves thinking of reasons why we should not send them our support? Do we reach for excuses, or do we reach for our credit card? Perhaps generosity is easier when we have no personal contact with the need. What do I do when I am walking down the road outside my church and I'm accosted by some needy individual? It's always easy to think of an excuse for dodging past them and going my way. After all, I'm busy – I have messages to write about giving to the needy! There is a story told about an American seminary where they ran one of those psychological tests. They announced there was going to be a seminar on the subject of the Good Samaritan – Jesus' parable about the man who was left beaten up and bleeding by the side of the road. They had an actor lie down outside the building with fake blood all over him; and they watched to see what would happen. Most of the people on the way to the seminar walked straight past him. They were so busy going to talk about helping the needy that they walked right past the need. Could that be any of us?

How do we react to a grievance?
This question is more searching. What is your instinctive response when someone offends you? To the kids who throw rubbish into your front garden, or the teacher who talks down to you at a parents' meeting – how do you feel? Perhaps you hear that someone has spread gossip about you, or misrepresented you, maybe in the office, maybe in your street; and you know it's not trivial, it's going to damage your career or your reputation. It's an injury. It's a slap in the face. It's violence. How do we respond? Well, you know what Jesus is asking of you (5:39b)! In all such situations, we have a choice. We claim retribution, our beloved 'rights'; or we show love. We turn the other cheek. I love these words of Martin Luther King, spoken at the height of the civil rights campaign in the USA. This is a man who knew what it was to be attacked: maliciously accused, physically assaulted, widely detested, betrayed by some of his friends.

'Through violence you may murder the liar, but you cannot murder the lie, nor establish the truth.... Returning violence for violence multiplies violence, adding deeper darkness to a night already devoid of stars... Hate cannot drive out hate: only love can do that.'[33] There was a man who understood and practised what the Lord Jesus is telling us. And what an impact his life had because of it!

How do we react to ourselves?
This is where Jesus' words strike the deepest. The sinful nature which still lurks inside us is always crying, Me! Me! Me! Look at me, listen to me! I've been insulted, I've been hurt – demanding its rights, demanding attention. That old, sinful nature, with all its insecurities and worries, that demands its place at the centre of the universe. How *dare* people not respect me; don't they know who I am? I'm going to get them. I'm going to have my rights! What are we going to say to our sinful selves? The spirit of Jesus in us says loud and clear, *No.* How can we say no to the claims of our sinful nature? We can, if we are *meek* – if we are secure, if we know we have complete and utter security in Christ, if our joy comes from him and not from our pride and self-esteem and success. That leads on to the final question.

How do we react to Jesus Christ?
It is Jesus who is calling us to all this. How do you respond to *him*? If you are not a Christian, don't you see how much you need him? These

demands are impossible. No-one can read these words, decide to live this way and then go out and do it. The only person who can begin to live like this is the person with a new heart, a new creation inside. That is what only Christ can give you.

You have heard it said... Enemies

One Monday not long ago, two men stepped out of their spacecraft onto the surface of Mars. Italian Diego Urbina and Russian Alexander Smoleyevsky had been confined in their capsule along with the other four crew members for the past 257 days, but now the long voyage to the red planet was over and this at last was the moment they had been waiting for. If you never heard about this, there's a very simple explanation. *It wasn't really Mars.* The steel capsule had remained for all of those 257 days exactly where it started, in a Moscow research centre, and the surface of Mars was really just a bit of floor. The truth is, this was just an experiment, a simulation. What would it be like to send a real mission to Mars? Well, here's the closest we can get. The astronauts locked in their steel capsule could communicate with earth like real astronauts, eat the same food as real astronauts, and shower only once a week like real astronauts. But for all that, they never got to Mars. The problem is that a real mission to Mars remains far beyond our reach. It is something we will probably never see.

And when we read the Sermon on the Mount, we might well feel we are facing the same kind of problem. Here is Jesus, setting up all these standards and here closing the long section we have just been working through with this almost casual instruction, 'Be perfect, just like God!' Isn't this something that's entirely beyond us? We read this and think, I can't get anywhere near this! We have as much chance of reaching these exalted standards as those guys in Moscow have of reaching Mars.

We have come to the last of six case studies which Jesus sets out for us in Matthew 5 and which expand on the statement he made in verse 20. Jesus has been gradually painting a picture of what this 'righteousness' looks like in practice. In verses 43-48 he takes the demand about retribution (5:38-42) one stage further. Yet again there is the familiar structure.

The Kingdom Manifesto

'You have heard'
Look at verse 43. As we have moved through these six case studies, we've found that sometimes the people's understanding of the Law is accurate, and sometimes it isn't. In this case, it certainly isn't. 'Love your neighbour' – yes, that directly quotes Leviticus 19:18, although at once we notice a difference. The Law says 'love your neighbour *as yourself*', which as we all know is a very high standard of loving indeed. It seems the demand of the Law has been somewhat watered down. But the bigger problem comes with the second half of what they've heard – 'hate your enemy'. The Law of Moses never says that. There is no command to hate your enemy. In fact, the Old Testament contains various encouragements to *care* for those outside your circle of friends. The same chapter in Leviticus also contains verse 34. Exodus 23:4-5 is even more striking. So already there is a strong suggestion in the Old Testament that we should care for those for whom naturally we would not feel inclined to care.

However, by the time of Jesus, it seems that the Law is being understood in this way: Love your neighbour, hate your enemy. Meanwhile the religious leaders have defined 'neighbours' in a very precise way. A 'neighbour' means your fellow-Jew – as long as he is someone who obeys the Law properly! By definition, everyone else is not your neighbour, and they are to be hated. When a pious Jew returned from a trip that took him outside Israel, he would stop at the border and very carefully wipe his feet, so that not one speck of Gentile dust should pollute the pristine land of Israel, an example of the arrogant nationalism which was far from the spirit of the Law.

The words Jesus quotes are echoed in contemporary documents. In particular, there was the religious community at Qumran, which produced the Dead Sea Scrolls. This sect had taken themselves off into the desert in order to pursue an even purer form of religious observance. Their governing document, known as the Community Rule, contained a command to 'hate all the sons of darkness', which would include unenlightened Jews as well as every Gentile. So the words 'hate your enemy' are certainly well-known; but they seriously misrepresent what the Old Testament actually says. Now, it's true that the Old Testament does contain some very negative messages about enemies, so we had better look at those. They come especially in the so-called 'imprecatory' psalms, the ones that perhaps we don't like to read so often. Look at Psalm 139:19-24. It's shocking stuff, which is why you sometimes hear people stop at verse 18 when they are reading this psalm! But if you look more closely at what David is saying here, the picture changes. It's not his own enemies he is concerned with here – it's God's. David is speaking of the people who rebel against God, who refuse to submit to him, who blaspheme his holy name – and they have become *his* enemies only because they are God's. David is not defending his own rights or reputation here – he is not protesting against his own injuries or suffering – he is speaking like this out of his love for God and for *his* reputation. In fact, he turns at once to ask God to examine him to confirm that his own heart and attitudes are pure. David willingly submits his own motives, his own heart, to the Lord's gaze.

So in these embarrassing psalms, the writers are calling on God to carry out his work of judgment. The fact is that God is one day going to judge everyone who has remained in rebellion against him – and it is right that he does so. It may not be a truth that we like, but it *is* the truth, and an essential part of the Bible's message. Everyone who insists on being God's enemy will eventually pay the price; and the price of enmity against God is very high. But to come back to Matthew 5: it is one thing to affirm the rightness of God's ultimate judgment against rebels, but it is quite another to hate those we think of as our enemies because they have injured or offended us. Jesus now goes on to make that clear.

'But I tell you'
Look at verse 44. What Jesus is doing here, you see, is moving us on from verses 38-42 – it's not just that we must not *retaliate* against an attacker, or claim our rights; it's not sufficient that we give more than is demanded of us; it's not enough that we should be generous to an enemy – now Jesus is saying we must actually and positively *love* him[34]. Here's the simple headline statement: 'Love your enemies'. As we've seen, the Old Testament doesn't say 'Hate your enemies'; but it doesn't actually tell us to love them either. But Jesus does! For Jesus' listeners, there on that Galilean hillside, enemies are easy to find. They might think first of the Roman soldiers and their local auxiliaries, whose occupation of their beloved land is so brutal. They might think of the landlords who oppress them, the tax-collectors whose demands are so extortionate; or perhaps they think of the sort of enemies we might think of: at work, the unpleasant manager who is so down on you, the subordinate who resents your success and refuses to co-operate, or the team member who is so disruptive. At home, the infuriating neighbour; or the woman

at the toddler group who has taken a dislike to you; or even a member of your family.

Jesus says – whoever they are, *love* them. And show that love by *praying* for them. After all, he says in verse 45, that's what God is like. God does not deprive evil people of daylight: the sun shines on them just the same. And when it rains – remember rain in a place like Israel is always a sign of blessing, whatever we might think of it! – it doesn't mysteriously fall only on the homes and fields of God's best friends. Jesus says, This is what God is like; and this is what you must be like as well. Make sure that you are. Love them: that is, forgive them, wish them well, do them good with a genuine heart. Take that enemy of yours – you know who it is – and *love* them. Once again, just as we have found repeatedly in the Sermon on the Mount, it is Jesus himself who gives us the most powerful example of what he tells us. When Jesus goes to the cross, when his hands are being nailed to the wooden beam, when the hatred of his enemies is surrounding him in such bitterness, he loves his enemies and prays for his persecutors (Luke 23:33-34).

Dietrich Bonhoeffer was a German pastor who spoke out against Hitler and the Nazi regime and who was later imprisoned and finally executed. During that time of courageous resistance, while he was still free but could see what was coming, he wrestled with the demands of the Sermon on the Mount in his book *The Cost of Discipleship*. He clearly believed that this issue of praying for our persecutors is the heart of Christian obedience: 'This is the supreme command. Through the medium of prayer we go to our enemy, stand by his side, and plead for him to God'[35]. Who is your enemy? It may be an issue of long standing, a relationship full of poison that has accumulated over many years; or it may be only some minor offence. Whatever it is, you need to pray for them. Pray until you begin to love them and then keep praying for their good.

Now Jesus drives his message home with two illustrations which would be very pointed for his original hearers (5:46-47). 'Tax collectors' at this time are proverbially evil people: not only are they characteristically corrupt, but also by doing business with the Roman overlords they make themselves ritually unclean. So to think of 'tax collectors' is to describe the most detested people in Israel. And 'pagans', as our translation has it here, is literally 'Gentiles', people from other lands. Remember that at this time the Jews generally regard Gentiles as dogs. In these two verses Jesus is really saying the same thing twice. The point is not that all tax-collectors are impossibly evil, or that all Gentiles are really pagan dogs. The point is that even the most debased specimens of humanity are capable of living their lives by a certain code. They give as good as they get. They return favours. Yes, they love those who love them; yes, they greet their own family and friends. So, Jesus says: If that's all *you* do, my people, what's so special about that?

We too have our circle of friends and family – the people we naturally do favours for, the people we feel we owe something to, whom we try to treat well. Then there's the rest of humanity – and we don't feel we owe them anything. After all, charity begins at home! Jesus is telling us that we must not set boundaries like that. Remember the parable of the Good Samaritan (Luke 10:25-37). 'Who is my neighbour?', someone asks Jesus. In reply he tells the story of the man beaten up and left for dead by the roadside – and the one who comes to rescue him is not the religious professional, not the priest from the temple, but a foreigner – one of the hated Samaritans. Who is my neighbour? Anyone you're in a position to help, that's who. And if everyone in the world is my neighbour, then there is no-one left for me to hate!

The book *The Hiding Place* tells the story of Corrie ten Boom and her sister Betsie, Christians who are captured and imprisoned by the Nazis in occupied Holland because they are sheltering Jews. The most striking aspect of their story is not the horrors they went through as they were taken from one prison to another and finally to the concentration camp at Ravensbruck. It is the way that first Betsie, and then Corrie as well, are given the ability to forgive and to love their persecutors and enemies. There is the scene when they are first arrested and Betsie, beaten up by Gestapo, tells Corrie how sorry she feels *for her attacker*. Then later, in one of the camps, they discover who it is who betrayed them. Betsie speaks.

> 'Corrie, do you remember, the day we were arrested, a man came to the shop? You were sick and I had to wake you up. Apparently, everyone in Ermelo knew him. He worked with the Gestapo from the first day of occupation.' His name was Jan Vogel. Flames of fire seemed to leap around that name in my heart. I thought of Father's final hours, alone and confused, in a hospital corridor. Of

the underground work so abruptly halted. And I knew that if Jan Vogel stood in front of me now I could kill him.

Days go past as Corrie is filled with this rage, and then:

'Betsie!' I hissed one dark night. Three of us now shared this single cot as the crowded camp daily received new arrivals. 'Betsie, don't you feel anything about Jan Vogel? Doesn't it bother you?' 'Oh yes, Corrie! Terribly! I've felt for him ever since I knew – and pray for him whenever his name comes into my mind. How dreadfully he must be suffering.' For a long time I lay silent in the huge shadowy barracks restless with the sighs, snores and stirrings of hundreds of women... Wasn't she telling me in her gentle way that I was as guilty as Jan Vogel? Didn't he and I stand together before an all-seeing God convicted of the same sin of murder? For I had murdered him with my heart and with my tongue.

'Lord Jesus', I whispered into the lumpy ticking of the bed. 'I forgive Jan Vogel as I pray that you will forgive me. I have done him great damage. Bless him now, and his family...' That night for the first time since our betrayer had a name I slept deep and dreamlessly until the whistle summoned us to roll call.[36]

If we are Christians, we know that we have been forgiven when we deserved nothing. So how can we fail to forgive? Can we look at the Lord Jesus, who prayed forgiveness for his enemies even as they drove the nails through his hands – and not forgive, and not love, our enemies too? But Jesus isn't finished yet. In verse 48 he brings this whole extended section to its climactic conclusion. Step by step we have seen this coming together. We have heard the call – that it is not enough that we do not murder, there must also be no anger in our hearts. It's not enough that we do not physically commit adultery, there must also be no lust in our eyes. Not enough that our divorces should be properly managed, rather we must build our marriages with unswerving commitment and unfailing love. Not enough that we obey the rules about taking oaths, rather we must be people of complete and transparent integrity. Not enough that we should seek our proper legal rights, instead we must treat our attackers with generosity. And now, not enough that we should love our nearest and dearest, instead we must love even our sworn enemies. These are no ordinary standards. We've realised little by little that the level Jesus is setting, and now he confirms it, is in short to be perfect, just like God!

Surely this is impossibly far beyond us. We might as well try and fly to Mars! It's a hopeless quest. Or is it? Did you notice that in verse 48 (and also in verse 44, actually) Jesus doesn't use the word 'God'? Instead, he speaks of our heavenly Father. That's significant because, as we have kept saying, these demands are not for everyone. They are only for people who have God as their Father.

Let's be clear: Jesus is not saying that we will ever achieve sinless perfection in this life – when we get to 6:12 we will find that he's expecting us to keep on asking for forgiveness throughout this life on earth. But he *is* saying that when God is our Father, we will show the family likeness. We've all looked at babies and wondered and commented how much or how little they look like their parents. I can look at my own children and see myself in their faces – for better or for worse, there is something of their father about them! Jesus says, *you* are to look like your Father in heaven. So do we show the family resemblance? Our Father showered unconditional love on his enemies, on rebels, on men and women who had defied his rule and authority – on us. The measure of that love is that he sent his own dear Son to die a death of unimaginable horror, to set us free from the consequences of our own actions. How justly, how reasonably he could have said, They are my enemies, I will simply finish with them? Instead he chose to set his love on us through Christ.

Do we show the family likeness? Is there anything about you that would remind someone of the character of God? Something that just can't be explained in purely human terms? If God is your Father, you have his Holy Spirit in you. You will be a special person! You will find that you can show love to the undeserving, that you can pray for your enemies, that you can resist the temptations of anger and lust and lying and retaliation. We can – if God is our Father – and we will. Christians are special people, because the Lord is making us that way. As we hunger and thirst for righteousness, little by little we will find that righteousness, incredibly, appears in our lives. At times it will feel painfully slow, but it is God's work in us, to make us like our heavenly Father, and he will do it.

Questions to reflect on or discuss

1. Can people trust you? Think through the various places where you interact with others – home, the work-place, your wider family, social

gatherings, church, and so on. Are you known as someone whose word is always completely trustworthy? If not, how can the example of Jesus and the power of the Holy Spirit help you here?

2. How can we resist the constant claims of our sinful nature to assert ourselves and our rights? To demand retribution when we have been wronged?

3. Whom do you find it difficult to love? Why do you think that is? How can the grace of Jesus help you to love them?

4. Think through all six examples or case studies in 5:21-48. Which of these do you find the greatest struggle? Where do you see the Lord helping you to make progress? Do you look more like your heavenly Father than you did a year ago?

Chapter 8
Giving up hypocrisy
Matthew 6:1-4

It would seem that he knew just enough to be convincing. For around twenty years, William Hamman enjoyed a successful career as a cardiologist, presenting himself as a highly experienced heart specialist with several medical degrees and a Ph.D. He led seminars, he ran symposiums, he gave lectures in prestigious places – to the American Medical Association, Northwestern University and the American College of Cardiology. Then, very suddenly, William Hamman's career fell to pieces. When officials of the Beaumont Hospital checked his credentials in the course of examining a grant application he had made, they discovered that he had no medical degrees, no Ph.D., nothing except for a few years at medical school on a course he had never completed. He knew just enough to pass himself off as the expert he claimed to be. Hamman's former colleagues were astounded. They remarked how competent he appeared, how confident and smooth his presentation style. 'I was shocked to hear the news', said Dr Douglas Weaver, president of the cardiology group at the hospital which had given Hamman a training contract of $250,000 plus expenses. 'He was totally dedicated to what he was doing.' That's what they thought!

The only good news in the story is that Hamman did not endanger any patients, because he had not actually attempted to treat anyone. But what Hamman's story shows us is that you can fool an awful lot of people an awful lot of the time! That is exactly what Jesus is talking about in Matthew 6, as in three stages he warns us of the terrible danger of hypocritical religion. The key expression that runs through from verse 1 to verse 18 is this: Don't be like the hypocrites. Be genuine. Be *real*.

The Kingdom Manifesto

So far in the Sermon on the Mount, we have encountered eight Beatitudes (5:1-12) and six case studies (5:21-48) showing how Christ fulfils the Law and what that means for the attitudes and behaviour of his people. Now in 6:1-18 we find three examples of Christian practices, as our new identity as kingdom people is worked out in our giving, in prayer and in fasting. This ordered arrangement again suggests that the Sermon on the Mount is deliberately structured to be easily taught and easily remembered. Whether the arrangement originates with Jesus, or at least in part is due to Matthew's editing, we cannot be sure. 6:1 is an introduction to the whole section: in this chapter we will look at that introduction and the first of the three examples which follow (6:2-4).

Let's begin with verse 1. The NIV translation 'acts of righteousness', which is placed in quotation marks, sounds a little awkward! That awkwardness reflects the difficulty of expressing what is meant here by the ordinary Greek word for 'righteousness' – a word which has already been used in 5:6, 20. The context demands a slightly different meaning here: this 'righteousness', clearly, is something that we *do*, as an expression of what we *are*. It refers to the way that the state of our heart is expressed in the specific actions which Jesus goes on to describe in verses 2-18: acts of religious devotion, we might call them. For the true follower of Christ, these actions flow from a renewed and righteous heart. And such actions can be done either publicly or in secret.

It may be this slight difficulty which led some of the early manuscripts to substitute 'acts of mercy' at this point (the same word that is used in verses 2-4)[37]. That would make verse 1 part of the opening paragraph, instead of standing on its own as an introduction. However, the best manuscript evidence and the flow of the section strongly suggest that the reading 'righteousness', though more difficult, is correct – in which case, Jesus is giving us the general principle in verse 1 before moving on to three specific examples. And in this opening verse he is warning us to be very careful about our motivation. It is so easy, Jesus says, to do the right things for the wrong reasons. And in God's eyes, if we do that, they become the *wrong* things: they cease to be acts of righteousness.

Jesus has already mentioned the Pharisees and teachers of the law, or scribes (in 5:20). The case studies of chapter 5 have opposed the scribal interpretations of the Law. It is clear that in chapter 6 Jesus has these characters very much in his sights, not now in their legal rulings

Giving up hypocrisy

but in their religious practices. We can confirm this from the parallel with chapter 23, where Jesus denounces the Pharisees and teachers of the law; and in particular 23:5, where he accuses them in the words 'Everything they do is done for men to see'. We need to remember that these are very religious people, steeped in God's Word and regarded by the general populace as the pace-setters in all matters of religion. If we keep that image of them in mind, it will help us to realise how great the danger is for any of us who regard ourselves as committed followers of Christ. We must be very careful not to make the disastrous mistakes they made.

Jesus speaks of God as 'your Father in heaven'. Again, just as in the previous verse (5:48), he reminds us that we are part of a unique and special family, fathered by God himself. These words are not intended as a general statement for all of humanity; they are instructions for the family. Jesus is telling us, as he does constantly throughout the Sermon on the Mount, that we are to be *different*: in this case, different from anyone whose religious motivation is merely to impress people.

So this is the message of verse 1, which will then be unpacked in greater detail. The true measure of our spiritual life is what we are like in private, not where others can see us: not in church, with scores or hundreds of people looking on, but at home on our own, where the only audience is God our Father. We might wonder whether this message contradicts 5:16, where Jesus tells us to 'let our light shine before men'. Are we to live out the Christian life publicly or not, we may ask. The answer is that Jesus is addressing two different problems. In 5:14-16, he warns us against a cowardly retreat from the non-Christian world. We are not to drop out of sight from a desire to avoid trouble, or in a misguided attempt to keep ourselves pure of worldly contamination. No, we must be boldly willing to shine the light of Christ into the many dark corners of the world around us. In 6:1, however, the potential problem is that we deliberately show off to spectators – especially Christian spectators – so that they will think more highly of us. No, says Jesus, you are not to promote yourself in that way! In both cases, Jesus' commands have the same final aim – the praise and glory of God.

Jesus' three examples – giving (6:2-4), prayer (6:5-15) and fasting (6:16-18) follow a similar pattern, though the second is much longer because it includes the 'Lord's prayer' as a concrete outworking of what he is teaching. Each of the three begins with an expression like 'When you... do not be like the hypocrites'. This is followed by a description of what the hypocrites do and the statement that they have already had their reward. Jesus then explains the righteous alternative and assures his hearers of their Father's reward if this is true of them.

As I read 6:1-18, I am immediately driven to examine myself, and I hope the same is true of you. Jesus' message is an urgent call to spiritual reality. So: am I genuine, or am I one of the hypocrites Jesus is condemning here? Martyn Lloyd-Jones puts it so well, writing of the whole of chapter 6: 'I sometimes think that it is one of the most uncomfortable chapters to read in the entire Scriptures. It probes and examines and holds a mirror up before us, and it will not allow us to escape. There is no chapter which is more calculated to promote self-humbling and humiliation than this particular one. But thank God for it. The Christian should always be anxious to know himself.'[38] If you are ready for that process of searching and humbling, then read on!

Giving for real

My colleague Mark Detzler tells an alarming story of the 1950s, when his father, Wayne, was training to be a minister. He was on placement with a certain church in Chicago. At the start of the service, everyone received an envelope for their offering, with a space to write their name. When the time came, Wayne placed his marked envelope in the bag like everyone else. But what happened next was rather unexpected! The preacher extracted all the envelopes from the offering bag, and one by one read out each name and what each person had given. Great enthusiasm greeted the impressive sums that were announced – but for a poor trainee minister, it was a highly embarrassing moment when his own rather paltry contribution was revealed!

At a safe distance, the story is amusing, but it has a serious side. In 6:2-4, Jesus is telling us that our giving should be done in secret. As far as possible, no-one should know what we are doing – in fact, in a remarkable expression, Jesus implies that we should barely even know it ourselves! This is the first illustration of the terrible dangers of hypocrisy. As we open up these verses, we will discover that the issue is more profound than merely the amount of publicity we should pursue. Once again, Jesus' words will go to the depths of our hearts and attitudes. So we will begin by working through this short passage, before applying its challenge to ourselves. It begins with a 'therefore' (NIV 'so'), confirming that verse 1 was a general introduction which now leads into a specific case.

Jesus begins 'When you give to the needy' (6:2); and the 'when' is really a 'whenever'. It is certainly not an 'if' – this giving is something Jesus expects us to do on a regular basis. The Greek word for 'giving' refers to giving to those in need – it is derived from and connected to the word for 'mercy'. Previous generations knew this as 'almsgiving'. Thus it relates specifically to giving to the materially poor, rather than more generally to all forms of giving. For the Jews of Jesus' time, bearing the massive economic burdens imposed by the Roman occupation, financial support for the needy was vital. It was highly structured, too, with collection arrangements in every village; so as the crowd listens in, they are on familiar ground. As an aside, this command reminds Christians today that while there are many calls on our giving, caring for the poor should never be forgotten, as evangelical churches are sometimes prone to do.

The other word we need to explain is 'hypocrite', which is so prominent in 6:1-18. Originally, the Greek word *hupocrites* meant an actor in a play. Jesus, of course, is not referring directly to actors! The point about actors is that their words are not to be taken at face value. They are telling a story which bears no relation to what the speakers are really like. In a drama, where the audience understands the conventions, that is all well and good; in real life, it is deception. And that is the essence of hypocrisy: to present an image, to tell a story, to the outside world, which is unconnected with the true state of our hearts. In the case of giving to the poor, Jesus warns his people against 'announc(ing) it with trumpets', whether in the synagogues or in the streets. Either of these locations could refer to the regular arrangements for giving alms, or to a more spontaneous act of mercy: the synagogue was, after all, used for many community purposes as well as meetings for worship. It's highly unlikely that anyone literally blew a trumpet to announce their generosity, although it's a plausible illustration because trumpets were used for all kinds of public announcements. Jesus is using extreme language to highlight the absurdity and inappropriateness of drawing any attention to our giving. 'Don't create publicity', we would say – but this is exactly what the Pharisees and scribes were doing. We can imagine the scene in the narrow, crowded street, as one of these white-robed gentlemen condescendingly and very visibly favours a beggar with his cash; or in the synagogue, as he sweeps through the building and flourishes his wallet. He would be delighted with the arrangements in that Chicago church – as long as had advance warning, of course, so that he could stuff the envelope appropriately!

Jesus' solemn statement at the end of verse 2 will be repeated word for word in verses 5 and 16. These people's reward, he says, is the praise they will receive for their ostentatious actions. It's what they wanted, after all. But if they think there will be any further reward, they are mistaken. If they hoped to impress God, they are wrong. The praise of men is all the reward they will receive. The term used here is the normal commercial one for receiving a complete payment and issuing the corresponding receipt. It's as if these hypocrites are collecting their reward in tangible form and signing papers to confirm they have actually received it!

Jesus has made the attitude and recompense of the hypocrites very clear. Now he turns to the alternative with two simple words: 'But... you' (6:3). How strikingly different this is. No outward show; no publicity at all; instead, while one hand is giving, our other hand should not even guess what is going on! It's deliberate hyperbole, of course, meant to drive home the point that not even *we* are to reward ourselves with so much as a pat on the back for our giving. It's a memorable proverb, which is why it has passed into the English language.

So this is the attitude the Father commends (6:4). Our giving is to be done 'in secret'; and our Father, who unlike a human audience sees 'in secret', will reward us. We might well ask what this reward will consist of. The King James Version adds the word 'openly' at the end of verse 4 (and at the corresponding points in verses 6 and 18), suggesting that while our giving (and praying and fasting) might be in secret, God will vindicate our devotion in public, in full view of the very audience we have so carefully avoided. However, the evidence of the best manuscripts points decisively to omitting the extra word. Jesus is not saying that the reward for secret giving will be public recognition.

It would seem most natural to the context if Jesus is speaking, throughout this section, of rewards in this life, rather than eternity. In each of the three cases, it is likely that the prize is something appropriate to the action that has prompted it. So in this case, the reward is to know that we have given in a way that pleases God and which reflects his own self-giving grace to us. By giving in this way, and not for the applause of others, we show that we are growing in the family likeness, which as we saw in the previous chapter is God's desire and plan for his children. And thus we grow into a deeper and truer relationship with our Father, which is a great reward indeed. The reward, like the original motive, remains hidden in our own hearts.

Should we feel concerned about being motivated by rewards? Some people have thought so. The answer depends, once more, on our motive. There is nothing wrong with seeking a reward like this! Seeking to grow closer to God and enjoy a more intimate walk with him is exactly what he wants from us. It's a desire Jesus has already promised us he will fulfil (5:6, 8).

It's not 'how much?', it's 'why?'

We have seen how Jesus draws the contrast between the attitude of the hypocrites and kingdom people. He has shown us what we are to be like when it comes to the issue of giving. Let's now see how this message applies to us. The attitude of the world we know is that what matters is *how much is given*. The headlines after disaster appeals or charity telethons are always about the amount that has been raised. That is perfectly understandable. After all, the sum raised is the only thing that it's possible to measure! And as Christians, we are certainly commanded to give generously (see 2 Corinthians 8 and 9 for the New Testament's fullest treatment of the subject, especially 9:6-7). But from what Jesus says here, the amount given is *not* what matters most. What matters most is the state of our hearts – just as in verse 7, the value of our prayers is not measured by the number of our words or the length of our speaking!

The word 'love' is not actually mentioned in 6:1-18, but it is clearly present in the background throughout. Jesus is constantly posing the question, What do you love most? The applause of men and women, or the approval of God? As far as giving is concerned, the only motive the Lord will accept is love. Paul makes this explicit in one of his best-known chapters (1 Corinthians 13:3). Without true love in our hearts, without that longing to please God and to walk more closely with him, even the most apparently generous giving is worthless in his sight. What are the motives of your heart when you give?

I don't believe that Jesus' words in verse 3 are opposed to the kind of carefully planned giving which Paul calls for in 1 Corinthians 16:1-2 and 2 Corinthians 9:7. The whole emphasis of what Jesus says is on the attitude of our hearts, not on spontaneity versus forethought. Yes, we should think and plan our giving. If we are married, we certainly need to discuss and agree our giving with our spouse, and we should pray over it together. More than that, we should work together to see how we can give more! If we are able to make arrangements to recover tax on our giving (in the UK this means using Gift Aid) then we should do so, even though it will inevitably mean that one or two other people will know something about our giving. It is perfectly possible to do that with complete discretion and without disobeying what Jesus is telling us here.

It's not for 'them', it's for 'him'
This second application is closely linked to the first. In the world's eyes, it's fine for givers to be recognised and publicly applauded. There is simply no problem about people's generosity being paraded; and it's something we frequently see. For the most part, the recipients of their largesse are unlikely to know or care. But God does both know and care. Giving for the sake of a human audience is so appealing. And the appeal is very subtle. Commenting on this passage, Don Carson points out that there are several different types or levels of hypocrisy in the world. Some hypocrites are genuinely evil people who pretend to be good; but the people in this passage are not like that. They may truly believe they have the best interests of the needy at heart. Yet what really motivates them to give is the thought of the gratitude of those they are helping, or the approval of onlookers. How pleased with me they will be!

There are all kinds of ways we can quietly seek this approval. Even if we have managed not to publicise the original act of giving, there are hints we can drop into conversations at church, ways in which we can subtly let it be known, and thus we fall foul of what Jesus warns us of here. What reward are we really seeking? If what we want is human praise, we can have it. We can even arrange for people in our church to get the impression that we are not only generous givers, but humble and secret givers as well! We can make sure we are known as not only generous, but also spiritual! What a warm glow we feel when our reputation for godliness is reported back to us – what a reward that is! Or perhaps we merely long that our generosity will eventually be

Giving up hypocrisy

discovered accidentally. We never intended for it to be known, of course – but wouldn't it be wonderful if the news got out? A good practical test of this is to ask yourself, Am I as happy to give anonymously as to have people know that I am the giver?

Even more subtle, perhaps, is the delight we take in ourselves when we give generously. Perhaps I have completely avoided letting anyone else know. There will be no approving audience for me, either now or in the future. And yet there is! I myself will be the approving audience. How well I have done, keeping this between me and the Lord! Yes, it was tempting to let it be known how much I'd given to that special collection, but I resisted the temptation. Haven't I done well! But that is hypocrisy. We must never underestimate the desperate deceitfulness of our sinful hearts, which are perfectly content with the lesser and fleeting reward of the praise of men. God's reward – the reward of knowing him, of enjoying his smile – is much more worthwhile.

Mark records a very significant story right at the end of Jesus' public ministry (Mark 12:41-44). Jesus is in the temple watching people place their offerings in the large receptacles which are placed there for the purpose. The wealthy are tossing in large amounts; and many of them, no doubt, are doing so with a great flourish, relishing the sound of the coins clinking on the metal of the trumpet-shaped openings as they fall into the boxes. Then Jesus sees a poor widow who drops in a couple of tiny coins. His verdict on what he sees is striking. In stark contrast to the world's outlook, he says that it's this woman who has made a bigger contribution than any of the others. They have given more, certainly; but she has given all that she has. Her story, and Jesus' comment, underline his teaching about giving in Matthew 6. Yes, she gave – generously and far beyond what she could safely afford, though the amount was tiny. Yet it is not the amount she gave, but the reason she did so, that matters to the Lord. She has not done it for show, for the audience reaction, but for him. And it is her example that Jesus calls us to follow.

Questions to reflect on or discuss

1. What false motives do you struggle with in the area of giving?

2. Does your giving to the poor qualify for a 'whenever' (6:2) – in other

155

words, do you give regularly and generously? If not, how could you change?

3. More generally, are you guilty of hypocrisy in any area of your Christian life? Because this sin can be so subtle, it would be good to ask the Lord to show you more of the state of your own heart.

Chapter 9
Spiritual reality
Matthew 6:5-18

In the previous chapter we saw how Jesus begins to warn us against the problem of hypocrisy, which is the theme that runs through the first half of Matthew 6. In verse 1, he introduces the issue; then verses 2-4 set out the first example – giving to the poor: how hypocrites give, and how kingdom people are to give. In this chapter we will look at Jesus' other two examples. The first of these is prayer. Within that subject, we will give the Lord's prayer (verses 9-15) a section of its own. The second example is fasting – more foreign to most of us, but clearly regarded by Jesus as important, so we mustn't overlook it!

Praying for real

A few years ago I paid a visit to one of our church's overseas workers, who at the time was based in Tibet. Entering Tibet was quite a fraught experience; it was very difficult to get in without being part of an officially recognised tour party. That meant that an inescapable part of the trip was a few days' compulsory guided tourism. So I got to see the sights, including several of the Buddhist monasteries and temples. For me, one of the most memorable features of these places is the prayer wheels. Row after row of them – metal cylinders, mounted vertically just at a convenient height so that as you walk past you can run your hand along and give them all a spin. The idea is that as you spin the wheel you are releasing the prayers that are inscribed on it. You gain merit from spinning the wheel just as if you had spoken the prayer out loud – in fact, if the prayer, or the mantra, is written many times on the wheel, then you get the benefit multiplied accordingly! At the same time, you are radiating spiritual peace and harmony to everyone within range. That's the theory. More prominent still in the Tibetan landscape are the prayer flags. On every hilltop, across many a hillside, you see them draped in great profusion – small squares of cloth and paper which flutter in the breeze, all with prayers written on them, so that as the wind blows, the flags flutter and the prayers are automatically spread far and wide. The more flags, the more prayers. The more prayers, the greater the effect.

These prayer wheels and flags illustrate many of the ideas that people have about prayer: that prayer is a mystical force for good; that the benefit of prayer is proportional to the quantity of prayer; that praying gains you merit, especially if you say just the right words at just the right times. In some form or another, these are actually the beliefs that most of the world's religions hold about prayer! Whether it is Muslims with their five daily prayers, most of them with fixed wording and meticulous preparation and washing, and the merit that it gives you; whether it is Hindus with their ideas of *karma*, gaining merit for the next round of reincarnation; or whether it is the folk religion of modern Britain where your friend might tell you they'll say a prayer for you, without any clue about what they mean – nearly everyone prays. But are they really praying?

If we are Christians, we probably think we have some idea of what prayer is and what we are doing when we pray. But a lot of us find prayer confusing; probably we all find it difficult; and all of us would love to have a better prayer life. So what is real praying about? In Matthew 6:5-15, Jesus addresses just this question for his followers. First, we'll see what prayer is *not*; then we'll see what prayer *is*; and then we'll ask, So what must we do?

Prayer is not...
If you look at these verses, you will soon see there is a simple structure or layout: Jesus says in verses 5-6, Don't do that, do this; and then again in verses 7-8, but a bit differently, Don't do that, do this. So prayer is not *to impress other people* (6:5). Once again, Jesus uses the word 'hypocrites' – this word that basically means an actor, someone who pretends to be what he is not. So what is wrong with their prayers, that Jesus would call them hypocrites? It's not that they are standing up; that

was the standard posture for praying. It's about what they are trying to do when they pray. In the synagogues, when they meet for worship, the practice is to ask a man to come up and lead the public prayers. The temptation is to pray for the benefit of the audience, to pray long, flowery prayers with clever and polished language, to adopt a very reverential tone of voice – in the hope that after the service, people will come up to you and say, What a wonderful prayer! Wow, that was good. Jesus says, That's what the hypocrites love. It's all about impressing people. Or, he says, they love praying on the street corners where they can be fully seen. We might wonder why anyone would do that. It could be because there were certain times appointed for praying – this is yet another area where the religious leaders have laid down stringent rules about when to recite the set prayers[39] – and when the time comes, you are on your way somewhere, and so you just have to stop in the street and pray. Or perhaps they just like to do it that way; but either way, they are praying for show. Of course, the advantage of a street *corner* is that you can be seen from two streets, not just one!

Now, the idea of praying standing on the corner of the street sounds strange to us today. But the principle is obvious enough. If you pray to impress other people, you will probably succeed. They will be impressed, and that will be your reward – your *full* reward. For those of us who lead prayers in public, there's a clear warning here. When we are up at the front of church, or in some other place, who are we really praying for? When we are in a prayer meeting, who are we really praying for? Jesus says, Prayer is not to impress other people. That's hypocrisy – because you're pretending to pray to God, but really you're praying to the audience, or even to yourself!

Then, prayer is not *to impress God* (6:7). It's perfectly possible to impress *people* with your prayers, but it is certainly *not* possible to impress God. The word translated 'babbling' is a strange one (Greek *battalogeo*); it's almost unknown outside this passage, and it seems to refer to a mindless, repetitive burbling. It's not necessarily meaningless, it's just talking for the sake of more talking. It's what people from the surrounding nations would do – the pagan Gentiles. They worship many gods and when they pray they will want to cover all bases, so they pray to each god in turn in the hope that they'll all be satisfied, and they'll all be pleased. The idea behind this is that the more you pray, the better you're doing. The more words you can string together, the better it will be. The more prayer flags you can set flying in the wind, the more times you can spin the wheel, the more hours of meditation you can put in, the more blessed and peaceful thoughts you can think, the better it will be for you – and God, if there is one, will be impressed.

Jesus is saying, Thinking like that misses the point. God is not impressed with your words, or with the quantity of prayer, or with your effort. Jesus is not forbidding long prayers. He's not saying, Five minutes, absolute maximum, then he'll stop listening! Jesus himself prayed all night at times (see Luke 6:12). No: the point is that real praying is not about the form of the prayer, the exact words that you use, or the number of times you can say those words. God is not interested in that. He is interested in only one thing in all this – and that is the state of your heart.

In Luke 18:9-14, Jesus tells a parable about this very subject. Here is a Pharisee – and it's undoubtedly the Pharisees that Jesus has specially in his sights in Matthew 6. He's respectable and smartly-dressed, and he knows how to pray. He is so full of himself, so pleased with himself – and how it shows in his prayer! Then there's the tax collector. Remember what we've said about them (see on 5:46). No Pharisee would go anywhere near one of those dirty collaborators – it's just as well that this one stands 'at a distance', further back, far out in the temple courts. He just pleads for God's mercy. And it's his prayer that is heard.

Prayer is...
Prayer is about a *relationship*. Did you notice how the word *Father* is used here, twice in verse 6 and once in verse 8? Look at the picture in verse 6. You want to pray. You go where you can't be seen, not just into your house but into the *inner room* (an emphasis the NIV misses), which is a place completely concealed from view. You close and lock the door so no-one can disturb you or see you. And there you are closed in with God your Father, and you *pray*. No-one else can hear what you say: it's just you and the Father. No-one is going to be impressed with your words now, so there's no reward there. God himself will take care of your reward. Once again, the *nature* of the reward is not specified. I think Jesus means that in this case, the reward is simply the great reward of knowing God himself. The relationship is the reward – and what a great reward it is! But the main point is that God will look after it.

Spiritual reality

Prayer is about a relationship. One reason we struggle with prayer is that we make it so complicated. Yes, there is a lot we could say about prayer, but basically prayer is very simple, as we will see again in 6:9 and in 7:11. It's a child going to his father and talking! Really understanding this helps us with so many of the problems we have with prayer. You don't conduct any *genuine* relationship for show – unless you're a rich businessman with a trophy wife, I guess! It's the same with prayer – it's not for show. And just as with our relationships, the key moments take place in private. That's true in a marriage, it's generally true in the one-to-one times we spend with our children or with our close friends – and it's certainly true of our relationship with the Father. Praying for real is about getting real with him, one to one; that's what we need to do. Talk to him about whatever is on your heart – the people you love, your worries, things you don't understand, the world news – everything. Now, does this mean that in order to pray, we must literally, always, find a totally secluded and private spot where no-one can see us? Does this actually forbid all public prayer? No: we need to understand the principle behind what Jesus is saying. After all, we can pray in private and still be hypocrites. It's possible to make sure people know exactly what we are doing, even if they can't actually see us.

Shutting ourselves away simply means being aware only of yourself and God. And that can happen anywhere. Often a quiet, empty room is the best place to pray, for obvious reasons. But it's not the only place we can pray. You may know the famous story of Susannah Wesley, mother of John and Charles but with about fifteen children to look after altogether, who would simply sit in the kitchen with her apron over her head, which meant *Do Not Disturb*. That was the nearest to a peaceful spot she could get! Mothers of young children will sympathise – please note, she still prayed even though she had a whole horde of kids to juggle! The point is, this is about relationship, having a communion with God that doesn't watch the clock. If you need to, you too can shut yourself away while you're sitting in your kitchen, or on the bus or train to work, or walking the dog – then and there we can, as it were, go into the inner room, close the door, and open our hearts to our heavenly Father. Even when you are leading prayer in a church service, you can (in a sense) cut the congregation out of your mind – because even though you are leading them, you are not praying to them, you are praying to your *Father*!

161

The Kingdom Manifesto

This is the answer to all thought of using special, flowery language, or carefully polished phraseology, when we pray. How does a little child speak to her father? How does she ask him to read her a bedtime story? Can you imagine this? 'Dear father, whereas it has been found pleasing unto you on sundry preceding days to read unto me from the volume whereof the title is, *Noddy goes to Toytown*, even so as the shades of evening do descend upon the earth do I herewith humbly beseech thee to extend the like favour unto me this eventide.' Really? Have respect, yes, reverence as we come to the God of the universe, of course – but be real! He is our Father.

Then, prayer is about *confidence*. Look at verse 8. Of course he knows! The implication, by contrast to all those people who are trying to impress God with the wordiness or volume or format of their prayers, is that you can pray with confidence because he is your Father God, so he already knows exactly what you need. Even an earthly father, and not a very good one, doesn't need to be asked a hundred times before a request gets through to him. He enjoys giving what is good to his child, and he knows what is best for him anyway! How much more with God! What a wonderful God we have: he is infinite, he made the world and everything in it, the stars and planets, the remotest corners of space, and yet he is interested in knowing you and me! What a loving God, too, who wants a relationship with sinful, broken men and women who live in this poisoned world! He knows what we need; like a human father, he wants to be asked; and he will give us what is good. It's his promise! Not a stone, but *bread*; not a snake, but *fish* (7:9-10)! This is the Father we meet when we come to pray – and when we see him like this, doesn't it make us want to run into his presence? Here on earth, fathers get tired: God is never tired. Here on earth, fathers have to stay late at work, or go looking for work, or may even walk out and disappear: God is always there. Human fathers get cross, petulant, selfish: God is not like that. He always wants to hear from us, welcomes us, has time for us, loves us. Now, if we have taken this passage to heart, what should be our response?

What we must do

1. *We must recognise our deep sinfulness.* As we reflect on what Jesus says here, surely we are horrified at what it tells us about the depth of sinful deceit in our own hearts. We cannot know ourselves as human beings until we understand about sin. We have to realise that sin is not

just about doing certain things we should not do: sin is a polluting force that has infected and ruined every part of our lives, every single aspect of our existence. So much so, that as we see here, sin even infects us in the highest of all human activities – our prayer. We just can't get away from it. As Martyn Lloyd-Jones puts it – and he writes very pointedly on this passage – 'Sin follows us all the way, even into the very presence of God'[40]. If you are a Christian, you know this is true. You can be deep in prayer and suddenly your mind will explode with all kinds of evil thoughts. I can be in that shut-away place and still I can be thinking, I bet they'd be impressed if they could see what I'm praying for now! She asked me to pray for her today, and aren't I clever, I've remembered! I finish praying, and I think, Wow, look how long I've prayed for! Our hearts are so deceitful that even our prayer is poisoned by sin and pride. Even when we are praying, even perhaps in the moment when we are repenting of one sin, our hearts are throwing up another one. In this sense we are all hypocrites – not just the Pharisees swanning around on the street corners. This sin is so deceitful, so insidious, so powerful, it gets us even when we are praying. How we need a rescuer! How we need our Saviour!

2. *We must be in the relationship.* It's vital to point this out here. Most people, not just Christians or 'religious' people, admit that they pray at times. When there is a crisis, a sudden illness, or your teenager goes missing, or the plane hits some bad turbulence, almost everyone admits they pray. They cry out to a God, whether they think they know him or not. Sometimes they complain if there is no answer – but if you are not in the relationship, you can't really pray! God is not your Father, and this wonderful gift called prayer is not for you. You can go and shut yourself away and talk all you like; your 'prayers' will get no further than the ceiling. You need to come *into* this relationship, through the Jesus who died to take away the barriers and offer us a relationship with God; to make God our heavenly Father and you and me his children.

3. *We must pray!* For some Christians, the pitfalls of praying simply don't arise. Maybe, even if you are a Christian, all this has flown over your head because you hardly ever pray at all. But just as you can't have a human relationship unless you communicate, so you can't have the Christian life unless you keep in touch with your Father through prayer. Perhaps you have never realised what God is really like. Perhaps you think of him as someone who would want to keep you at arm's length,

or who will always be angry with you. Or perhaps you have let the pressure of time steal your prayer life away from you. If that's true, can you admit it and ask someone you trust to help you?

One more point to make about this. The very last thing anyone should do as a result of this study is to think, It's true, I *can't* get my attitudes straight, my motives *are* screwed up, I *do* try and impress people – I'd better stop praying! No: Jesus says, twice here, '*When* you pray' – remember, that 'when' is more of a '*whenever*' – just as his words about giving assume we will definitely give, so his words about prayer assume we will definitely pray. Of course, if you're in the kingdom, you will give generously. It's assumed. Of course, if you are in the kingdom, you will pray all the time. It goes without saying. The message is this. Keep praying. Pray, and seek God for the right attitudes, the pure heart and mind, the true motives. Ask him about that! Pray, and enjoy getting to know your wonderful, loving Father. He wants you to come. Pray, and lose track of the time. Pray, and don't count the words. Pray for real!

Pray like this

It's at times of great crisis that the biggest questions are always asked. Whether it's a crisis that affects only ourselves, our own family; or whether it is a great disaster that dominates the news headlines for weeks, the same kind of questions are heard. Where is God in all this? *Is* there a God? What is he doing? And more personally, closer to home – does he care about *me*? Can I trust him? If we are Christians, it's at these times of crisis that we find out what our faith is really worth. We pray, or we try to; but we find ourselves wondering, What am I really doing? The issues seem too vast, or too impossible – what difference can praying really make? What is the cash value of this thing called faith, this thing called prayer?

The wonderful truth which the Bible tells us is that if we know Jesus Christ, then we have God as our Father, and there is nothing outside his control. Jesus has given us the principles of praying: what it is and what it isn't. Now in 6:9-15 he will put some flesh on the bones by giving us a model prayer. And of course, this is one of the best-known parts of the whole Bible, a prayer that's been prayed who knows how many billions of times down all the years since Jesus first spoke it. This is what's always been known as 'The Lord's prayer', because it's been given us by the Lord Jesus. In these famous verses is an outline that shows us what praying should really look like. Most of us probably find these words very familiar; but we must make sure we take them in their context. You may have learned these words by reciting them in church or in a school assembly, but we have to remember that Jesus first says them as an illustration of what prayer *is*, and is *not*. After what he has just said about empty babbling, wouldn't it be crazy to think that prayer is about mindlessly reciting these particular words! Jesus says, This is *how* you should pray, not *what* you should pray. The Lord's prayer is a template, a pattern, not a fixed formula. So let's work our way through the prayer, so that we are clear about what Jesus is telling us; and then pick up three key lessons about prayer and how as God's people we are meant to pray.

So Jesus begins in verse 9: 'This, then, is how you should pray'. That 'then' is a 'therefore' – in other words, this model prayer is tied in very closely with what Jesus has just been saying. And this prayer begins with God and who he is, and where he is. That word 'hallowed' is rare in English these days. It means to keep something *holy*, to keep it special. These days people might talk rather tongue-in-cheek about the 'hallowed turf' of Wembley Stadium or Lord's Cricket Ground – and what they mean by that is that those are special places, and that if you step out onto those playing surfaces you are doing something quite out of the ordinary. People are in awe of those places. That gives us a faint idea of what the word means. God's name is already holy, it is special, and we are praying that it will be known and recognised for what it is. The word 'name' meant far more to Jesus' first audience than it does to us. We hear this and perhaps think Jesus is talking about not swearing in God's name, not blaspheming. It does include that, but for the Jews, a 'name' meant much more than just the label that gives people something to call you. Your name stands for your identity, the person you are. So 'hallowed be your name' is no trivial expression! We are praying that people will recognise the true nature and character of our God, his majesty, his sovereign power, his glory, his love, his truth and justice – for people to recognise all that and to give him all the honour he deserves.

We stay with God as we pray verse 10. We pray that God's kingdom will come. Maybe that's a little confusing. Haven't we said that Jesus has already brought in the kingdom, that that's what he came to do – so what's this about praying that the kingdom *will* come? That's a good question. The kingdom of God is all the people, and all the places, where the rule of God and of Christ is accepted and acknowledged, everywhere people say, Yes, Jesus is King. Jesus came to earth to inaugurate this kingdom, to show by his miracles that God's power was breaking in, to begin with his small group of disciples and to prepare them to take the message of the kingdom out across the world. In that sense, the kingdom has come with Jesus. But that's not the end of the story. Ever since those days, the kingdom has been spreading and growing. It's been growing through *us*, as we live lives that trust and follow Jesus Christ. Every time we share our faith in Christ, every time we preach his truth, every time we see one more person beginning to follow him, we are extending God's kingdom a little bit further. So as we pray this prayer, we are praying for all that.

Even that is not the end of the story. The time will come when Jesus Christ returns in his glory and his triumph and brings in his *eternal* kingdom. On that day everyone will acknowledge his rule and his kingship, whether they like it or not, when as Paul writes in Philippians 2:10-11, every knee will bow at the *name* – there's that word again – of the Lord Jesus Christ. So as we pray this prayer, we are praying towards that day. Your kingdom come![41] Then, 'May your will be done'. In heaven, God's will is already obeyed perfectly. We are praying that his will, his purposes, will be obeyed fully here on earth, just as happens in heaven. We pray for that now, as we look out on the world and see so many places where God's will is being blatantly and violently defied; and we pray for the day when his perfect rule is established here on earth. Again, doesn't this show up the rottenness of the human heart? We are so concerned about our *own* name, *our* reputation, *our* plans, *our* will, *our* little empire. Jesus puts his finger right on our problem when he says – you pray first for *God's* name and honour, *his* kingdom, *his* will! That's what matters most.

Now at this point, having begun with God, his glory, his holiness, his kingdom and his will, the prayer moves on to our own needs – verse 11. Don't you think this is amazing? We seem to have gone from the sublime to the ridiculous, from the lofty heights to the utterly trivial. Lord, establish your kingdom, enforce your great purposes throughout this world, come back in your glory and bring about justice and judgment – oh and by the way, please don't forget my sandwiches! In fact, some of the early commentators were so struck by this that they thought Jesus couldn't literally be talking about bread that you eat. That was just too mundane. They thought this bread must refer to Communion; or perhaps it was a reference to us feeding on God's Word. But no, it means bread! And, by implication, it includes everything else we need to feed our bodies and to keep ourselves alive. The word translated 'daily' (Greek *epiousion*) is a famously tricky one, by the way. It's one of the very few words in the Greek New Testament where we can't be sure what it means, because it seems to be found nowhere else apart from here and the similar passage in Luke's gospel. It could mean 'necessary', that is 'give us the bread we *need*', or it could mean 'for today', or possibly 'for the *next* day'. Whichever of those precise meanings is correct, it comes out much the same. We are to pray for the food we need to live, to trust God for the needs of the day. We are praying that God will meet our *needs*, not our every desire! Jesus will have more to say about this in 6:25-34.

Next, Jesus says, pray for forgiveness (6:12). Every time we sin, we create a debt that we owe to God. Some have found this verse a real problem – is Jesus saying we will be forgiven only if we have completely forgiven everyone else? We will come back to this shortly, but no, what he is saying is that if we are truly God's children, we *will inevitably be* people who forgive. Then verse 13. The two halves of this verse are really two sides of the same coin. We know God never tempts us to sin (James 1:13). What we are praying here is that God will keep us far away from sin. We know we are weak. We are not good at standing up to temptation – so we pray that the Lord will keep us safe. Whether these final words should be 'from evil' or 'from the evil one' it's hard to be sure, but again it doesn't make much difference[42]. As Christians, we have an enemy who is out to get us. Satan is prowling around looking for a chance to attack, and we pray that the Lord will keep us safe.

So Jesus encourages us to make these three kinds of requests for ourselves. I like John Stott's suggestion that these three requests have a very Trinitarian flavour – it's the *Father* who provides for all our daily needs; it's the *Son*, the Lord Jesus, whose death on the cross brings us forgiveness; and it's the *Holy Spirit* who gives us power for the spiritual fight and protects us from the evil one! So as we pray we are engaging with all three Persons of the Trinity! You are probably familiar with the traditional ending of the Lord's Prayer – 'for yours is the kingdom and the power and the glory for ever, Amen'. Those words are usually included when we say the Lord's Prayer in church, and they are in many of the Greek manuscripts, but it's unlikely they were part of the original text. The words are certainly true, and there is nothing wrong with saying them, but as far as the actual text of the Bible is concerned they probably don't belong.

That, then, is the prayer; and that's what it means. Now let's turn to what this means for us and our own praying. Jesus is not saying that our prayer life should simply consist of repeating this little prayer. I think there are three important lessons here that could transform our prayer lives.

1. *The right priorities.* Look again at verses 9-10. It's vital that we notice that this prayer does not begin with us, but with God. When we come to pray, we often rush in, full of our own concerns, the anxieties that are filling our minds, the problems that have accumulated during the day, and our instinct is simply to pour them all out. Lord I'm so worried about tomorrow. Lord, I'm so anxious about my family. Lord, I feel so angry with that guy at work. Jesus says, *Hold on.* The time for that will come, but you must begin here. You must begin with God. Now here's the challenge: which is greater: your problems, or God and his glory? I do not say this lightly, but however serious your situation may be, you have to begin with God – and not just with him, but with his *name*, with all that he is – and with his priorities for the coming of his kingdom. That has to be our highest passion. Revelation 11:15 gives us the picture of a great declaration at the end of the age, the day when this prayer, this longing for the kingdom to come, is finally answered in full, and heaven responds with worship. So as we pray, we need to begin by lining ourselves up with God's great purposes. This is for our own sake too. We can never really pray until we recognise the character and the nature of the God we come to. Then that perspective on God enables us to pray.

So we pray – Lord God, I ask that your name would be honoured in this situation that I'm struggling with, because I know that is what matters most: that the people I love, the people I'm concerned about, would acknowledge you as the great and wonderful Lord that you really are. Lord please advance your kingdom – in the world's troubled places, may your kingdom come as people bow the knee to King Jesus. Lord, may the rulers of this world understand that they are accountable to you, that they only hold their power because you have given it to them.

Lord, would you please work in the great disasters to bring despairing men and women to know you and the true life that only you can give them. Are you willing to pray, Your will be done – not just out there in the world but in your own personal life, whatever it is you are facing? Do you remember someone who prayed that prayer (Matthew 26:39)? Do you remember what it cost the Lord Jesus to pray like that? But for the joy of obeying his Father, he did, and so must we.

2. *The right relationship.* The first two words of the Lord's Prayer are 'Our Father'. This *prayer* is the *family* prayer, as some have called it. As Martyn Lloyd-Jones puts it, 'The only thing that really matters for us is that we know God as our Father'[43]. That's true – because everything else flows from this. Again, we must understand that this is an exclusive relationship. If you don't know Jesus Christ, then God is not your Father, and you cannot pray, and this is not for you. The world may talk about the 'brotherhood of man', or the universal fatherhood of God, but the Bible shows us plainly that that is all false. The only way to know God as your Father is to come to him through Jesus Christ, to ask him to forgive you and put you right, and to start living this new life under his control – the life that the Sermon on the Mount is describing, all the way through.

As Christians, we remember this is a Father we can trust (6:11-13). Praying like this helps us to remember that we actually depend on God for everything. How foolish we are if we think we are in control, if we don't realise that it is our heavenly Father who gives us all we need. That's why it's such a good custom to give thanks to God as we sit down for every meal, as long as that doesn't sink to the level of meaningless ritual, because food on our plates is such a vivid and visible representation of his goodness to us. We need to remember that we are dependent on him not just for every meal, but even for every breath we take – but meal-times are good times to start with! We can trust our heavenly Father to take care of all our daily needs – our *needs*, notice, not our luxuries – and there is a difference! The prayer asks for bread, not caviar. We can trust him to forgive us. We can trust him to keep us clear of evil – not out of trouble, for Jesus never promised us that. In fact he promised his people a life of challenges and trials – the Christian life is not like being wrapped up in a huge roll of cotton wool. In this life we will know trials, and God is faithful in them. But we need not know *evil*. God is our Father; he wants our good – and he will do us good.

3. The right spirit. There is just one section of the prayer that Jesus adds a comment on – verse 12 (see verses 14-15). These verses have really troubled people. Does this mean that I have to forgive everyone, perfectly, before God will even think of forgiving me? Am I lost if I haven't been able to forgive? I thought salvation was all about God's unconditional grace, but these verses seem to place conditions on it. We need to remember that this prayer is for people who are already in the family, part of the kingdom – and therefore already *forgiven.* Jesus is not talking here about the act of salvation, he's talking about the experience of living as a Christian. And in the Christian life, as we know, we still need to ask God's forgiveness for the sins we commit each day – for we are still sinners, as the Bible makes clear and as we ourselves know all too well. Jesus' point is this. If we are not forgivers, it casts serious doubts on whether we have ever genuinely repented and been forgiven ourselves. If you say about anyone, I could never forgive him, the question must be, Have you ever really been saved? In case you think that is going too far, read the parable Jesus told on just this point (Matthew 18:23-35). The point of the parable is what Jesus says at the end. If we do not show a forgiving spirit, it shows that we are not forgiven and we will not be saved.

Our problem is that we do not understand how much we have been forgiven. In the parable, the servant is forgiven a fortune. I suppose for us the nearest parallel would be one of those rogue traders who manage to lose billions of pounds on the currency markets. Imagine that was you and you personally owed billions of pounds! And then suddenly, it was all written off. We think our sin is trivial – but it isn't. Have you looked at what it did to Jesus on the cross? We think our sin is normal, it's natural, because we've been surrounded by sin since the day we were born. We don't see that what we've been forgiven through Christ's death is vastly greater than anything we could be asked to forgive. It will cost you – but it won't cost you what it cost him. If we really understand this, if we have reached that point that Jesus describes in the Beatitudes of mourning over our sin (5:4), there will be *no-one* we cannot forgive. There will be no grudge that we cannot drop. Forgiveness is the one crucial element of the Christian life that Jesus singles out here. The spirit of forgiveness is right at the heart of the Christian life. As Christians, as people of the cross, we are *defined* by grace; and we must be *people* of grace. Forgive, as you have been forgiven. If we can pray this prayer from our hearts, then we will truly have learned to pray.

Spiritual reality

When you fast

'Because you're worth it' is famously the advertising slogan of L'Oreal, the major cosmetics company. Women are urged to buy its products, to pamper themselves with the promise of beauty which the commercials hold out, apparently on the grounds that it would simply be unfair to deprive themselves of something so beneficial! The slogan sums up the attitude of commercialism: whatever we can obtain that will do us any good, give us any pleasure, enhance our life experience – we must acquire it at all costs. We are worth it! In such a world, a message that features self-denial does not immediately appeal. Yet in Matthew 6:16-18, Jesus is devoting valuable time to explaining to his followers that he *expects* them to deny themselves; he *expects* them to do without certain things that do them good and give them pleasure. He is talking about fasting. However the practice has been abused by others – and it certainly has been – the people of the kingdom are to fast, just as they are to give to the poor and to pray. Fasting is to be a normal part of their lives. How counter-cultural, for us! And so these words pose a challenge to all Christians today. In our hearts, which world are we part of? Or to put it another way, how much is following Jesus really worth?

In verses 16-18 we come to the third and last of these 'religious activities' which Jesus is describing. He approaches the issue of fasting just the same way as giving and praying. He assumes his followers will *give*, he assumes they will *pray*; he assumes they will *fast* as well. He doesn't say, Just because the hypocrites do it falsely, steer clear – any more than you would tell me, Because there are fake £5 notes in circulation, don't ever touch a fiver! You would say, Make sure you stick to the genuine article! That's what Jesus says here; and this time we will tackle the issue by asking a series of questions.

What is fasting?

We need to ask this question because, frankly, for us, fasting is a pretty obscure subject. What are we talking about here? Fasting does not mean going on a diet or losing weight! It's not about starving yourself for the sake of your health – although fasting can do your health a lot of good. No, fasting means *abstaining from food for spiritual purposes*. It is a deliberate action to deny your appetite to eat, in order to focus on prayer and worship. Actually, it can apply to things other than food as well (in 1 Corinthians 7:5, Paul is talking about fasting from sex for similar purposes), but to keep it simple we will stick to that one idea. You fast to help you to seek God and to deepen your relationship with him – and we'll come back to that later.

There are at least two reasons why fasting seems weird to us! First, because in the past the idea has been taken to such extremes. That was especially true hundreds of years ago, in the medieval church – and many Christians and Christian movements have been reacting against that excess ever since. If we think of fasting at all, we probably associate it with monasteries, with cold stone floors and sleep deprivation – in other words, we associate it with *asceticism*, the idea that giving yourself a really hard and miserable life is a good thing in itself. So back in the recesses of our minds, fasting has bad associations and a bad name. As a result, fasting was rare at least among British evangelicals until quite recently; thankfully, there has been something of a re-discovery in the last thirty years or so.

The second reason is almost the opposite, and we have already mentioned this: it's because of the world we live in today. We are constantly bombarded with the idea that a good life is about satisfying every physical desire we have, as fully as we can. We get that most obviously from advertising, which works mainly by persuading us to buy stuff we don't need. But it's there in the culture in many more subtle ways as well. Whether it's food, sex, or holidays, the assumption is always that you should get as much as you can, whenever you can. And in a world that mocks celibacy and thinks people who keep sex for marriage are either sad, repressed or stupid, it is hardly surprising that fasting from food should also be thought bizarre. As Christians, we are far more influenced by thinking like that than we usually realise.

Where did fasting come from?
In the Bible, there is only one fast that is actually commanded. That fast came on the Day of Atonement (Leviticus 16). 'Deny yourselves' (verses 29-31) is understood to include fasting (see the NIV footnote). This was a day of national repentance when the people were to focus on their sins and the wonderful way that God rescued and forgave them. Then as time went by, other fasts were added – Zechariah 8:19 mentions four regular fasts, in different months of the year. Overall, the Old Testament gives a positive view of fasting and provides plenty of examples of *voluntary* fasts for special reasons. For some reason, perhaps because

of the repeated and pressing need to seek the Lord's guidance at this time, many of these examples cluster around the end of the Exile, when the Jews were returning to their own land. There were three types of occasion when people would decide to fast. One was times of *crisis or special need*, as in Ezra 8:21-23. Ezra is about to lead a great throng of Jews back from Babylon to Jerusalem after the Exile. It's a great occasion; it's also a time of danger. So he calls a fast and prays urgently to the Lord. Or see Nehemiah 1:3-4. Nehemiah receives disastrous news from Jerusalem. It's a time of crisis; he needs to know how he should respond, so he fasts and prays.

A second occasion for fasting is at times of *repentance*. There's a good example in Nehemiah 9:1-3. The scene is Jerusalem: the people stand together, confess their sin and fast; and you see also how fasting is tied up here with worship. Then the third kind of occasion is a time of *specially seeking God* in prayer, as in Daniel 9:1-4a. Daniel is praying like this. Lord, you said this exile would last seventy years – and seventy years is up. Please have mercy on our people, please forgive, please restore us! It's a wonderful prayer, if you read on through Daniel 9. He is fasting because he wants to focus everything on meeting God and discovering his will.

For these reasons, then, godly people would fast – sometimes as individuals, sometimes together as the body of God's people. However, by Jesus' time the situation has gone sharply downhill. The religious landscape is now dominated by the Pharisees, and as they do in so many other areas, they take something good, push it, add to it and then freeze it in a rule-book. So by Jesus' day, the Pharisees are observing regular fasts, not once a year, but twice every *week* – see Luke 18:12 for biblical confirmation of that. And they don't fast as a voluntary response to God, they do it to prove their own righteousness. That's the background to this passage in Matthew 6.

What does Jesus say?
Look back to verses 16-18. Once more, as he did with giving to the needy, and as he did with prayer, Jesus begins by warning his people against hypocrisy. Don't be like them, he says. Evidently, the hypocrites go round with very long faces, looking sad or gloomy to make it obvious that something's going on. Even more, they 'disfigure their faces'. It's not clear exactly how they would do that, but most likely it means

that they wouldn't wash, they might smear dirt or ashes over their hair and their face, and generally they would make themselves a bit of an eyesore. Of course, they won't make themselves unrecognisable, because if no-one knows who they are, they won't get any credit!

Jesus says, Don't be like that. For the third time, and in just the same words as before, he says that they already have their full reward. People are impressed – great! – that's the reward. That is *all* their reward. Let's hope they enjoy it. No, when *you* fast, act completely normally! Putting oil on your head was the normal custom; Jesus isn't saying they have to make an effort to look splendid! He's saying – if you are fasting, just do whatever you normally do when you go out in the morning. Have your shower. Brush your hair. Put on your moisturiser. Do whatever you would do – so that *no-one but your Father God* will have any idea what you are up to! He will look after your reward, too. Once again, I think the 'reward' that's in view is simply the high reward of the relationship he has brought us into, the relationship we are building all the time when we seek him wholeheartedly, like this. You seek God with all your heart, and the reward is that day by day you know him better and you become like him.

The clearest commentary on this passage is actually found back in the Old Testament, in Isaiah 58:1-9, where we find both a solemn warning against hypocrisy and a wonderful promise relating to fasting. The prophet is telling people just this, Don't be hypocrites! Don't fast and expect God to hear your prayers, when all the time your lives show that you are a million miles away from him! You're exploiting people, you're oppressing them, you are fighting among yourselves – do you think the Lord is pleased with you? True fasting can only come from a genuine heart. True fasting is tied up with justice, and compassion, and caring for the poor. If you want to enjoy a real relationship with the Lord, your heart must be right, and your actions must prove it.

We might be asking at this point – Does Jesus actually tell us we *should* fast? No, he doesn't – and that is not the point of this passage – but the 'whenever' at the start of verse 16 implies that we will. Matthew 9:16 confirms that Jesus expects fasting to be a normal part of our Christian experience – although it seems, from the same passage, that Jesus and his disciples did not keep the frequent, regular fasts. Jesus himself certainly fasted, as we read in Matthew 4:2. This crucial time, just before his public ministry begins, was marked by a most serious and extended period of fasting. And if Jesus needed to fast at such a time, why don't we?

What about the early church?
How did Jesus' followers pick up his teaching and example? Did they fast? They certainly did. They clearly understood Jesus to mean that fasting was still normal and appropriate. In Acts 13:1-3 we read how the church in the multi-cultural city of Antioch, seeking God's direction for their future, pray and *fast*. The Lord answers them in what is probably a very surprising way – send out your two best men on a mission I am calling them to. So they fast and pray some more, and they send them out. Fasting here is closely integrated with the church's worshipping life. Soon afterwards we find the same Paul and Barnabas in the churches they have established on that mission (Acts 14:23). This is a key stage in the lives of the young churches – for the first time, they will have leaders of their own; humanly speaking, these churches are now stepping out on their own. As they commit these new leaders to the Lord, no doubt with a lot of nervousness on all sides, they pray and they *fast*.

To summarise where we have got to: we have found that fasting runs all through the Bible; and we've found Jesus teaches about it and assumes we will do it too! But there is still a difficulty.

One big problem
It's exactly the problem that Jesus identifies here. Fasting lends itself so easily to hypocrisy and pride – in fact, more so than either giving or prayer. All Christians give their money. All Christians pray – it doesn't immediately sound super-spiritual to talk about giving or prayer. But *fasting* – well! Fasting today is so easily seen as something that's on a higher spiritual plane. If you even hint that you've been fasting, you are likely to get some funny looks. But you will also find people believing you are some kind of super-saint – and then, if you are not careful, you will find yourself agreeing with them!

What is more, fasting is so easily turned into a rigid law. The Pharisees had already done that. Sadly, it wasn't long before it happened in the early church as well. There is an interesting document called the *Didache*, which was probably written within the first few decades of the church's existence. It's a kind of teaching manual for churches, and it already shows signs of this kind of rule-book mentality. Here's what it says about fasting: 'Let not your fasts be with the hypocrites, for they fast on the second and fifth day of the week [Monday and Thursday]. Rather, fast on the fourth day and the Preparation [Wednesday and Friday]'. In other words, the way to avoid hypocrisy is simply to pick different days to fast! They entirely missed the point of what Jesus is saying – but that is so easily done.

When we fast
Finally, let's focus on ourselves. Is fasting for Christians today? The Bible's answer is clear: Yes, absolutely. Fasting is appropriate on just those occasions when God's people fasted in the Bible – both for us as individuals, or together as a church, as a body. It's appropriate in times of crisis or special need. When, like Ezra or Nehemiah, we are aware that some great challenge or some great difficulty is in front of us – perhaps some unexpected news has arrived, or perhaps we are preparing for a new phase of our lives – a new job, or even marriage, or a new ministry – we will respond with prayer and with fasting. There are also times when leaders need to call the whole church to fast and pray. It may happen when we realise that we have sinned. In some very serious way we have failed God, we have turned away from him; and we know that we need our relationship with him to be restored. Then, like the people of Jerusalem in Nehemiah's time, we will come to him with *fasting*. When we know we specially need to seek God, when we are uncertain about our future, when we believe he might be leading us in a new direction, then like Daniel, or like the church in Antioch, we will seek him with fasting. These verses are ones we so often ignore – and that's to our loss.

Is fasting as important as prayer? No – you can't live a Christian life without prayer, but you can live it without fasting. If we can think in terms of family life, prayer is like the daily conversations, the connection that builds and cements our relationships, and you can't do without that; fasting is more like the special occasion, the outing with your kids, the special treats. Now you can have family life without those times – but ask yourself, would you want to?

Fasting has some great fringe benefits. It is good for your physical health, especially if you fast for a day or more; it is good for mental clarity, which is specially helpful at times of decision; more important, fasting shows what really controls us. If you want to know what drives you, try fasting; and you will soon discover how far you are ruled by your appetite and how deep your pride is as well. Fasting asks us the question: What do I need to be truly content? Do I have to have all my physical appetites met before I can be content – or have I learned what it means to be content in Christ alone? This is what Paul talks about in Philippians 4:11-13 – being content in any and every situation, in plenty or in want.

Of course, there are practical issues to be considered. You should not fast if you are ill, if you are diabetic, if you have a history of eating disorders or if you are pregnant – but that still leaves most of us who *can* fast! For a person in normal health, the physical impact of missing food for a day is not great. But above all, fasting is not to impress people – and it is certainly not to impress God. In a sense, fasting is more to prove to *yourself* that you are serious about him. Are you serious about knowing God? Can I challenge you with this: If you say you are a Christian, and you don't ever long to be closer to him, whatever it costs – then what is wrong with you? If you would not consider fasting as part of building that relationship with your heavenly Father – why not? If even skipping a few meals is too much effort, what is knowing him really worth to you?

As we reach the end of this section of the Sermon on the Mount, Jesus' message rings out loud and clear. It's a call to be real. It's a call to be genuine! If you are a believer, have you heard the call to seek the Lord, to seek your Father, with all your heart and in all you are doing? Never mind what other people think of you, their good and bad opinions. There is only one opinion that counts – and actually, if you are in the family, he has already given it. He loves you, more than you can possibly imagine. So enjoy knowing him. Enjoy his love.

Questions to reflect on or discuss

1. In what ways do you find prayer a struggle? Can you trace those difficulties to your own sin or do you think the problems come from elsewhere? What have you found most helpful?

2. The right priorities; the right relationship; the right spirit. Which of these areas do you need to work on if you are going to have a more effective prayer life?

3. What experience do you have of fasting? If, like most Christians today, you have very little experience of it, are you prepared to try it? What might encourage you to fast – and what might put you off?

4. How much are you troubled by thoughts of other people's opinions of you – especially other Christians' view of how good a Christian you are? What is the answer to this problem?

Chapter 10
Where is your heart?
Matthew 6:19-34

In the first half of Matthew 6, Jesus has been teaching us about the importance of being real, not hypocrites, specifically with reference to giving away our money, praying, and fasting. All these relate to the attitude of our hearts as we live the spiritual life. In the second half of the chapter, the Sermon on the Mount takes a new turn as Jesus begins to talk about how we relate to this world, what we own, what our priorities and ambitions are. It's very challenging, because we love to think of ourselves as being in control of our own lives, and what we do; but Jesus' perspective is different. He presents us with some inconvenient truths which a non-Christian will certainly find hard to accept. He is telling us that most of what people put their efforts and energies into is ultimately futile; that we are *not* masters of our destiny; and that we need to stop worrying and trust God our Father to take care of all our needs.

Treasures in heaven (Matthew 6:19-24)

Not long ago, I went back to college – not to study, this time, but for a grand reunion. Everyone who was around long ago, in the early 1980s, was invited back. So there was a big formal dinner, and drinks before and after, which went on into the early hours of the morning; and an absolutely deafening noise of conversation as everyone caught up on the news of the last few decades! As you do at these occasions, I spent a lot of time looking round the room, seeing who was there, spotting the people I wanted to see and perhaps one or two that I didn't; and simply observing, seeing and hearing how people had changed and what thirty years had done to them. There was a lot of grey hair – or in some cases, not very much hair at all. Some of the women, and many of the men, were quite a different shape from what I remembered. All of us had aged; I derived some satisfaction from seeing that most had aged more than I have!

Some of them, you might say, are very high achievers. A couple of my old friends are now professors. Two more have married each other: *he's* high up in the oil industry, *she* breeds alpacas! Academics, bankers, teachers, civil servants – and one of my best friends, who simply brings up her two boys and works a couple of hours a week in the local library. But however they had aged, whatever they had been doing, however high or low they have flown, all these people had something in common. For the last thirty years, they have all been investing. They have all been accumulating treasure, pursuing their priorities – and very often you can tell what kind of treasure it is from the way that they talk. For some of them, their great treasure is their career. For others, it's their family. For some, it would seem, their supreme treasure is themselves. And for some, their treasure is somewhere else altogether: some of them have what Jesus calls *treasure in heaven*.

This is what Jesus is talking about in Matthew 6:19-24. He confronts us with the fact that all of us are investing, building up a portfolio of treasure either on earth or in heaven. He calls us as his people to make sure we are investing wisely – not in the transient and temporary treasures of this world, but in the permanent and unfading treasures of the world to come. This passage consists of three little sections, which at first sight might seem to be rather disconnected. But in fact they all focus on this central challenge about our *priorities* and our *treasure*. Jesus is telling us that we have three fundamental choices to make.

Your treasure – in heaven or on earth?
Look again at verses 19-21. Jesus is assuming that everyone is storing up treasure somewhere. He identifies two options. One option is storing up treasure on *earth*. In Jesus' day, there are a number of ways you might do that. Some are similar to today, others a bit different, because there are no banks or financial investments of the kind we know. One kind of treasure is splendid clothes, perhaps inlaid with gold or jewels; you might store your wealth that way. Or you might own fields full of sheep

or cows, or fields of grain, or vineyards, or a fishing boat on the Sea of Galilee. You might own houses. You might not manage to accumulate very much at all, but it would still be your treasure. Jesus says, Don't you realise what is likely to happen to that kind of stuff? Moths can get at those fancy clothes of yours and reduce them to ruin; rats can munch through your crops – the word 'rust' (6:20) simply means 'eating' and it describes any way in which vermin, or decay, could consume your valuable property. Even if you escape all that, there is still the possibility of theft. Since homes are generally built out of mud bricks, breaking in to a house would generally require little more than a spade.

For us today, treasure tends to take a slightly different form, and a thief is more likely to break a window than dig his way in through the walls – but otherwise the picture is exactly the same. Do we really think our property is immune from decay, destruction and theft? You are deluding yourself if you do. In fact, you must have slept through the recent financial crisis, ever since it began with the fall of Lehman Brothers, America's fourth largest investment bank – and that trail of dazed employees we watched on television, departing company headquarters with their belongings in little cardboard boxes. Following that, many of the world's great financial institutions and even entire national economies have faced collapse. When a whole country can move from 'tiger economy' to near-bankruptcy in the space of a couple of years, do we really think *we* are immune from financial disaster? Banks fail; pension funds collapse; jobs are lost; cars rust; houses are repossessed; our money is eaten away by inflation or by taxes. Wherever we live in the world, and whether we have much or little, we should know that we cannot rely on money!

Exactly the same applies to anything that gives us status and worth: our career, the friends we surround ourselves with, our sporting obsessions, anything that gives us status and identity; yes, even our family. How foolish we are if we place any confidence, any security, in any of those – in other words, if we store up for ourselves treasures on earth. They are all destined to disappear; and even if they don't disappear before you die, you certainly can't take any of them with you. When you are lying on your death bed, you will not be making a packing list of all the possessions you will take into the next life. The Greek words literally say, Do not treasure up for yourselves treasure on earth. Jesus is *not* saying, You can't *have* any of this stuff – some of it is a necessity, after all – but he *is* saying, This must not be your *treasure*. It must not be your security. In reality, it is no security.

Now he tells us, There is a far better alternative. Instead of pouring out your energy and your love on that kind of stuff, treasure up for yourselves treasures in *heaven* (6:20). That comes with an unbeatable advantage. If you have treasure in heaven, it doesn't decay, or get consumed or destroyed, or lose its value. It can't be stolen. What is this 'treasure in heaven'? We need to be careful here, in case we start thinking that anyone can earn credit with God that they can later cash in, like supermarket vouchers, to buy their way into heaven. No, we have to keep remembering that Jesus is talking to his own followers here, people who already belong to his kingdom. So he is *not* saying that anyone can accumulate credit with God by doing good deeds, or that we can build up heavenly credit every time we give to charity. No – the Bible is clear – until you belong to Jesus Christ, you are permanently and for ever in hopeless debt.

This message is for his own people, for Christians. Every time you serve others for the sake of Christ, you are storing up a little more treasure in heaven. Every time you lovingly share your faith with someone, or grow your Christian character so that you become more like Jesus, or sacrifice something precious because he calls you to do it, or willingly face abuse or persecution because you love his Name, your heavenly treasure grows. Look at the way Paul puts it in 1 Timothy 6:17-19. You see, what Jesus is saying here is really common sense. If you're a Christian, you can have treasure here, if you want to. It will last a few years; it won't satisfy you anyway; you will either watch it disappear or worry that it will; and with unfailing certainty, it will last no longer than your earthly life. Alternatively, you can build up your treasure in heaven, where nothing can get at it and where you will enjoy it for ever. The choice should be what we call a 'no-brainer'.

What is more, making earthly treasure your priority is dangerous (6:21). Wherever you build up your treasure, wherever you pursue your priorities, that is where your heart will be. If your treasure is in the bank, your heart – your love, your devotion – will be in the bank. If it's in your comfortable, secure lifestyle down here, whether that means property or career or meeting up with your friends – your heart will be there. But if you are building up treasure in heaven – then that's where your heart will be too.

Where is your heart?

Your vision: light or darkness?

Look now at verses 22-23. At first sight, these verses may be puzzling. It's an illustration about eyesight. Your eyes are what you see with: they are like a lamp that shows you the way to go. If your eyes are sound, working properly, you can see clearly what's in front of you. You don't blunder into obstacles or fall down the stairs. But if your eyes are *not* working properly – if you are blind – then you might as well be in pitch darkness. Of course, the point Jesus is making is not about physical eyesight. What is true physically is also true spiritually. He is talking about how we perceive reality – what today, using similar language, we would call our world *view*. And when our English translation reads 'if your eyes are good', there is actually a play on words in the original, because the word translated *good* literally means *single*[44]. So Jesus is saying, the kind of view of the world you need is one that is very focused, very clear. We would say, not single-eyed, but single-*minded*. That's what he means.

Or think of it like this. If you have ever experienced double vision, perhaps after a blow on the head, you will know that for as long as it lasts, double vision makes normal life impossible. Jesus says, What you need is a single, focused vision: a single set of priorities. You can see how this connects with what he has just said. You need to be investing in heavenly treasures – that should be your one priority, your single goal – not pouring your energy into temporary and passing toys and trivia down here.

Recently, my wife and I were at the theatre. A man sitting in front of us spontaneously started telling us his life story – unusual among us reserved British, but that's what happened! He told us he was born with a severe defect in his eyes, which had grown worse and worse until he couldn't read and in fact he could barely see. His view of the world was both limited and distorted. And then a couple of years ago, he had a cornea transplant; suddenly he had one eye with almost perfect vision; and his life was totally transformed. Suddenly the light had come on. What we need, as Christians, is a simple, undistorted vision, so that we see the world as it really is, and so that we can look, undistracted, towards our Lord and eternity.

Jesus ends this illustration with a warning about deceiving ourselves (6:23b). It's bad enough to be in the dark, to be spiritually blind – but to think or to claim that you can see when really you are blind is the worst state of all. If you were physically blind, but acted as if you could see, and told everyone you could see – well, you can imagine the consequences! Or if you had double vision and tried to live normally, you would be heading for disaster. Similarly, if you claim to be single-mindedly following Christ, when in reality you have never known him, then you are hallucinating, you are fooling yourself and you are heading for disaster. Yet again Jesus is asking us the question: Are you genuine? Are you for real?

Jesus will have more to say about this in 7:21-23. There are many people who claim they are following Christ – or maybe even believe that they are – because they come to church, spend time with Christians, or know how to use the right words; but in fact they are nothing of the kind. They think they have the light, but actually they are still in the dark. Could that be you? Don't fool yourself that you are in the light when the truth is that you are still in darkness. And so we come to the third and final choice.

Your master – God or money?
Look at verse 24. Again, Jesus lays this out very bluntly. You can serve only one master at a time. Wait, you might say – what's this about serving a master? I don't serve any master: I'm my *own* master! Plenty of people think that: Jesus says otherwise. The word translated 'Money' in the NIV is written in some English versions as 'Mammon'. Originally, mammon meant something you put your confidence in. Because so many people do put their trust in wealth, it came to mean wealth or property. The reality is that the power of earthly treasures is so great, we end up enslaved to them. You might think you are running *them*, but in actual fact they are running *you*. So we move into our dream house, and immediately we find we have to work harder or longer than ever to pay the mortgage, or to put the new bathroom in; or we have to put aside weeks of our time to working on the house so that it doesn't get damp, or rot, or leak: who is really in charge here? Mammon fills your mind, fills your day, grabs your attention – it's your master. The same happens with anything else we are devoted to – be it sex, or food, or sport, or socialising – they end up as our masters.

There is a very good reason for this: *sin*. The power of sin, which has corrupted us all, has weakened us so much that these good things which God put into the world to be enjoyed actually become our gods.

Where is your heart?

They take control, and we become their slaves: enslaved to what we possess, to sex, to pleasing our friends. Their demands are absolute. They are totalitarian dictators: not at all interested in the well-being of those who serve them, they are concerned only with their own power over you. Yes, we put this in extreme terms – and you may tell me that you are not driven by such extreme obsessions. But if we are honest, many of us are: ruled by our appetites, our longings for more of what we like; and these things are not good masters. There is only one good master out there, who will love us and care for us – his name is God, and his Son is Jesus Christ. Ultimately you can serve only one master – so which is it to be?

Jesus has set out three choices for us – three searching questions which demand an answer. Where is your treasure (verse 21)? You can tell where your treasure is by what you give your time and attention to. What do you think about most – building your relationship with the Lord because you love him the most, or building your career, your bank account, your social network? When you get up in the morning, which is most important to you – making yourself look good for the day, or opening your Bible? What's the most important date in your diary – time with God's people or time to indulge yourself? If money gets a bit tight, what is the first thing that goes – your giving to the Lord's work or your Sky Sports subscription? It's not hard to tell where your treasure is. Here is the challenge. Where is your treasure? Where is your heart?

Jesus talks about serving two masters. Many Christians think they *can* serve two masters – or more than two! Some of us think we can serve God on a Sunday and serve Mammon the rest of the week. Some of us, sadly, pretend to serve God on the outside, but inside, in our hearts, we are really serving Mammon and its insatiable desire for more, more, more. What about you?

Here is a test. This one's tough. If someone robs you on the street, how do you feel about it? After the initial shock has passed, how do you feel? Don Carson quotes this story about Matthew Henry, the great Bible commentator of the early eighteenth century. When he was robbed, Henry returned home and wrote something like this in his diary: *Lord, I thank you that I have never been robbed before; that although they took my money, they spared my life; that although they took everything, it wasn't very much; that it was I who was robbed, not I who robbed.*[45]

That was a man who knew who his master was, a man whose heart was with his treasure in heaven and who knew his true identity as part of the kingdom, as a child of God. Is that you?

Don't worry! (Matthew 6:25-34)

Anyone who travels from one country to another across the world must be constantly struck by the diversity of human cultures and the places people live. They speak different languages, they belong to different social structures, they follow different religions and they observe different customs. But here is something that they all have in common. Wherever you go in the world, you will find that people worry. It's a universal human problem.

In many places, people worry because they are suffering the pain of real poverty. They lie awake at night worrying about where the next day's food is going to come from. They are worried about their children's chances in life. Can they go to school? Will they grow up healthy? Will there be a job for them? In some places, the question is, Will they survive to grow up at all? We might think worry would be less of a problem in richer countries. After all, no-one there (or very few) should be worrying about whether there is a school for their children, or a doctor, or food to put on the table! But apparently not. In a 2000 survey quoted by Britain's Office for National Statistics, for instance, one in seven people had considered committing suicide during their lifetime. In the work-place, stress is the second most serious reported cause of ill-health.

Meanwhile in America, which some people think of as a paradise, consumption of mood-altering drugs is astonishingly high. To those accustomed to struggling with poverty, this might seem ridiculous, but it seems that being well-off doesn't stop you worrying – you just worry about different things. Will I lose my job? Will my country's economy survive? Can I afford the payments on my house? What will happen to me when I get old? In Britain, for instance, society is very fractured, family units are very small and many people live alone. Loneliness is a huge problem and that certainly makes people worry. Sometimes we look with envy at Africa, where they operate in extended families, where everyone is looked after and you don't have to worry about growing old and being all alone. But although the extended family can be wonderful, I know from speaking to people who have experienced it that it brings its own pressures and worries – especially if you are the one member of the family who has done well in life and find that you are expected to provide for all the others!

I read a few years ago that the happiest place in the world is actually a small island in the South Pacific. It's part of the nation of Vanuatu, and the name of the island itself is Pentecost. On Pentecost Island, the people have few possessions, the outside world has not intruded very far and they use a very strange form of currency for buying and selling. Instead of money, they use pig's tusks! In the island's banks, it seems, instead of your deposits being bits in a computer memory, your account is held as a big pile of pig tusks. Perhaps that gives us some clues that wealth is not the answer to worry. But I can guarantee that even if you went there, you would still find people worrying about something – maybe that someone will break into the bank and steal their pig tusks!

The problem of worry is universal. If you are poor, you worry about whether you will have any clothes to wear. If you are better off, you worry about choosing exactly which clothes you should wear to create the right image and impression. Now here is Jesus telling us, Don't worry (6:25, 31). How can Jesus say that? Doesn't he know what my life is like? Doesn't he know how much I have to worry about? Before we go any further, notice what Jesus is *not* saying. He is not saying, Don't plan for the future, or, Don't go to work to earn money, or, Don't be responsible. There are things in life we need to be concerned about. Of course we need to look after our families, provide for our children, work hard at our jobs, fulfil the ministries the Lord has given us. We should certainly be very concerned about the sin that still remains in our lives. Jesus is simply saying, In all of that, my people, *don't worry*. Don't panic. In this passage he is implying that we can actually be free from that kind of worry. Jesus has just been warning us that material possessions are a terrible snare, because they can capture our hearts and enslave us. Now, in 6:25-34, Jesus is still talking about the material world and what we think about it, but now the emphasis shifts to worrying about what we *don't* have. Jesus gives us four reasons why we shouldn't have to worry.

The Kingdom Manifesto

Because worrying ignores our true identity
Look at verses 31-32. The Bible calls us to *live* differently because we *are* different – because God has given us a new identity. We are not the people we were before we were saved; and we are called to live as the new people we really are. That is the call of the Sermon on the Mount. The message is, You can do this because you are already a child of God; and children of God are not worriers. Pagans, Jesus says, are worriers. Pagans are obsessed with the material world and their possessions, because that is all their life consists of. Actually, the Greek word[46] means Gentiles, but in the time of Jesus, Gentiles were all pagans – thank God that is no longer the case for us! Pagans *have* to be obsessed with this world and what it has to offer, because they know nothing better. But we do (6:25)! Yes, we know life is more than all this. We know that life is about the relationship we have with God. If we worry, we are ignoring our true identity, because we are the children of a heavenly Father, who has brought us into his family through the Lord Jesus Christ. Think about the position that puts us in!

We have already reflected on this relationship in the Lord's Prayer (6:9-15) and Jesus will say more about it in 7:7-11. As Christians, we have the Creator of the universe for our Father. We can step into his presence and speak to him at any time, day or night. We know him as our Father and we can trust him to do us good, every time. If you are a Christian, do you understand the new identity that you have in Christ? You are part of God's family, you have a heavenly Father who will always care for you and always provide for you. So don't worry!

Because worrying reveals a lack of faith
Look now at verse 26. I love watching the birds: maybe you do as well. Perhaps as Jesus is speaking, he too is glancing up at the birds flying around that Galilean hillside. Look at them, he says. Do you see any farming activities going on there? Any sowing, any reaping, any storage arrangements? No? But they seem to be doing all right, don't they? Why – because your heavenly Father feeds them! Note that Jesus says *your* heavenly Father, not theirs. Our Father keeps them alive, and we are worth far more than they are (Matthew 10:31). Jesus is making an argument from *lesser* to *greater*. If God looks after small, insignificant creatures like sparrows, surely you realise that he will look after you, his children! 500 years ago, Martin Luther put

it like this: 'You see, he is making the birds our schoolmasters and teachers. It is a great and abiding disgrace to us that in the Gospel a helpless sparrow should become a theologian and a preacher to the wisest of men... Whenever you listen to a nightingale, then, you are listening to an excellent preacher... It is as if he were saying, I prefer to be in the Lord's kitchen. He has made heaven and earth, and he himself is the cook and the host. Every day he feeds and nourishes innumerable little birds out of his hand.'[47]

Then, in verses 28-30, Jesus gives us a second illustration. First the birds, now the flowers. Solomon was the great king, the son of David and the wealthiest individual Israel had ever seen. 2 Chronicles 9:22-27 describes something of the glory of his reign. Can you imagine what he looked like when dressed in his full regalia? Jesus says, That's nothing. Look at those flowers over there! See how beautiful God has made them. Look closely at the beauty and intricacy of any flower and you will see the skill and the care that he has lavished on it. And they look like that without doing anything at all! Have you ever seen a lily spinning or sewing its own clothes? But there it is! Even the grass, which the farmer will shovel into the fire tomorrow to cook his dinner, is beautifully clothed! Again Jesus says, If God lavishes such care and attention to clothing the grass and the flowers, which last for a few days at most, don't you think he will *much more* clothe you? Of course he will!

At the end of verse 30 Jesus uses the expression, 'O you of little faith' – in the Greek original, by the way, that is just the one word *oligopistoi*, something like 'littlefaithers'. It's a word that comes four or five times in Matthew's gospel, and Jesus always uses it to describe his disciples. He doesn't use it of the world in general, only of his own followers, because they are the people who should know better. They should have known enough to trust God, and so should we. Can't you see from the birds, can't you see from the flowers and the grass – how can you have so little faith? How can you worry? Peter summarises it so neatly in 1 Peter 5:7: 'Cast all your anxiety on him because he cares for you.'

We should note two points, before we move on. One: Jesus is talking about providing for our *needs* here, not our *luxuries*. If we are people who are materially better-off, we have to take note of that. This promise to provide does not mean a big house, two cars, the world's biggest TV set and a huge salary. It means what we actually need. Two: the point of these illustrations is *not* that we don't need to work! Think of those birds again. God feeds them, yes – but they go out and find the food. The point Jesus is making is simply this: *God provides*. He has all sorts of ways and means for providing – but he does provide. Let's move on to reason number three.

Because worrying is pointless
We are now focusing on verse 27. In fact, if you look more closely at verses 25-31, you can see an interesting structure. In verse 25 and again in verse 31, Jesus says, Don't worry – about what you will eat, drink, or wear. So those two very similar verses enclose this little section. Inside that, you have the two illustrations, first in verse 26 about the birds and again in verses 28-30 about the flowers and grass – each time with the message, If God looks after *them*, he will look after *you*! And right in the middle here, sandwiched between the two illustrations and the repeated command not to worry, we have verse 27. This structure suggests a strong emphasis on the verse in the middle. Its message is simple. *Worrying is pointless!* Literally, Jesus is saying, You can't add a cubit to your height. A cubit was a length of around half a metre. Many commentators think that Jesus is using this 'cubit' as a figure of speech – that is, you can't add a very small span of time to the length of your life. As the NIV has it, 'a single *hour* to his life'. That makes more sense, for two reasons. Firstly, a cubit would be a very large amount to grow; very few of us would want to add half a metre to our height! Secondly, extending our lifespan is precisely what millions of people wish they could do.

Jesus has chosen the most powerful illustration possible to reinforce his message about worrying. Longer life is just what people wish for: every year, billions are spent pursuing the goal of a longer life. But Jesus says, Worrying about your lifespan achieves nothing. Worrying can't lengthen your life even by an hour. In fact, it may well shorten it – there is such a thing as worrying yourself to death! Now of course, just telling someone not to worry because it's pointless doesn't help very much. You can't stop someone from worrying just by telling them not to worry! Jesus does more than that. Already he has reminded us of our new identity, the people we really are in him; he has shown us how our loving heavenly Father provides for us; but now there's more, a fourth reason not to worry.

Where is your heart?

Because there is a wonderful alternative!
Look now at verse 33. The alternative to worrying is to set your heart on God and his ways. 'Seek first his kingdom and his righteousness'. Those two goals, the *kingdom* and *righteousness*, are very closely connected. What does it mean to seek God's kingdom? First of all, it means seeking the king, the Lord Jesus himself. And of course, that means making him *your* king. It means submitting to King Jesus absolutely and in every way. You put yourself under his rule, you become part of his economy, you allow him to run your life unconditionally. Secondly, it means to seek the character of the kingdom, which means being just like Jesus: as we saw in 5:6, that is what 'righteousness' means here. So Jesus is saying, Seek me, and seek to be *like* me. The Beatitudes, especially the trio in 5:7-9, lay out clearly what a Christ-like character looks like. It means being *merciful* (5:7) – just as we have had God's mercy lavished on us, so we will show mercy to others. It means being *pure in heart* (5:8) – striving to be pure and clean, not through some external activities or religious ritual, but clean from the heart, from the inside outwards, people of utter integrity, never pretending to be what you are not. It means being a *peacemaker* (5:9) – so that we will go out of our way to bring peace in a world that is broken and torn by sin, just like Jesus. Do you want to be like that? If your answer is yes, if that really is what you long to be, then you know something about seeking first his kingdom and his righteousness.

From beginning to end, the Sermon on the Mount sets forth the distinctive life of the man or woman of the kingdom, the righteousness that means being like our king, the Lord Jesus Christ. Set your heart on that – this kingdom is what you belong to, and this kingdom is where your heart should be – and here is the promise: 'all these things will be given to you as well'. That's the promise. Set your heart on the Lord and being like him, and he will look after all those things that you are worried about. So when you find yourself worrying, seek him and his ways. This is the message from David in Psalm 37:4. If we do delight ourselves in the Lord, then of course he will be the number one desire of our hearts! It is also the message from Paul, in Philippians 4 (verses 6-7, and then verse 19). Don't be anxious, but seek the Lord and he will take care of it! Remember that as Paul writes that letter to the Philippians he is in prison and facing a probable death sentence. So this is real. It works!

Of course, it is not only Paul who proved this attitude by experience. It is also the Lord Jesus himself. If we can express it this way – just think what he had to worry about! Ahead of Jesus, as he speaks these words in Matthew 6, stands the cross and all that it will mean for him: the abuse, the false accusations, the physical suffering – and supremely, the unimaginable experience of the wrath of God poured out on him, hour after hour, alienation and fury from his beloved Father. In Gethsemane, the horror of what is about to happen sweeps over him like a tidal wave. But he faces it by seeking God in heart-felt prayer. He wins his battle, there in the garden, and goes to that bitter cross in prayerful, humble trust in his heavenly Father. So don't worry – because there *is* a wonderful alternative!

Dealing with our worries
Worry affects different people in very different ways, depending on our situation in life and also on our temperament and character. First, there are people who naturally don't worry at all! Their response to this passage might be to say, Yes, quite right, worrying shows a lack of faith, and it's pointless, and that's why I never worry about a thing! Well, if you genuinely never worry, I am very happy for you! But you must be careful. Maybe when you say 'I never worry' what you really mean is 'I am irresponsible'. You don't worry, because you don't care. But when Jesus talks about not worrying, he doesn't mean we should be lazy, that we should ignore the needs of others – especially our own families – or that we should never think about the future. The peace and confidence Jesus promises us here comes from knowing who we are in Christ and seeking him with all our hearts, not from being selfish, uncaring or irresponsible.

Secondly, there are the natural worriers. This is definitely the group I fall into! Some of us naturally worry all the time. It's part of our personality. If there's nothing to worry about, we worry about that too. If you are like that, then your response might be, Yes, that's right, that's me, I worry too much – and then that becomes one *more* problem to worry about! Listen to what the Lord Jesus is saying to you and me from this passage. Remember who you are. You are a child of God – you have a wonderful, loving heavenly Father who has promised to look after you. With him, you're safe and secure. You belong to the king – do you know that? Let's relax a bit, let's enjoy the relationship we have with the Lord, and let's seek the kingdom with all our hearts. There is this wonderful alternative to worrying. Seek the Lord and his ways, and let him look after the rest.

Thirdly, some of you who read this know what it means to be poor, to struggle to have enough to get through each day and each week. What

Where is your heart?

you worry about is not the luxuries that some of us take for granted, but the simple needs of life. Jesus promises that your heavenly Father will provide for you. One of the main ways he will do that is through his people in the church. God does not call each local church to solve the problem of world poverty, but he certainly does call every local church to look after its own. As God's people we are called to provide for one another and share the good things he has given us.

The Lord has many ways of providing for us. Let me tell you this story, well-known in Britain, from my own home town of Bristol. It comes from the life of George Muller, who lived in the nineteenth century at a time when there were huge numbers of destitute children on the streets and no way of caring for them. Over the years, George Muller built and ran five great orphanages housing thousands of children, solely on the basis of faith. The buildings still stand there in our city today: they are used for other purposes now, but whenever I see them, I remember Muller's work. At the same time as running the orphanages (and this is less well-known), he was sending funds to hundreds of missionaries and supporting a hundred schools as well! Every need was brought straight to the Lord in prayer. The burden of caring for thousands of children must have been enormous. Muller wrote: 'But God, our infinite Treasurer, remains with us. It is this which gives me peace.'

The story comes from the earlier days of the very first orphanage. One morning, as the children came in for breakfast, there was no food on the table and no money to buy anything. Muller prayed in his usual way, Father, thank you for what you are going to give us to eat. Suddenly, there was a knock at the door. The baker was standing there. 'Mr Muller', he said, 'I couldn't sleep last night. Somehow I felt you didn't have bread for breakfast and the Lord wanted me to send you some. So I got up at two o'clock and baked some fresh bread, and here it is.' Almost at once there was another knock on the door. This time it was the milkman. His milk cart had broken down right outside the orphanage. He had to empty the cart so that he could repair it – so would they like some cans of fresh milk?

It's a powerful story, and we need to hear both sides of it. Some of us certainly need to be more like George Muller, and trust the Lord to provide for us in wonderful ways, as he will. That is the point that is usually made from this story. But some of us need to be like the baker, who heard the Lord calling him to get out of bed and go and provide for his people. The Lord will provide – and very often he will provide through *us*!

The fourth and final group are those who don't know the Lord at all. If you are not a Christian, all these wonderful truths about not worrying, and trusting in the Lord to provide, can mean nothing to you. If you are not a Christian, then you are outside the kingdom, God is not your Father, and at this moment he is not smiling down on you. When you have seen that clearly, then you must come to the cross of Jesus and confess your sin. It's the cross and the death of Jesus alone that can make you acceptable to God. Accept Jesus as your king so that you will live under his rule and his control. Then you will be part of the kingdom and know God as your heavenly Father to love you and to provide for your every need. Then you too will have nothing to worry about!

We conclude this chapter with verse 34. Don't worry, Jesus says. Let tomorrow take care of itself – by which he means, of course, that the Lord will take care of tomorrow. But you notice that he is very realistic. Jesus doesn't say there will be no trouble, or guarantee that no Christian will ever be hungry. He never even suggests that the Christian life will be comfortable. In fact, he says, there will be *plenty* of trouble. As a faithful, trusting, God-honouring Christian, you may still be poor. But you will have enough. You will still get ill. But that will be an opportunity to prove God's faithfulness. We will still suffer, as long as this earthly life endures. Jesus did, why shouldn't we? And that will be an opportunity for us to become more like him. Some Christians will suffer a great deal for their faith, even to the point of shedding their blood. But even then, we should not worry. It's pointless anyway! Remember your identity – you have a heavenly Father, you belong to the king. Seek him, seek his ways, seek his righteousness, and he will look after all that you need.

Questions to reflect on or discuss

1. What kinds of 'treasures on earth' are the greatest temptation for you? Why do you think those are particularly a problem in your case?

2. Think about your own priorities, as reflected by the way you spend your time and money. Is there anything about your lifestyle that needs to change?

Where is your heart?

3. I have suggested that Jesus gives four reasons why we should not worry (because it ignores our true identity, because it reveals a lack of faith, because it is pointless, and because there is a wonderful alternative). Are any of these reasons more important or more powerful?

4. Which of the groups mentioned at the end of the chapter best describes you? Are there any of those four reasons that you specially need to hear?

5. In the story about George Muller, do you need to focus more on the faith of Muller or the obedient response of the baker?

Chapter 11
Life in the family
Matthew 7:1-12

The chapter divisions in our Bibles are not always as useful as they could be – they aren't part of the original text, of course! In the case of Matthew 7 we could really do with a 'chapter division' after verse 12, because verses 1-12 finish off the main message of the Sermon on the Mount, while verses 13-27 contain an extended challenge to receive the message and put it into action, and verses 28-29 give Matthew's description of the crowds' response[48]. So we will divide Matthew 7 into two chapters of our own. We begin with verses 1-12, which are about relationships in the kingdom family – how we relate to others, in verses 1-6, and how we relate to our Father God, in verses 7-12.

Sound Judgment

One Monday morning in 2011, the world woke to the news that Osama bin Laden was dead. An American special forces team had landed in his secret compound, broken in to his living quarters, and finished him off with two shots to the head. The families of his many victims can now feel that some measure of justice has been done. Osama bin Laden spent the last two decades of his life denouncing the western world and calling in the most vivid and bloodthirsty language for its destruction. Some words from 1998, speaking to his followers in Afghanistan: 'It is far better for anyone to kill a single American soldier than to squander his efforts on other activities'. Again, from the same year: 'In today's wars, there are no morals. We believe the worst thieves in the world today and the worst terrorists are the Americans. We do not have to differentiate between military or civilian. As far as we are concerned, they are all targets.' And after the suicide bombing of the USS *Cole* in 2000: 'The pieces of the bodies of infidels were flying like dust particles. If you would have seen it with your own eyes, you would have been very pleased, and your heart would have been filled with joy.' The ideology led to action – the attacks in New York and Washington in 2001, the bombs in London, Bali, Nairobi, Dar-es-Salaam, Madrid, year after year – killing thousands; and as that last quote tells us, he was exultant. But now he was dead. The judgment he poured out on others had been served on him.

It's not that everything bin Laden believed was necessarily wrong. Sadly, much of what he said about the West was true, but in writing us off as condemned, hopelessly evil and fit only for death and destruction, he was putting himself in the position of God. He judged and condemned in a way that none of us has the right to do; and for that sin, he paid the ultimate price on earth. But in fact, Osama bin Laden is simply an extreme case of what Jesus is warning us against in Matthew 7:1-6. 'Do not judge, or you too will be judged.' You might think the comparison is far-fetched, but the truth is that many of us have something of the spirit of Osama bin Laden in our hearts. If that's the case, we need to know how to deal with it.

We have already seen that relationships in the kingdom family are a crucial part of the new life we are called to, because the Christian life is not just a cosy thing between me and Jesus – we're a community, we are a family. Here in verses 1-6 we are looking at the way we as Christians see and relate to others with sound judgment. We will look at this in three stages.

Don't judge harshly
Look at verses 1-2. Now the word 'judge', like many words in Scripture, can have a range of meanings: so what exactly does it mean *here*? It's not immediately obvious just from verse 1 what Jesus means by not judging. When we looked at 5:39 and not resisting the evil person, we mentioned the somewhat eccentric views of Leo Tolstoy. Well, he had some rather distinctive views of this verse as well. He read it like this: 'Christ totally forbids the human institution of *law courts*' and 'he could mean nothing else by these words'[49]. But in fact, Jesus cannot possibly be talking about law courts and the like, because he is not dealing with

the way nations are governed and run, he's talking about the personal relationships of his own people in the kingdom. Tolstoy is making the same mistake he made with chapter 5.

Alternatively, we might take Jesus to mean, Make no judgments at all – that it is not for us to have opinions about anyone, that we should assume everyone we meet is nice and friendly and we should treat them accordingly – don't judge them. But the context of what Jesus is saying proves that that can't be right either. In this very passage, in verse 6, Jesus is going to assume we can identify the 'dogs' and 'pigs' he is talking about – and we can't do that without making some *judgments*. Later on, in verse 15, he will be warning us against false prophets; and he says, They will sometimes be very hard to spot, but you must watch out for them. Obviously, that too implies that we must make *judgments*.

This is a good example of why we should always study what the Bible says in its own context, so that we don't go barking up the wrong tree. In context, it's clear that what Jesus means here is judging *harshly*, or censoriously; to condemn people – acting as if we have a divine right to pass judgment, when really we have none. In everyday life, we hear this kind of judgment all the time, as one person or another makes confident and sweeping statements where they simply write someone off. 'I can't stand so-and-so, she must be the laziest/ most selfish/ unkindest/ most arrogant/ most full of herself person in the world.' They are miniature Osama bin Ladens, busily writing people off as fit only for the scrap-heap. Our human nature loves to do this, because every time we push someone else down, we are pushing ourselves up. I can feel better about myself by declaring that you are useless. Tragically, you sometimes hear that kind of talk even in church. But only God has the right to make judgments like that. Only God has all the facts – we don't – and only he has the right – we don't.

Jesus says, Don't do it. Why? Because if you do, just the same judgment will rebound on you (7:2). What does he mean? On one level, it's simply about how other people will see you. If you are generally warm and friendly to others, usually they will appreciate it and they are more likely to treat you well in turn. But if you are very judgmental, people will want to get their own back. That's true (as a general rule!), but it's not the main point. The only opinion, the only judgment, we should seriously be concerned about is *God's*, and what *he* will think of us. Not for the first time, we find Jesus' words here echoed by James, in this case in James 5:9.

Is Jesus, then, referring to the final judgment? No, I don't think so. Remember, this is written for Christians, and Jesus is certainly not threatening us with losing our salvation. He is talking about how the Lord will deal with us now, during this life. The way we look at other people, the way we treat them in our words and even in our thoughts, is so important. We saw that in 6:14-15, where Jesus puts forgiveness at the very heart of Christian living. In the same way here, Jesus is saying, If you condemn others harshly like this, the Father will deal with you strongly. He loves you, and he does not want you to continue in such a serious sin – so, lovingly but firmly, he will tackle it – through rebuke, through discipline, through judgment. Condemning others is not trivial. God doesn't take it lightly, and neither must we.

Don't judge blindly

If the first point concerned our attitude towards everyone, this now is about our relationships with our brothers and sisters in the Christian family. Look again at verses 3-5. This is an intentionally humorous picture. Imagine the scene: you've got this little speck in your eye and someone comes along and says, My friend, let me sort that out for you. But you can see that he has a massive plank sticking out of his own eye, so quite apart from the fact that he can't see what he's doing, before he gets near you he's hit you round the head with this plank! Or imagine an optician peering closely into your eye, trying to see round this great block of wood strapped to his head that's completely blocking his own vision. I don't think even his most loyal customers would stick around for long! It's a ridiculous picture, the idea of trying to put someone else right when something far worse is wrong with us – and we can picture Jesus smiling, and his listeners chortling away; and then in verse 5 he hits them between the eyes with the damning word, *Hypocrite!* That word recalls its repeated use in chapter 6 and reminds us that Jesus would have had the attitude of the Pharisees particularly in mind.

Now, this case is a little bit different from the first one. This is not a case of condemning someone harshly, writing them off. This is about trying to sort out someone's problem – which might be a very good thing to do. The problem here is that you can't help someone else to see when you yourself are blind. You can't help someone deal with the sin in his

Life in the family

life when there is something far worse going on in yours, something which you know about perfectly well, or you should do. That's hypocrisy – because you are pretending that you can help when really you can't. You are pointing out the sin in their life and trying to correct it, while blatantly ignoring your own.

So what does Jesus say? Well, hypocrisy is not incurable. You need to get the plank out of your own eye – and, with God's help, you can. Please note, Jesus does *not* say we should never correct one another! He does *not* say that the speck doesn't matter, that it's not serious. Actually, having a speck in your eye is painful and irritating, and it's great to get rid of it. And having even the smallest sin in our lives should cause us pain, and we should certainly long to be rid of it. How do we do that? Again, let's put ourselves in the situation. You become aware of something that a brother or sister in the church is doing, which you know is wrong, but they seem unaware. It may be the way they are treating someone else in the church, or the way they talk that is compromising their witness or the church's witness.

The first thing to do is *pray*. If you have any thought of correcting this brother or sister – which is a good thing to do – you should examine yourself prayerfully. Are there any planks, large or small, in your own eye? Are there even any specks? Is it a real issue that you have seen in your brother, or is it that you are so blinded by your own sin that you're really just imagining it? Check that it's not just you being picky or fussy or irritable. Ask the Lord to deal with *you* first. Repent of any sin in your own life. Wait, be patient, don't rush in. Then go. Be straight. Deal with the person directly. Eyes are sensitive places, so treat them accordingly.

We call this, *Speaking the truth in love*. We need both the truth and the love: we can't do without the truth, and we can't do without the love. When it's done right, it's a great blessing. I am very grateful to people who have done this for me. I can't claim I was always very grateful at the time – that's why it is so hard to criticise a friend, because it may take them a while to appreciate it! – but looking back, I am grateful for it now. They have helped me to grow, to be more like Jesus. Isn't that a great ministry to have? It's a great fallacy, and very popular today, that a friend always agrees with you and supports your viewpoint unconditionally. No, a real friend, a true brother, does not pretend you are in the right when in fact you are in the wrong. He comes to you and helps you to deal with your sin. But don't judge blindly.

The Kingdom Manifesto

Don't judge stupidly

Now, having spoken of relationships within the Christian family, Jesus turns to relating to outsiders. Look at verse 6. These dogs, of course, are not the cheerful, friendly, well-behaved animals which some of us have at home. When I was growing up, there was a hymn in our hymn-book with a line thanking God 'for dogs with friendly faces'. I don't think we ever sang it, but it stuck in my mind! No-one in Jesus' day would be thanking God for dogs with friendly faces, because the dogs they know are fierce, half-wild, hungry scavengers that hunt in packs and will bite you as soon as look at you. Similarly, 'pigs' here are not cheerful, snuffling porkers: to the Jews they are unclean animals they would have nothing to do with, probably pretty fierce and wild as well. Picture yourself, confronted with a pack of these dogs, or a herd of these pigs. You have, for some reason, a bag of pearls in your hand and you decide to offer them to the animals. It doesn't make a lot of sense. Dogs and pigs don't eat pearls, and they won't be very impressed when they find out they can't chew them. In fact, they will be so unimpressed that they are likely to turn on you. The pearls will end up trampled into the mud, and it will be *you* who gets chewed up.

That's the picture that Jesus puts in their minds. Now, what does he mean? What are these 'sacred' things? Some in the early church thought he was talking about Communion, but it isn't that (although it might be an indirect implication). The most sacred thing for a Christian, the pearl of great price as Jesus calls it in a parable (Matthew 13:45-46), is the gospel of the kingdom, the good news of our salvation. That's what's in the bag of pearls. Jesus is talking about people who will respond to the gospel only with abuse, or even violence. He is saying that we have to be *discerning*. This is the balance to the preceding verses which warn us not to be too *judgmental*. This verse warns us not to be undiscerning – not to be stupid, in fact.

The New Testament gives us various examples of what this means in practice. In Matthew 10:11-14, Jesus instructs these same disciples when he sends them out on their first mission. He tells them, Look out for people who are welcoming, those who are friendly. If people persist in refusing you, then warn them and get out. Don't waste your time, don't let your message be abused, go elsewhere. Then see what Paul does in Corinth in Acts 18:5-7. When the Jews of Corinth become abusive, he no longer offers them the pearls of the gospel – he goes next door instead.

In fact, something similar happens in several other cities he visits (Acts 13:46-51, 19:8-10, 28:23-28).

We need to be discerning. Everyone we meet with the gospel is not the same, and there are some who will be hostile, contemptuous and abusive. Be careful how you take this, though: Jesus is *not* talking about people who are slow to understand, or who don't seem interested, or who might laugh at you a few times. That would describe the response of almost every non-Christian. Jesus is speaking of those few who will meet us persistently with nothing but abuse, or worse. In those cases, move on, because there are plenty of other people who need the good news. In general, we are called to persevere in our witness, to be patient. As Don Carson points out, Jesus takes *five* verses to warn us not to be judgmental, and just *one* verse to warn us not to be undiscerning, which points to where the main danger lies for most of us! Don't be harsh, be generous.

Finally, let's pull together what this passage means for us. If we look at the positive side of this passage, it gives us a beautiful vision for what a church should look like, the way we see each other and can help each other. If we take Jesus' words seriously, the life of our churches will be beautiful and people will be drawn to the Lord as soon as they get to know us.

1. *Don't write people off* – whether that's people inside or outside the church. It's not for you to condemn people. 1 Corinthians 13:6-7 tells us what love does for our relationships. It means we don't give up on people, however difficult they are, however many times they have failed. Think: are there people, is there one person, you have written off as useless or impossible to deal with? Then you must be warned: that judgment is sinful, it will rebound on you, and you need to repent. Love them, always hope the best of them; don't write them off.

2. *Don't ignore your own sins.* None of us is perfect – in fact, we are all a long way off our destination, which is glorious, beautiful perfection as the Bride of Christ. Most of us have some fairly large planks in our eyes, yet that does not seem to stop us from wanting to sort out everybody else's life. There is a time for helping other people sort out their sins – but your priority is your *own* sins. Are you asking the Lord, every day, to show you the planks in your own eye, and to help you by his Spirit to take those things out and put them on the bonfire? That's what the

normal Christian life should be like – daily searching, daily repentance, daily moving on to be more like the Lord Jesus.

3. *Don't fail to be a brother.* If you are coming before God each day like that, if you are genuine about rooting out your own sins, *then* you are in a position to be a true brother to someone else who is struggling. If you are dealing with the planks in your own eye, *then* you can bless your brother by helping him with the speck that's in his eye. Actually, we all need that kind of help.

4. *Don't refuse the gospel.* All this is written to people who are already Christians – but what if you are not? What if you are still outside the kingdom of Jesus? Don't put yourself with the dogs and the pigs who abuse this valuable message. Don't reject what Jesus has done for you, because the offer will not be there for ever.

Good gifts

Of all the words Jesus ever spoke, these must surely be the most popular. 'So in everything, do to others what you would have them do to you' (7:12). It's what is known as the *Golden Rule*, and to this day millions of people and most of the world's major religions would acknowledge the Golden Rule as one of the best possible descriptions of the way human beings should behave to one another. Jesus said it, but in a sense it was not particularly new. Five hundred years earlier, as far as we know, the Chinese teacher Confucius put it like this: 'Never impose on others what you would not choose for yourself'. Even earlier, in the Hindu classic, the *Mahabharata*, the god Brihaspati is quoted as saying, 'One should never do that to another which one regards as injurious to one's own self'. And around the time of Jesus, the great Jewish Rabbi Hillel gave his view of the matter. Here's the story from the Talmud:

> Another Gentile came to Shammai saying: "Convert me on the condition that thou teach me the whole Torah while I stand on one foot". Shammai pushed him away with the builders' measure he held in his hand. He thereupon came to Hillel, and the latter accepted him. He told him: "What is hateful to thee, do not unto thy fellow; this is the whole law. All the rest is a commentary to this law; go and learn it."

Life in the family

Many others in the ancient world made similar pronouncements. But do you notice the difference? According to those various authorities, the way to live is to avoid inflicting anything nasty on someone else. If *you* don't want to be beaten up, don't beat your *neighbour* up. If you don't like being insulted, don't be rude about anybody else. Fine – but actually you could keep to that rule by staying at home and doing absolutely nothing! Jesus' standard is higher. Jesus says, Think how well you would like to be treated: now go and do *that* for others. So Jesus puts the Golden Rule in a positive form, a much more challenging form. But then he says, in fact, even this is not really new. The second half of verse 12 says 'for this sums up the Law and the Prophets'. In other words, if you really want to know how God wants you to live, if you want to understand the underlying meaning of all that he taught his people Israel in years gone by, this is it. Do to others as you would have them do to you. After all, Leviticus 19:18 does say, 'Love your neighbour as yourself'. That's positive![50]

With this Golden Rule, Jesus brings to an end the main body of the Sermon on the Mount. It's not quite the finish, but what is left of the Sermon after this is not more teaching but a challenge to *respond* to the teaching. If you recall, the main body of the Sermon on the Mount begins in 5:17, where Jesus says: 'Do not think that I have come to abolish the Law or the Prophets; I have not come to abolish them but to fulfil them.' And it ends here as he says, 'This sums up the Law and the Prophets'. This is what we call an *inclusio* – these two references to the Law and the Prophets are like a pair of brackets, and everything inside the brackets shows *how* Jesus is fulfilling the Law. Jesus never contradicts the Old Testament. Instead, in his teaching he brings out the true meaning of the Law and takes it to new heights. Jesus' teaching sets a standard that, if anything, is even higher than before. We can see how that works as we look back over some of the things Jesus has been saying – and in most of these we can see straight away how the Golden Rule summarises it all.

For instance, we could look at 5:21-26. Jesus says, Don't just avoid murder, don't just avoid anger – that's good, but it's not enough. What you must do is actively seek reconciliation and peace. Or 5:38-42, where Jesus says, Don't demand your own rights: you must do positive good even to those who treat you badly. Isn't that how you would like them to treat you? Or 5:43-47, where Jesus says, Love your enemies –

positively, actively *love* them. Or think of 7:1-6. Don't condemn people, Jesus says; but again, you can do better than that. You need to go out of your way to help your brother to deal with his problem, this speck in his eye. Now Jesus reaches the end of this great block of teaching and he gives us 7:12. The Golden Rule calls us to live in a way that is utterly selfless, totally self-sacrificing, focused on the needs of others, loving our neighbour as ourselves. This is the way Paul expresses it in Romans 13:8-10[51].

We reply, Fine! Yes, I can certainly see that is what I need to do. That is exactly how I should live. But I can't do it! So we are confronted straight away with our own weakness and inability – and in fact we have seen this over and over again as we have moved through the Sermon on the Mount. We read these instructions, and we apply them to ourselves, and we say – at least if we are honest – This is beyond me! These demands Jesus makes are impossible. He has already told us we must be perfect, and here he is saying that if we want to meet what God lays down we have to follow the incredibly high standard of the Golden Rule.

Once again, this proves beyond doubt that the Sermon on the Mount is not something for anyone to pick up and have a go at. People have often taken it that way – a sort of general code of ethics for the world at large – but if we understand it properly we can see that that's ridiculous. Today, most of the world's religions, philosophers and teachers, humanists and atheists included, would freely acknowledge something like the Golden Rule as the heart of their moral and ethical teachings. They say this is exactly right. You might think the same. But I don't hear anyone claiming, Yes, I can *do* this. So how can we live like this? Well, once more the Sermon on the Mount has driven us back to our desperate need for help – our need for the grace of God. And this is why Jesus actually offers us the answer right here. Just before he concludes with the Golden Rule, he gives us this little section in verses 7-11. The answer is the relationship we can have with God through prayer. Here's the point. The Lord has not left us with some frankly impossible teachings and told us to get on with it – as if he were just one more dead philosopher!

Does someone who follows Confucius have a relationship with Confucius? Are any of the great philosophers of Greece available to guide us today? Is Muhammad still around to enable the Muslim to keep his teachings? Those men are all dead and gone. Here is the difference: our Lord is *alive!* God is alive, Jesus is *alive* – and that makes all the difference, because it means we can know him and experience him today. Prayer is the way we communicate, get to know him and call on the help we need so much.

We will look now at this prayer relationship that Jesus tells us about in verses 7-11, and then we will see how that connects with the Golden Rule. In these verses, Jesus speaks about prayer very simply. He speaks of prayer that relates, prayer that persists and prayer that trusts. Let's look at those in turn.

Prayer that relates
Look at verse 11b. Here is the first priority about prayer: it is a *relationship*. People who can pray are people who have God as their Father. Not everyone can pray. Many people think they can, but if you do not have God as your Father, if you have never entered into that relationship, then you cannot pray like this. It's another reminder that the Sermon on the Mount is for the family, for people who already belong to Jesus and his kingdom. As his people, we are a family – and God the Father is the head of the family. Remember how the Lord's prayer starts – 'Our Father in heaven, hallowed be your name' (6:9). Prayer is a child talking to his dad and asking for what he needs. Basically, that's it.

Of course there is more to say about prayer than that. We need to take this passage alongside other New Testament teaching on prayer – which tells us that we must pray in faith, and according to the will of God – but the emphasis in this passage is very simple. Pray – and your prayer will be answered, every time, because God is your perfect Father. We have a Father who is infinitely strong, infinitely loving, wonderfully good.

Prayer that persists
Look at verses 7-8. Jesus uses three different words: ask, seek and knock. Now perhaps these three have a slightly varying or progressive emphasis, as some commentators suggest, but they are not really very different. Taken together, the main impression they give is *persistence* – and the form of the commands in the Greek reinforces that. This is asking that *continues*, seeking that is *determined* to *find* what it's looking for, knocking that is *repeated*. Sometimes people pull these verses out of their context as if they were describing a general spiritual quest – that

everyone is on a journey of discovery and the important thing is simply to keep persevering, keep exploring until one day you arrive at the place that is right for you. 'Climb every mountain, follow every rainbow, Till you find your dream', as the Mother Abbess sings in *The Sound of Music* (though it is hard to imagine a real abbess sharing these sentiments!). 'Seek and you will find.' But again, that's nonsense. Jesus is speaking about prayer that is set squarely within the relationship we *already have* with the Father.

You notice how Jesus uses such simple, everyday words as he teaches us about prayer. Prayer is as simple as asking, searching, knocking on the door – and as long as we know God as our Father, anyone can do this. Again, don't let's make it too complicated. Our Father is there and he wants us to pray. He wants us to keep praying. When we recognise how much we need him, how empty and desperate we are without him, then we will pray, and we will *keep* praying.

Prayer that trusts
Look at verses 9-11. Just imagine it: 'Dad, Mum's away for the weekend, can we have fish and chips, please dad?' 'OK, here you are, son – catch hold of this' – tossing him a live snake! Jesus says, *You* don't do that. You are far from perfect – in fact, like everyone else, you are evil, you are still fallen and sinful human beings even though you belong to me – but you know not to treat your own kids like that[52]. And so Jesus argues, from lesser to greater: Isn't God a better father than you? Don't you think you can trust him to give you what is best? In verse 8 Jesus said, Everyone who asks receives, and so on: yes; but he does not say, We will always get what we ask for. Very often, we ask for the wrong thing.

Let's push Jesus' illustration a little further. In China there is a tourist attraction called the Istone Mineral Park. One of the displays at this park is a table laid out with a huge banquet of wonderful food – or at least, that's what it *looks* like. But the fact is, every single item on that table is made of stone. Now imagine you're taking your little son around that park. As kids do on such days, very quickly he starts feeling peckish, and just as you get to this display he decides he is starving. Dad, give me some food! There – I want that one – it looks fantastic! You have only to reach over and pick up a bread roll from the display and he will sink his teeth into it. Actually, if he tries, he won't have teeth for very long! Do you give it to him? He wants it, he has asked for it, he is very sincere, he believes you can give it to him! Do you do it? Do you even have to think twice about it?

Life in the family

Very often when we pray, we think we are asking for bread, but we are actually asking for a stone. With our little understanding, very often we can't tell the difference. We see something that we think is good, we are very sincere, and we know the Father can give it to us; but in fact it would break our teeth. That's when our Father *won't* give us what we ask for. He knows better than we do – and we can trust him. What he gives his children is always good, even when it doesn't look good to us. Sometimes what the Lord gives us does not feel at all welcome. Sometimes it comes with pain and heartache. But he is still our Father; and even at those times, what he gives us is *always for our good*.

The first and best thing we should pursue is always the Lord *himself*. Remember 6:33. Seeking the kingdom means seeking the King. Look at the promise in Jeremiah 29:13. God our Father wants to give us more of himself. He has already given us his own Son, the Lord Jesus. He has given us his Holy Spirit to live in us and make us more like Jesus. And whatever situation we are in, whatever we are facing, what we need most of all is to have more of him. Is that what you want? If you have a clear view of God as your loving heavenly Father, the Father who always wants the best for you, then you *will* want more of him. You will *ask* for more of him, more of the character of Jesus in your life; you will *seek* for more of him, not for other stuff he can give you but simply for himself, to know him better; you will *knock* at the door to come in closer to him.

You see how praying like this gives us the perspective that we need. This is where we get back to the Golden Rule. What does it mean, to pray like this? It means we have put ourselves in the place of absolute dependence on God. We have said, Yes, you are my father, I am your little child, and I depend on you for everything. I need you, because there is nothing else. Then we look round at other people and see that they need God in exactly the same way. We look at our brothers and sisters, Christians, who have come to the same place as us, knowing God as their kind and loving Father, who are also learning to depend on him. And we look at people who aren't Christians, and we see that what they need is exactly the same – they just don't know it yet. The more we pray, the more we can see it[53].

Prayer doesn't change God, but it does change us. The more we pray, the more we see ourselves as we truly are. We're not so special after all – except that God has given us his grace. If he has dealt with us like that, then we can treat other people in the same way. He will give us the power to do it. 'Do to others what you would have them do to you' – yes, because I am just a little child, a sinner saved by God's amazing grace. I owe everything to him, so how can I act as if I'm the centre of the universe? And if this is how my loving Father has asked me to live, then surely he will give me all that I need to do it.

The Golden Rule: what a beautiful way to live! By the way, Jesus doesn't say, Do good to others *so that* they will do good to you. They may not. He says, Do good to others because that's what I am calling you to as members of my kingdom! So: shall we do what Jesus calls us to? It doesn't mean keeping our heads down. It isn't a formula for staying out of trouble – quite the opposite, in fact. It might mean many things for you, but it will certainly mean taking all that Jesus has been teaching us through the Sermon on the Mount and putting it into practice. It might well mean seeking God to help you with the sins of your own heart – the anger, the lust, the enmity, the deeply-rooted selfishness which cries out for its own rights and its own self-importance, the hypocrisy which longs to look good however empty we are on the inside, the pride in our own judgment – exactly what Jesus has been addressing in these chapters. Do you want to suffer those things from others? Hardly! Then seek the Lord to change your heart so that you don't live that way yourself!

Questions to reflect on or discuss

1. Do you have any tendency to be judgmental, writing people off because they don't fit some ideal picture in your mind? How does the example of God's attitude to you help here?

2. When it comes to helping and correcting others, what do you find most difficult? Is it having the honesty to face your own sin first, finding the courage to speak up, or using genuinely loving words? Think and pray it through – with someone else, if you have the chance.

3. How can you trust God more fully to give you what is good? Have you had experiences that make that more difficult? Can you think of times when you have had special reason to thank him that what he gave you was the best – even if it didn't seem that way at first?

Chapter 12
Decision time
Matthew 7:13-29

We've reached the point in the Sermon on the Mount where Jesus has completed the main body of his teaching – he has really said what he wants to say. As we saw in the previous chapter, the heart of the Sermon on the Mount is bracketed between 5:17 and 7:12, the two place where Jesus mentions 'the Law and the Prophets'. After that, there's a full stop, a big pause; and Jesus turns to his followers, and to the great crowds who are thronging the hillside around them, and he says: This is it. Now: what are you going to do about it? Here's the message: I've told you about my kingdom; I've told you what my followers' lives will look like; I've shown you what it means to have a live and genuine relationship with God, to know him as your Father; now, will you take it or leave it? Are you going to be part of my kingdom, have me as your King, and live like this, or reject me and stay outside?

So the rest of the Sermon on the Mount, the second half of Matthew 7, is really a repeated challenge to respond to the call of the kingdom. From here on, we find a series of comparisons which emphasise the gulf between those inside the kingdom and those outside, and at the same time stress the urgency of decision:

- A narrow gate and road versus a broad gate and road (7:13-14)
- Good trees and fruit versus bad trees and fruit (7:15-20)
- People who do the Father's will versus people who claim much but are evil (7:21-23)
- A wise builder and a foolish builder (7:24-27)

The Kingdom Manifesto

And even after the Sermon is completed, in Matthew's conclusion:

- Jesus' teaching versus the scribes' teaching (7:28-29)

Decision time

Imagine the scene. You are in the office where you work, sitting at your computer. The morning is the usual mixture of real work, chat at the coffee machine, and just the occasional glance at Facebook! It's a perfectly ordinary day – then suddenly, someone says, Do you smell that? Does that smell like smoke? Absorbed in what you're doing, you take no notice; in fact ,you hardly hear the words. Then a few minutes later, someone the other side of you says, That *definitely* smells like smoke – I'm going to have a look. But you've found an interesting website and you're just not listening. The smell grows stronger but you choose to ignore it. There is a faint crackling sound in the distance. Then the fire alarm sounds. It's ear-splitting. Still you sit at your desk peering at your screen and wishing the infuriating noise would stop. Now coils of smoke are clearly visible drifting in through the door. You're not interested – but you can't help starting to cough. Above your head, the lights flicker and die. Then the computer screen goes dark. As you look round, you can see the fire breaking in from the corridor. And you can see that there is one doorway in the far corner of the room that is still clear. There is still one way of escape. You have two options. You either stay and face the smoke and flames, or you run for the doorway and escape.

In Matthew 7:13-14, Jesus confronts us with a choice just as stark as that one. After all the teaching he has given, after all that he has explained to his listeners, it is now decision time. The worst thing we could do is to read or to hear the Sermon on the Mount and think, That's great. I like the sound of that: you know what, I think I'll try and do it. These two short verses make it absolutely clear that *that will not do*. Jesus is calling us to respond. When the fire alarm goes, and you smell the smoke, you do not focus on tidying your desk or checking your emails, or even debating the evacuation plan – you make for the escape route, or you stay put and face the consequences. See how Jesus closes the Sermon on the Mount. It's not with some vague philosophical observations, or some intellectual theory that we can calmly evaluate and then pass our own judgment on. It's not even by urging us to try harder, but with this inescapable summons. We will break this challenge into four simple statements.

Decision time

There are only two options
Look at verses 13-14 again. Here's the really shocking thing. According to Jesus, there are only two options, only two pathways through life. Doesn't that come as a shock? A lot of people would say differently. They would say, Thanks very much, but I am on my *own* journey through life, and I'm sure everyone else is on theirs – the possibilities are endless. Don't tell me there are only two options! But that's not what Jesus says. Whether he speaks, in these verses, of gates, of ways, or of destinations, there are two and two only. Just as in a burning building, there are two options – and no middle ground between. According to Jesus, all the world's philosophies and religions, every belief system you come across, whether it's five thousand years old or was dreamed up yesterday, all boil down to two simple options: do you follow Jesus Christ, do you submit to him as Lord and King; or do you reject him? You may not like that message, but you can't deny that it is what Jesus says.

There are only two destinations
Perhaps, like me, you have been up Snowdon in North Wales. Now many people think that the spiritual journey we make through life is rather like climbing Snowdon. It's a wonderful mountain, and there are many ways to reach the top. There are so many paths to choose from: there's the Watkin path, the Llanberis path, the Pyg Track, the Miners' Track, there's Crib Goch, the Snowdon Ranger path, or several others – or, if you prefer, you can even go up on the train. Some of these routes are harder, and some are easier: some steeper, some gentler; some longer, some shorter; and the views on the way up are different; but in the end, they all lead to the same place. They all start from *different* points, all the way round the mountain, but they all end up in exactly the *same* place, which is the top of the mountain, the summit of Snowdon. And that's what life is like, people think: we all climb the mountain in our own way, at our own pace, starting from different places – but in the end, we will all arrive at the top of the mountain.

Jesus says, It's not like that at all. In fact it's the *starting* point that is the same for all of us – it's the *destination* that is starkly different. There are two destinations. One of those options leads to destruction, while the other leads to life. It's a message that rings out all through the Bible. Long ago, Moses gave the same message as he spoke to the Israelites just before they entered the Promised Land (Deuteronomy 30:15,19). Moses, too, speaks of two destinations and calls on the people to choose life. Fifteen hundred years later, Jesus comes as God's full and final revelation. He presents *himself* as the crucial point in the choice that must be made – and he points out the same two destinations.

Jesus speaks first of *destruction* – a single word (Greek *apoleia*) with a huge and deadly weight of meaning. Jesus is talking about hell. Take one of these two options, he says, and you will end up in hell. It's absolutely essential that we hear and understand these words. The Jesus who lives the wonderful, loving, perfect life we read of in the gospels; the Jesus who heals the sick and raises the dead, who presents us with such profound and world-changing teaching; the Jesus who takes the children in his arms; this Jesus also speaks about *hell*, not once but many times, in order to warn people of where they will go, our final destination, if we insist on rejecting him. We are rebels against God, we are sinners, and according to God's justice hell is precisely what we deserve.

The Bible pictures hell in a number of ways, but most often as a fire – a lake of fire that never goes out. Revelation 20:10 presents this very clearly. If you are not listed in the book of life, this is your final destination. Yes, the image of fire is just that – it is an image, a picture. But the reality will not be easier to bear; it will certainly be worse than the picture. This is not comfortable to think about. It may not be a message you want to hear. It may be something you desperately want to ignore or deflect; but it is the solemn truth from the lips of the Son of God himself. Jesus bluntly warns his listeners that this fire, this destruction, is one of only two possible destinations.

Then he speaks of *life* – the other ultimate destination. Just as the experience of destruction will never end, so this life will never end – for this is *eternal* life, with Jesus, in a new, re-created world. We have found ourselves turning to the visions at the close of Revelation many times in this study of the Sermon on the Mount, and that's not surprising. Jesus has spoken of his kingdom – this is what the Sermon on the Mount has been describing – and this new world is where the kingdom will finally be perfected. Read Revelation 22:1-5 now for a brief description. It's a breathtaking picture of beauty, healing, light, the end of all evil, and above all the unending presence of the Lord Jesus Christ with us. Two destinations – one filled with tears of bitter despair, and the other where the only tears remaining are tears of joy.

214

Decision time

There are only two roads
Jesus speaks of a 'broad road' and a 'narrow road' which lead to these two destinations. The picture is of every member of the human race walking along one of these two roads. Each 'road' begins with a gate: a wide gate and a narrow gate[54]. So the first road is broad, it's wide. There is plenty of room on this road. You can carry as much baggage with you as you like and there is no need to leave anything behind. Although the word is not used directly, Jesus gives the impression that walking along this road is rather easy, the surface is smooth, there are no steep hills to climb. And the broad road, he says, is very popular. It's well-frequented. You have only to follow the crowd to find it and to keep moving along it. Stay on the *broad* road and you will have plenty of company. But there is room to spread out as well, so there is scope for differences of opinion, scope to express yourself.

The only real problem with this nice road is that it leads inexorably to the destination Jesus has just warned us about. As close as the next corner, perhaps, the sky will look darker, the threat of death will close in – and at that point, this road will have nothing at all to offer except for the company of thousands of others who are, in reality, just as lost as you.

But the narrow road is very different. It begins with a narrow *gate*. The word suggests it's hard to get through – in fact it's even hard to *find*. If you look at the two verses, you can see the descriptions of the broad and narrow roads are closely parallel, except at this one point: he doesn't say that few enter through the narrow gate, he says that few even manage to *find* it. The meaning of this is obvious: entering into the Christian life is not easy. It's a narrow gate: first you need to be shown it, so that you can see where it is; and then you need to squeeze through it. It's like one of those full-height turnstiles that you sometimes find at high security locations – we had them at the nuclear power station where I worked many years ago! You can't get through those gates carrying a big rucksack and a suitcase. In fact, if you want to get through, you have to leave things behind. On *this* road, you can't take it all with you.

In particular, to enter through the narrow gate, you have to leave behind your pride, your selfish ambitions, your desire to be running your own life. What Jesus has been talking about, all the way through the Sermon on the Mount, must be true of you as you walk this road. You won't be putting your own rights first any more, or striking back at people who hurt you, or promoting your own reputation. All that has to die, all that has to be left behind at the gate. There is a cost to beginning the Christian life. What is more, having begun with this narrow, constricted gateway, the road *continues* to be narrow. The picture this evokes is more like a narrow mountain path which climbs steeply, and is rocky underfoot – it's a challenge to walk this road. It's not at all like the broad open spaces of the other road. Let's be honest about it, just as Jesus is honest about it here: the Christian life is not the easy option. Do you want an easy path through life? Well then, stay on the broad road, follow the crowd – don't come this way. Christianity is not some crutch that will prop you up and make your life more comfortable. It is not a route to guaranteed prosperity or to perfect physical health, despite the teaching so popular in some parts of the church today. And it does not get easier as we go on. It starts narrow, and it continues narrow – and to pretend it is anything else is just deluding people. In the words of Christina Rossetti's poem, 'Does the road wind uphill all the way? Yes, to the very end.'[55]

Not only that, but the narrow road is not nearly as popular as the broad way. 'There are few who find it', says Jesus. Do you want to be popular? Then don't come this way. Many times Jesus speaks very strongly about the cost attached to going his way. He talks in terms of taking up your cross to follow him. He urges people to count the cost very carefully before setting out. This is a narrow road, a tough road. So if you are a Christian, if you are on this road, and the cost is feeling very high right now, don't be surprised. Trials and difficulties are exactly what we should expect on this road. Jesus told us about that (see John 16:33 for a very simple warning, but there are many others). But look at where the road is leading, and think of the alternative.

Of course, there is a wonderful aspect to this road as well. And as soon as we describe it as we have just done, in terms of following Jesus, we begin to see how wonderful it is. This is the great compensation, the great joy of the Christian life. Not only are we heading for the best possible destination, we are following in the footsteps of the Lord Jesus! As we walk this road, though it will not be easy, we are walking along behind Jesus, and as we do that, bit by bit we are becoming like him – more and more like the people described in the Beatitudes and the rest

Decision time

of the Sermon on the Mount, more and more like Jesus: more and more merciful, and peacemaking, and longing for what is good, and pure in our hearts; more and more getting rid of anger, and lust, and self, and hypocrisy; less and less trusting in the time-limited and decaying stuff we can accumulate in this world, and more and more pursuing the treasure that lasts for ever. The narrow road is steep, and sometimes it's specially painful – but it is *so much better* to be walking on this road! Again, if you are a Christian, when times are tough, just look back and see how far you have come. See how you have changed – see how he has changed you. See what he has been doing in your life since the day he brought you through that narrow gate.

Let me quickly deal with two possible misunderstandings about what Jesus says here. First, does he mean that very few people are actually on the road to life? Jesus says, Many are entering on the broad road, but few find the narrow way. The answer is, we don't know, and it's not really the point Jesus is making in this passage. Another time, he was directly asked this very question (Luke 13:22-24). Jesus doesn't answer the question – instead, he emphasises what is really important. You make sure *you* are on the right road. The point here in Matthew 7 is just the same. Don't count the numbers – you concentrate on where *you* are. Elsewhere, Jesus does speak of 'many' being saved (Matthew 8:11 and 20:28). When we come to the great vision of heaven in Revelation, we get the impression that there will be vast numbers around the throne of God (Revelation 7:9a), representing every group in humanity. We have to leave the numbers to God and listen to what Jesus is saying to us here.

The second misunderstanding is this. We might think about this picture of the two gates and imagine that we can loiter indefinitely outside both of them, wondering which one to go through – as if there is, in fact, a *third* option which is to do nothing at all, a neutral option. But that would be pushing Jesus' illustration too far. The problem for us is that in reality, we start life already embarked on the broad road. We are born at the wide gateway. We are sinners even at that point, rebels against God from the start. Or, to go back to the picture we began with, we are already sitting in the burning building, breathing in the smoke. As long as we continue to reject Christ, we are simply confirming our decision to stay on the broad road. There are only two roads: one leads to destruction, the other leads to life. Each of us is on one road or the other.

The Kingdom Manifesto

Therefore, we must decide
In verse 13 Jesus gives us this very simple command – 'Enter through the narrow gate'. At the beginning of the narrow way stands the narrow gate. If you have never done this, then a decision is required – *go through the gate*. The narrow gate is hard to find, Jesus says. But by the grace of God, you have found it – you are reading this book and at this moment you are standing at the gate with the opportunity to go through. To enter through the narrow gate means that we take a decisive step. We recognise that we are offenders against God, we have not kept his laws and we have not lived the life that he has told us to live. We recognise where the 'broad road' is leading us. So we decide to believe what Jesus says – not just the gentle stuff, but the hard words as well. We say yes, I know this is true.

This is the diagnosis. We are outrageous sinners. We need to be put right with God. That can only happen through the cross of Jesus Christ, where he died to pay the penalty for our sin and rebellion. The cross of Christ is where we can be reconciled to God; it's the only place where a lifetime of enmity can give way to peace. We recognise who we are and what we are like. We look at Jesus Christ and what he has done, and we ask God to forgive us; and because of Jesus, he will. That's what it means to enter through the narrow gate. Leaving behind our big ideas about ourselves – leaving behind our pride and our self-love, because they won't fit through the gate. This is radical, unconditional. Jesus Christ takes us through the narrow gate, and he will lead us all the way along the narrow road to the final destination – not *destruction*, but *life*. Have you been through the narrow gate?

True or false

It's generally agreed to be one of the very best children's books of the last fifty years. It is certainly one of the most popular. It's the story of how a small boy crosses the Atlantic in the company of some remarkably overgrown garden bugs, inside a remarkably overgrown garden fruit. The book, by Roald Dahl, is called *James and the Giant Peach*. James, the hero of the story, lives with his two cruel aunts, who give him the most miserable life you can imagine. In the garden of their house, where he is never allowed to play, there stands an ancient peach tree. It's worn-out and useless, and it never produces a thing.

Decision time

Then suddenly, one magical day, the two cruel aunts spot something astounding on the very highest branch. This tree, which has never even produced a blossom, has suddenly produced a *ripe peach*. The peach looks delicious, absolutely perfect. Before their astonished eyes, it is growing. Soon it's the size of a melon. The branch bends under the weight. Before long, the peach is so huge that it is the size of a small house and resting on the ground. And that's how the adventure begins.

Of course, the whole point of this is that it's completely ridiculous. It's an impossible start to an impossible story. How could a dried-up, ancient, useless tree produce any worthwhile fruit at all, never mind a giant peach? The answer is that it's utterly impossible. No: we know that only good trees produce good fruit – apples, pears, peaches or whatever. To find out if a fruit tree is any good, you have only to examine the fruit. If the fruit is no good – or if there is no fruit at all – then the tree is useless and you may as well get rid of it. Or, as Jesus puts it in verse 16, 'By their *fruit* you will recognise them'. Yes, but Jesus isn't talking about fruit trees. He is talking about us, tackling the vital question of whether people who claim to follow him are genuine or not – and how we can tell. Are people who claim to speak for God genuine or not? Are we, who say we are Christians, genuine or not? *True or false*, that's the question. Jesus is telling us that only those who are true and genuine will be accepted by God on Judgment Day. That makes this one of the most frightening and serious passages in the whole of Scripture. What could be more vital than making certain we are accepted by the Lord on the Day of Judgment? This is a life-and-death challenge for us all, whether we think we are Christians or not.

In verses 15-23, Jesus is expanding on the stark message he has just given. He is saying to his would-be followers, Be very careful. There are people who will try and keep you off the narrow road, by one means or another, and you must learn to watch out for them. Then there are people who think they are on the narrow road, and going to life, but the truth is they are not – and we must watch out for them as well, because that might be us – deluded and lost!

Watch out for false prophets!
Look at verse 15. Here's the picture Jesus is painting. There's a flock of friendly sheep out in the fields somewhere; and lurking in the woods there is a wolf. But this is a very cunning wolf, because he doesn't just

stroll up and say, Hi, I'm a wolf, let me eat you! This wolf dresses up as a sheep, so that for as long as possible the sheep, who are not the world's wisest creatures, will think he is one of them. So the wolf strolls out of the woods and meets the sheep, who promptly say, Welcome to the flock, it's good to have you! We're all one big, happy family here. But soon, sheep start to go missing; and the more gullible they are, the longer it will take the sheep to realise what their new friend is really like; and the more damage he will get away with. That is how Jesus describes these 'false prophets'. A prophet is not just someone who predicts the future. The point is not that these people make predictions which don't come true – although that is certainly possible, and the recent case of the man in America who foolishly predicted the so-called 'rapture' for May 2011 is a good example of that. Like the many others who have made similar predictions in the past, he has done a lot of damage by discrediting the whole Christian message.

Prophecy, however, is more than predictions. Let's look at a case in the Old Testament, in the book of Jeremiah. Jeremiah was a real prophet, a faithful and godly man, in the years just before Judah went into exile in Babylon. He is absolutely plagued by false prophets. Jeremiah 14:13-14 gives a flavour of his complaint about them to the Lord, and the Lord's response. Predictions of the future are one element of their message. A false prophet is anyone who claims to be speaking in the name of God, but in fact is speaking lies. They are false messengers, claiming to speak for God but actually leading his people astray. In the New Testament, the apostle Paul is plagued by a very similar group of people in Corinth. He nicknames them the 'super-apostles' because they claim to have special powers. He writes about them in 2 Corinthians 11:13-15. Paul bluntly attributes their message and their power to Satan.

These false prophets are by no means confined to biblical times. In fact Jesus himself, later in Matthew, warns his disciples of exactly this (Matthew 24:24). This is what it will be like until the day when I return to the earth, Jesus says. There will be this constant stream of deceivers, trying to lead you astray not only with their words, but even with dramatic miracles. Just like the 'super-apostles' Paul had to contend with, the false prophets of our own day may look highly impressive: polished, gifted, good on TV, smooth, persuasive. Jesus has told us. This is what we can expect.

Decision time

So who are the false prophets of today? Let's be clear: Jesus is not talking about people who are teaching something just a little bit different from us, differing on secondary issues. He is not thinking of someone who is just as committed to Scripture as we are, but has reached a different conclusion about baptism, or the order of events in the last days. That is not a false prophet; and we should not separate from our brothers over these minor differences. No, given what Jesus has just been saying about the narrow road, he almost certainly has in mind people who confuse that clear and fundamental message about this choice between two ways.

These false prophets are people who tell us that the broad road does not really lead to destruction after all – everyone will be OK in the end. That's dangerous, because it would mean we don't need to trust in Christ to be saved; and that's a lie from Satan. Or they tell us that the 'narrow road' isn't quite what we thought: in fact it's not narrow at all, it's not difficult, we can expect an *easy* time in the Christian life, full of health and prosperity. That's dangerous, because if we believe it, we are in for massive disappointment when reality hits and suffering comes – as it surely will. Other false prophets tell us that there *is* a narrow road, but it's not only Christians who are on it, and it's not only the death of Christ that brings you onto it. That's dangerous because it pretends that anyone who is sincere and religious is on his way to life; and that's a lie as well.

There are many ways in which this stark choice of two options, two roads, two destinations can be fogged, distorted or dodged. Anyone who misleads us in that kind of way is a false prophet. Watch out, says Jesus! Very often, in fact, the problem will not be about things these people *say*. The problem will be what they *miss out* of their message. False prophets are very good at talking about the *love* of God (though they will tend to describe it as a universal feeling of divine goodwill rather than his determination to save specific people in the way the Bible does). They are very good at talking about the life of Jesus, and the wonderful way he demonstrated God's love for the human race. But listen carefully, and you will find that they are not nearly so willing to talk about the seriousness of sin, our offences against God, the reality of judgment, and the fearful truth of an eternal hell. In other words, they don't want to speak about the holiness of God and the desperate hopelessness of men and women without Christ. They preach a truncated, cut-down gospel and they proclaim half a God. It's all very comfortable, very nice, very easy; it's what people prefer to hear – just like the men who so troubled Jeremiah. It has always been characteristic of false prophets that they give an easier, more comfortable message than those who genuinely speak for God. That was true in Jeremiah's time, in Paul's, and in our own.

We need to recognise the false prophets, because all this is dangerous. These people destroy the people of God just like wolves tearing into a field of sheep. Jesus doesn't pull his punches here – it's far too serious for that. Anything that distorts or confuses the gospel of life is very dangerous, because it can lead people to destruction. So we must recognise them – we must not be gullible, we must be aware.

As far as the church is concerned – and Christ has mandated local churches, in part, for precisely this protective task – this 'watching out' is especially a task for the elders. This is what Paul talks about in his farewell message to the elders of the church of Ephesus. I think this is one of the most moving passages of the New Testament – they certainly thought so at the time, given the number of tears that were shed (Acts 20:28-31, 36-37). That's the job of the elders – to keep watching out for the wolves. And of course, one of the vital qualifications for any pastor is that he should be able to do this, that he knows how to handle God's Word accurately and faithfully *and fully*, so that not only is his own 'prophecy' completely true, but also he is able to guard and protect us against the wolves. Far more important than whether he is friendly, or tells good jokes, or has management skills or anything like that, is this: Does he preach the whole counsel of God?

Watching out for the wolves is important for all of us. This is not to say that we should be going out of our way to hunt down heresy – and notice that Jesus is talking about people who come to us, that is, we become aware of their influence; we don't go searching for it. As church leaders, every time we faithfully preach the word, every time we refuse to duck the difficult doctrines and the more uncomfortable aspects of the Bible's teaching, we are building in 'wolf awareness' to our congregation. That's why we must do it – because we know the wolves are out there, and we are concerned about the sheep. The church of Christ has always been menaced by false prophets. It's just that in our super-tolerant age, where anything goes, we think it doesn't matter. It does matter, because eternity matters; and the Lord cares about the welfare of his sheep. A final summary of this comes from Paul, addressed to the church in Rome, the whole church, in Romans 16:17-19. Let that be true of us.

However, there is more to say. As Jesus continues, this test of whether people are true or false is not just about what they teach, what they say. It is also about their *lives*. Look at verses 16-20. You see the same words bracket this little section – 'by their fruit you will recognise them'. That's the simple message. It's not hard to understand, really. Do you get grapes off a thornbush? No. Figs off a thistle? No. Those are two impossible harvests. Then, changing the illustration slightly, can a useless, diseased tree produce good fruit, giant peach or anything else? No. What kind of tree produces good, tasty, healthy, nourishing fruit? A good, sound tree. What kind of person produces genuinely good fruit, the fruit of the Spirit? A man or woman who is genuinely godly, spiritually sound.

Undoubtedly, in these verses Jesus is telling us to test people *both* by their teaching and its results *and* by their lives. The two go together. The quality of someone's life is the ultimate test of the genuineness of what he teaches. Find out what his life looks like. This illustration of the fruit surely tells us that we need to look *closely*. You can't judge the fruit on a tree from half a mile away. You have to get close enough to smell it! Similarly, Jesus is saying, we need to be careful about people that we listen to. We should be slow to follow people, and slow to reject them. We need to test everything by the word of God.

For you, this might mean that you don't simply accept everything you hear when you switch on the 'God channel' on TV – that would be extremely unwise. You don't simply swallow everything you read in the latest Christian paperback or what you might find on the internet. There is a lot of rubbish out there, and some of it is dangerous rubbish! If you accept everything as easily as that, you are just being a silly sheep, and you are wide open for the wolves to come and tear you apart. Look carefully. Don't accept anything that just looks good from a distance.

Notice what Jesus says about the destiny of the false prophets (7:19). They are *condemned*. An orchard grower, faced with a useless tree that produces no fruit, will have no hesitation in chopping it down and burning it. The Bible tells us that teachers of God's Word will be strictly judged (James 3:1). Watch out for false prophets!

The Kingdom Manifesto

Watch out for yourself!

Look now at verses 21-23. Jesus is speaking generally here, not just about false prophets. He is speaking of the Day of Judgment – 'on that day' is all he needs to say – when everyone stands before God to be judged. The issue is whether people will 'enter the kingdom of heaven' (7:21) or not. We need to point out that Jesus is using the expression here to describe the final, perfected kingdom of eternity. Everyone who is genuinely part of the kingdom now, as they live on the earth (5:3, 10), will be accepted and welcomed on that day. But we now come to some of the most serious and solemn words Jesus ever spoke. He is telling us that on that day there will be people – and there will be *many* of them – who will stand before him, and they'll claim to know him and belong to him; and he will say, Go away – I never knew you. Go away to *destruction*. He describes them as 'evildoers' or (more literally) 'workers of lawlessness'. They are people who, whatever they claim, have never kept the fulfilled Law of obedience to Christ. And *we must watch out that this is not us*. There is a terrible danger of deluding ourselves, thinking we are secure, thinking we are saved, when in fact we are not.

Jesus' words show us that *having the right doctrine is not enough*. See what he says about these people. They call him 'Lord' (verse 21). They know what to call him. They know to address him by the name of God. That is very good doctrine[56], but we are not saved by doctrines, we are saved by knowing Jesus. Of course, if we are truly saved, it is hugely important to have the right doctrine, to have the clearest possible idea of what God is like and exactly what he has done to rescue sinful mankind – hugely important, but just knowing all about that *will not save us*. We are not saved by the beliefs we have in our heads, we are saved by Jesus. Do you know him? That's what counts!

What is more, Jesus shows us here that *words alone prove nothing* (7:22). These people claim to have spoken in the name of Jesus, and even to have done miracles in his name. We've already referred to the warnings that miracles can be faked, or done with the power of Satan, but these people claim to have done it all in the name of Jesus. Standing desperate on Judgment Day they will say, We did it all in your name! We did it for you! And Jesus will say to them, in effect, No you didn't! You might have thought so, you might have said so, but 'in my name' would mean you were doing my work on my authority. You weren't. I never knew you.

Decision time

Jesus says, There is only one test of whether you are genuine (7:21). The only test is obedience to God. What does your life look like? What is the fruit? You can have all the right ideas in your head; you can know the Scriptures; you can be steeped in theology; but if you do not know and love the Lord Jesus, this is what he will tell you. Of course all those things are important – but they are not the test. Does your *life* show that you know Jesus Christ? In your life, day by day, is there more and more of the character of Christ? What we have seen in the Beatitudes, this mourning over sin, this meekness, this pure heart, this longing for goodness – is that happening with you and me? What about this attitude of loving even our enemies? The challenge to be real, which we studied in chapter 6 – are you genuine, or are you a hypocrite, concerned only with looking good on the outside? What are your real motives for the good that you do? What is your real motive for serving God? What's in our hearts? Are we genuine or fake, true or false? This Sermon on the Mount has held up the character of the kingdom for us all to see – the character of Jesus himself – and if we really belong to Jesus, this is what our lives will be like.

When we see him, on that day, will we look at him and love him, or will we be scrabbling around for excuses and claims, like the people in these verses? Do you love Jesus? Does your life show it? Watch out for yourself! There is a great danger for anyone who has simply agreed to the Christian message – perhaps we grew up with it, and in our minds we have agreed that the Bible is true, and Jesus really came to die, and the gospel is the only way of salvation; and we've agreed with it in our minds, we've said that it's true; but it has never become part of us, it's never reached our hearts, we have never engaged with the Lord Jesus himself. If that is you, then you are in great danger. The Lord will say to you on that day, Go away – I never knew you!

I know that this message can be quite terrifying for some people who are naturally fearful and sensitive. You worry that this is describing you, when really it isn't. I would say this to you. If you know Jesus, if you know for sure he died for you – not as a nice idea, but in reality – if you are trusting him to take you to eternal life – then he will, and you have nothing to fear. Jesus has died so that on that day, you can stand before the Judge and he will say, Yes, you are real, and I *did* know you. Welcome in to the eternal kingdom! The way that we respond to the Lord Jesus will decide where we spend eternity. There is hope, but only if we respond to him. Nothing is more serious than this.

The Kingdom Manifesto

The ultimate test

A few years ago the Cornish village of Boscastle was struck by dramatic floods. At the time I was staying with my family at the cliff-top youth hostel in nearby Tintagel. I vividly recall looking along the coast that afternoon watching the rainstorm sweeping in; but it was still a shock to hear of what had happened four miles away in Boscastle as the quiet stream that runs through the village was transformed into a violent torrent that swept all before it. The Boscastle youth hostel was flooded almost to its ground floor ceiling; some of its occupants spent the night with us at Tintagel as refugees. Almost miraculously, no-one was killed by the flood. Plenty of cars were swept out to sea (including one whose surprised owner met it floating past as he returned to land in his fishing boat!); but the buildings, though many were damaged both inside and outside, stood firm. I suspect their survival had a great deal to do with their foundations.

In the closing passage of the Sermon on the Mount, Jesus uses just this illustration to give one last warning of the fate of those who reject him. Already he has talked of two gates and roads, of two trees and their fruit, and two claims: now he concludes by speaking of two builders and their two houses. As with the previous pairings, the two houses represent two different responses to the claims of Jesus Christ. Again we see that the distinctions may seem subtle, yet they are absolutely crucial. As with the fruit and the true and false teachers, it may at first be very hard to spot the differences, yet the differences are infinitely significant, for they determine where eternity will be spent. Both houses are destined to face violent storms; only one will survive.

Same environment – different response

Look at verses 24 and 26. Notice how Jesus uses exactly the same form of words to describe the builders and their work. That repeated form highlights the sharp contrast between 'wise' and 'foolish' and between 'rock' and 'sand'. But it also draws our attention to the similarities. Both these men hear Jesus' words. These are not people unreached by his message. He speaks of '*these* words of mine', indicating that it's the very words of the Sermon on the Mount that he has in mind. Both the men, then, have heard the call to humble themselves, to be poor in spirit and thus enter the kingdom. Both have been exposed to Jesus' searching exposure of the human heart and the uselessness of superficial religion.

Decision time

Both have heard him describe the genuine relationship he offers, with God as their Father who will love them, who will answer every prayer and provide for every need. Both have heard the warnings he has already given against refusing the message.

The two men, therefore, have heard the same words. Since both have been part of the same crowd, who have made a deliberate effort to go out from their homes and climb into the hills to hear Jesus speak, we can also say that they are both interested in the person and the teaching of Jesus. Hearing him has certainly been no accident. Probably they have both enjoyed listening. But now comes the difference. On hearing the words, one 'puts them into practice' (the Greek simply says 'does them') while the other does not. In the illustration, their responses are represented by the house that each man builds. Roughly speaking, the houses correspond to the life that each man lives and the decisions that he makes, but this analogy should not be pushed too far[57]. The houses may well look exactly the same: after all, the builders have much in common. There is just this one crucial difference. One builder has taken the time and trouble to excavate proper foundations. He has dug down to the bedrock to ensure that his house will be firmly attached to an immovable object, stable and secure. Meanwhile, his counterpart has simply found an empty plot and built straight on top of the sand he finds there.

Of course, in the short term there are advantages to building a house on sand. It is certainly quicker, uses fewer materials and is therefore cheaper. In Jesus' time, when tools are not very sophisticated, it will be much easier. Sand can easily be dug, shaped and moved. Rock is much less co-operative. Anyway, here are the two houses. Once built, the foundations are out of sight. There may be no way of telling that one man has built his house on the rock, and the other on the sand – as long as the sun shines and the weather remains calm!

Same threat – different outcome
Now look at verses 25 and 27. Once again, Jesus has used a very similar form of words. When the inevitable happens, and the weather changes, both houses face the same threat. The one change is that the word translated 'beat against' in the NIV is a different word in the Greek[58], but there is no significant difference in meaning. It is winter in the land of Israel. The dry countryside is suddenly being lashed by the rain. Down

227

from the hills the seasonal streams begin to flow. The sandy beds that are dry throughout the summer begin to fill (the Greek does not say literally 'the streams rose' but 'the rivers came'); and the unwisdom of the second builder's choices quickly becomes all too evident. The waters of the winter torrents reach the house. The sand that has been holding the inadequate foundations in place until now begins to wash away. As a further challenge to the beleaguered house, a gale has blown up. It would be no great problem for a properly-built home, perhaps, but it is for this one. Very soon, the house shifts, leans, totters, and collapses with a crash that is briefly audible even above the tumult of the river.

Meanwhile, just across the valley, the other house stands. It too experiences the rain, the floods, the violent winds. They are just the same in intensity, but here the result is different. Here, the stresses of wind and water are transmitted down through the foundations to the bedrock. The rock does not shift. The house does not shift. The house stands firm.

Clearly, the storms and floods Jesus describes represent the trials which everyone will face. Life is full of trials: some are trivial, like a shower of rain, while others feel more like a flood. We sometimes speak of 'keeping our heads above water' when life is tough! These trials are inevitable. It's important that we see what Jesus does *not* say. He does not say that the man who obeys his words gets to build his house where storms never strike, where the wind never blows. Obeying Jesus does not in any way spare us from trials. Rather, it provides us with a foundation that cannot shift.

But beyond the difficult and painful times we pass through in this life, Jesus' picture of storms and floods represents the ultimate test of final judgment; and in view of the context, this is certainly his main point. People who have not chosen to follow Christ may survive all that the present life has to throw at them. They may have other 'foundations' which will help them to do that: the support of friends and family, the convictions offered by another religion or philosophy, their own good health, financial prosperity or some other resources. Their 'house' may not fall while their earthly life endures. The really serious test comes after that. Just as the broad road (7:13) may be perfectly easy and enjoyable for most of its course, but ends in destruction, so the cowboy builder of verse 26 may thrive for many years but will eventually suffer the ultimate loss.

Decision time

The final judgment is a test that everyone will face. 'On that day' (7:22), we will all stand before the Lord Jesus Christ to be judged. Without Christ himself as our defence, we stand as much chance of surviving it as a beach hut in a hurricane. With him, with our foundations on the rock, we will most certainly stand firm[59].

Our own response
So Jesus concludes the Sermon on the Mount with a bang, leaving this final warning ringing in our ears. Where is our foundation – where is yours? How have you responded to these words of Jesus? Your eternal destiny depends on the answer. As you have read and contemplated his words, what has been the response of your heart? Do you accept the diagnosis that your heart is deeply sinful and urgently needs to change? Do you find yourself hungry and thirsty for righteousness, longing to be more and more like the Lord Jesus? Are you looking for a deeper and truer relationship with God your Father, and are you willing to sacrifice people's good opinions for the only opinion that matters? Are you constantly examining your own soul to ensure that you are on the road to life? These are good signs, excellent signs. But if you read Jesus' words and find yourself resentful, protesting that really you are not all that bad, or that a certain level of commitment is enough, or that it is foolish and impractical to take Jesus' words at face value, then you should be very worried. A response like that means that you are *not* putting Jesus' words into practice. It means that you are taking it upon yourself to decide what your life will be based on – but obeying the words of Jesus means submitting to them without conditions.

Listening to what Jesus says, or merely listening to any of the Bible's teaching for that matter, is not enough. Both the men in the picture did that, but clearly only one of them benefited. We can still find many people sitting in church services today – and you may even be one of them – who happily listen to sermons or read Christian books, and enjoy thinking them over and discussing them, but whose lives show that there has been no genuine response whatsoever. An intellectual response to Jesus is not enough. There have been many people who have carefully evaluated Jesus' teaching and given him their nod of approval, but that is not what he is calling for.

These verses are not proclaiming salvation by works. The message is not that you must listen to Jesus, go away and do your best. The message is the one familiar from other parts of Scripture, that faith without works is dead – in other words, it is not really faith at all (James 2:14-26). We are being warned against pretending – the pretence that religious people so easily fall for – that if we have heard about Jesus and what he said, and we have a clear picture in our minds of what Christianity is all about, and we go to the right places and say the right words, then we are going to be all right. So what are our lives based on right now? Are we merely hearers, or are we doers? Where have we been building?

Authority and astonishment
Matthew concludes his account of the Sermon on the Mount in a similar way to the four other great discourses he records (compare 7:28-29 with 11:1, 13:53, 19:1 and 26:1). These two verses, along with 5:1-2, comprise the 'narrative frame' of the Sermon: everything in between has been the words of Jesus, uninterrupted by any comment or explanation from the author. But what stands out here is the reaction of the crowds. From 5:1-2 we know that the primary audience of the Sermon on the Mount consists of the disciples, but even there at the beginning the crowds are not far away. We get the impression that as Jesus has been speaking, they have steadily been arriving, gradually thronging the hillside, until they are sitting on every rock and patch of grass within earshot. Thus many elements in the Sermon, especially towards the end, have clearly been directed beyond Jesus' immediate followers. The crowds too have been brought face to face with Jesus and his claims. And what has struck them so powerfully, to the point of extreme astonishment[60], is his *authority*.

In verse 29 we see that they are comparing him to the teachers they are most used to hearing, the scribes or 'teachers of the law'. What stands out about Jesus is that his style of teaching is so different. The scribes are their religious professionals. Their customary method is to quote an endless string of earlier authorities. They are prepared to use their own expertise to evaluate and balance these predecessors of theirs, but anything that smacks of innovation is very, very rare. Scribes do not speak for themselves. Their approach can be seen in the Talmud (which we have mentioned several times before), notably in Tractate *Aboth*, where the chain of teaching from the days of Moses to the current schools of Shammai and Hillel is set out. This sets the tone for the style of instruction throughout the Talmud. How different from Jesus, who speaks in his own name and in his own right. The most striking example of this is in 5:21-48, where he quotes authority and precedent only to say each time 'But *I* say to you'! He does not even trouble to lay out his own credentials – indeed, it will become one of the complaints against him that he has no official qualifications. He simply assumes the right to speak with this breathtaking note of authority.

Still more than his style, and beyond his speaking in his own right, it is the way that Jesus places himself at the centre of everything that impresses his hearers so strongly. Not only does he presume to advance and re-interpret their God-given Law, he actually presents himself as its fulfilment (5:17)! Here is someone who claims that God's age-long purposes and promises find their culmination and climax in him. And as we have just seen, it is people's response to Jesus' own words that will determine where they spend eternity. Likewise, in chapter 7, he presents himself as the Judge of humanity. It is Jesus himself who will send people away to hell on the grounds that he does not know them (7:23). This actually amounts to a claim of Deity, for it is well-known to the Jews that only God is the Judge of all the earth (Genesis 18:25).

No wonder the crowds are amazed. Whatever their further response may have been, they could not remain unmoved by Jesus' words and his claims, both open and implied. And so, as John Stott puts it, 'The main question the Sermon forces upon us is not so much "What do you make of this teaching?" as "What do you make of this teacher?"'[61]. I hope you have made your decision.

We cannot allow the Sermon on the Mount to be atomised into a series of individual sayings from which we can select as we please. What was true of the Beatitudes (see chapter 1) is equally true of the Sermon as a whole. This is a manifesto, coherent and complete. It reaches the depths of the human heart and it embraces every part of our lives and every kind of relationship. It concerns both the present and our future. We must accept it all, or not at all. Nor can we let it be written off as a collection of worthy sayings, issued by a teacher who could have been anyone – as so many have done. With other teachers and philosophers, that might be the case. Here, it simply cannot be. Jesus' teachings constantly point to himself. They cannot be separated from Jesus the man, for Jesus the man is Jesus the King. We cannot understand the Kingdom Manifesto without encountering and submitting to the King.

Finally, we cannot isolate the Sermon on the Mount from the rest of Scripture, or from Matthew's own account. The Sermon is part of the great Story that has brought Jesus to earth to become our Saviour, that will take him to the cross, that will see him raised from the dead, ascended and glorified and returning. So we do not 'put these words of mine into practice' except by coming to the cross, recognising our sinful nature, and finding forgiveness and new life. We embrace the crucified and risen King, we become part of his kingdom, we worship him now in our lives, and we long for his glorious return as Lord and Judge.

Questions to reflect on or discuss

1. The crowds are 'amazed at his teaching' (7:28). What about you?

2. As you have read through the Sermon on the Mount, do you find yourself submitting gladly to all that Jesus says, or are there things you struggle with? If the latter, do you think that's just because these are things you haven't yet fully understood, or is part of you actually in rebellion against the Lord Jesus?

3. How do the foundations that you have in Christ help you in specific trials? Think of some examples and reflect on how you responded. How would your response have been different without Christ?

4. Do you have a strong and secure assurance that your foundation in Christ will enable you to stand on the Day of Judgment?

Notes

1. In saying that the gospel writers had a role in selecting and arranging their material, we are not undermining either the inspiration of Scripture or its historical reliability. We are simply recognising that each of the four gospels has a distinct theological purpose. If this were not the case, there would be no good reason to have four of them at all! See, for example, my *A Ransom for Many* in the Welwyn Commentary series, which shows how the structure of Mark's gospel serves his specific purpose of progressively revealing Jesus' identity and mission as the suffering Messiah.

2. See the chapter 'Was Jesus Political' in *Tales of Two Cities*, edited by Stephen Clark.

3. Theologically, the only significant point of difference is the meaning of the word 'righteousness', where I am convinced we need to recognise the differences between Matthew's use of the word – generally with an ethical sense – and Paul's, where it is generally used with a forensic (legal) meaning. This becomes important in the way we interpret Matthew 5:6 and 5:20, where I shall have more to say about it.

4. Originally, the English word 'happy' meant fortunate – it meant that something good had 'happened' to you. In that older sense of the word, Jesus does indeed mean 'happy'. It's only more recently that 'happy' has shifted its meaning to describe feelings!

5. For example, at the outset of his ministry, Jesus in Matthew is quoted as preaching 'Repent, for the kingdom of heaven is near' (Matthew 4:17); at the same point in Mark the equivalent expression is 'the kingdom of God' (Mark 1:15); similarly, compare Matthew 19:14 with Luke 18:16-17.

6. Theologians say that the kingdom of God is both a space and an activity – meaning that it's defined not just by the people it includes, but by the fact that God is actively reigning there.

7. I owe the expression to John Blanchard in his book *The Beatitudes for Today*.

8. In *Studies in the Sermon on the Mount*, Vol. 1, p.18.

9. In *The Gospel according to Matthew*, p.96. Morris goes on to agree that there is an echo here of the Old Testament's teaching about God's care for the poor, but even then they are the *faithful* poor who look to God for deliverance.

10. Not everyone agrees with the line I am taking. In particular, Martyn Lloyd-Jones sees both meanings of righteousness here (*Studies in the Sermon on the Mount*, Vol. 1, pp.77ff). But I don't think he took sufficient account of the different ways that New Testament authors use the word 'righteousness' (Greek *dikaiosune*), nor the logic of the Beatitudes whereby at this point legal righteousness is already in our possession.

11. To be more precise, there is a slight difference between mercy and grace. 'Grace' is generally used of God's attitude to us as sinners. Thus *common* grace is his goodness to everyone on earth in spite of their sin, while *saving* grace is his intervention in the lives of those he is bringing to salvation through Christ. 'Mercy' is more specifically a response to human misery. But clearly there is a large overlap, and common grace is certainly one expression of God's mercy. 'Mercy' is sometimes defined as God 'not giving us what we deserve' but the references which follow show that it is more than that – it implies a positive response, not just holding back a punishment.

12. The story is told more fully in Robin Oake's powerful book, *Father, forgive*.

13. The clearest proof of this comes in 1 John 1:8-10. We should note that John also emphasises that sin is not normal for Christians, and we should never see it that way.

14. It is sometimes said that salt cannot lose its saltiness, and therefore Jesus is speaking hypothetically. But in its original setting, 'salt' clearly could lose its useful content.

15. In chapter 6, Jesus tells his people to make sure their 'acts of righteousness' are *unseen*. As we will see when we get there, this is not a contradiction: it all comes down to the attitudes of our hearts.

16. Interesting, then, that this is precisely what Jesus threatens to do to the unloving and unrepentant church in Ephesus (Revelation 2:5) – though the imagery is somewhat different.

Notes

17. 1 Corinthians 5:8, in the passage we shall refer to shortly, even applies the Passover law about yeast to Christians!

18. It is sometimes said that the food laws were also given for reasons of hygiene. This may be true in some cases but it certainly isn't the main point. Others have suggested that the division of animals into 'clean' and 'unclean' was related to the use of certain animals in pagan religious rituals or that there were other, symbolic associations. For further discussion, consult the relevant Old Testament commentaries or specialist material such as the fascinating article by Gordon Wenham, 'The Theology of Unclean Food', in *Evangelical Quarterly* 53.1, accessible at http://www.biblicalstudies. org.uk/pdf/unclean-food_wenham.pdf.

19. I am indebted to the excellent treatment of this passage by Chris Bennett in his paper *The Use of the Mosaic Law in the New Testament Church* to the 2009 Affinity Theological Study Conference.

20. A good example of this indistinctness is the Sabbath law. This is, of course, one of the Ten Commandments (Exodus 20:8) – part of the 'moral law', yet its detailed application in terms of exactly what can and cannot be done on the Sabbath is worked out in the 'civil law'. It is no accident that discussions of the place of the Law among Christians today often focus on the place of the Sabbath. At this point the Law simply defies neat classification. Further discussion of the 'Christian Sabbath' is, however, beyond the scope of this book, since the Sermon on the Mount does not mention it!

21. As we saw in Chapter 1, the 'righteousness' referred to here does not refer to the righteous status given to the believer by God (justification). In any case, such an interpretation would not be consistent with v.19, which is about keeping commandments.

22. The reference is actually to Gehenna, or the valley of Hinnom, a ravine near Jerusalem which was used as a rubbish dump. Because it was a place where refuse was dumped and where fires burned perpetually, its name became used as an alternative word for hell.

23. That is why many Greek manuscripts include the expression 'without cause' after the first 'brother' in 5:22. It almost certainly was not there in the original, but it accurately clarifies Jesus' meaning.

24. Origen never mentions this story in his own writings, which actually show that he did not follow a literal interpretation of these verses. However, there is good evidence that the practice existed: it had to be outlawed by the Council of Nicaea in AD 325!

25. *You can change*, p.81.

26. A reference to Deuteronomy 24:1.

27. In Jesus' time, divorce was probably obligatory in cases of adultery. This would explain why the other gospel writers do not include the specific 'Matthaean exception' about *porneia* – it could be taken for granted (Mark 10:11-12, Luke 16:18).

28. Instone-Brewer's book is called *Divorce and remarriage in the church*.

29. The force of this bald statement is not removed even if (as some would argue) the primary concern in Malachi is God's marriage to his people.

30. More recently, a similar view is expressed by the Mennonite theologian John Howard Yoder in his influential work *The Politics of Jesus*.

31. The Greek words in verse 39 (*to ponero*) could mean 'evil', 'the evil person' (generically, i.e. any evil person) or 'the Evil One'. The same choices of translation are available in verse 37. We have to decide from the context and from consistency with the rest of Scripture which is appropriate. In verse 39 the immediate context is decisive, since Jesus goes straight on to talk about specific 'evil people'.

32. *The Sermon on the Mount*, p.50.

33. In his book *Where do we go from here: chaos or community?*, p.64, published in 1967.

34. John Stott quotes Augustine: 'Many have learned how to offer the other cheek, but do not know how to love him by whom they were struck' (*Christian Counter-Culture*, p.122).

35. Quoted by John Stott in *Christian Counter-Culture*, p.119.

36. From *The Hiding Place* by Corrie ten Boom with John and Elizabeth Sherrill. The story has a wonderful conclusion, not told in the book. Jan Vogel was executed for his crimes against his fellow-countrymen; but a week before his execution, he committed his life to Christ and now stands in heaven alongside Betsie and Corrie in the presence of their Saviour – all as forgiven sinners.

37. This is the word *eleemosune*, which is used three times in verses 2-4 and is translated in the NIV as 'giving to the needy'. 'Righteousness' is *dikaiosune*.

Notes

38. *Studies in the Sermon on the Mount*, Vol. 2, p.11.

39. The rules are discussed in Mishnah tractate *Berakot*. As with other Pharisaic regulations and practices, there is a startling parallel with Islam.

40. *Studies in the Sermon on the Mount*, Vol. 2, pp.21-23.

41. I have gone into a little more detail about the kingdom of heaven in the Introduction.

42. The choice that has to be made in translation here is the same as in 5:37 and 5:39.

43. *Studies in the Sermon on the Mount*, Vol. 2, p.69.

44. Greek *haplous*.

45. *The Sermon on the Mount*, p.81.

46. The Greek word is *ethnos* (plural *ethne*) which means nations, and by implication non-Jewish nations.

47. Quoted by John Stott in *Christian Counter-Culture*, p.164.

48. The difficulty of tying the whole of chapter 7 together is underlined by the fact that John Stott identifies a loose connecting thread of 'relationships', whereas Martyn Lloyd-Jones was convinced that the underlying theme was 'judgment'. The latter certainly has a lot in its favour, but verses 7-12 don't really fit. It seems much better to accept that there is a clear break after verse 12 and treat the two halves of chapter 7 separately.

49. Quoted by John Stott in *Christian Counter-Culture* (p.175) from a collection of Tolstoy's works (*A Confession, The Gospel in Brief and What I Believe*).

50. So in fact, Rabbi Hillel was wrong!

51. It might be objected (both in the Sermon on the Mount and in Romans) that the Golden Rule and 'Love your neighbour as yourself' summarise the Law only in its 'horizontal' aspect – our relationships with other people – and not in its 'vertical' aspect – our relationship to God. Yes, but in both cases our absolute submission to God as the only God, whose worship is never to be compromised by idolatry and whose name is to be kept holy, is already assumed. Jesus is speaking in a Jewish context where these commands were well-understood (and see Matthew 22:37-40, where he makes the primacy of loving God explicit). Paul has addressed the nature

and character of God, and the roots of idolatry, earlier in Romans; and in 12:1 he has called on his readers to offer themselves wholly to God as their primary act of worship.

52. It is likely that Jesus' audience would be able to think of a fish they knew of that looked very like a snake. Morris quotes two suggestions for the identity of this fish, including Dick France's idea that Jesus might have in mind the eel-like catfish of the Sea of Galilee (*The Gospel according to Matthew*, p.171)

53. I want to acknowledge Martyn Lloyd-Jones' very helpful insights at this point.

54. Some commentators prefer to think of the road as leading up to the gate, but for two reasons I don't think that can be right. Firstly, Jesus mentions the gate first in each case. Secondly, finding and passing through the narrow gate fits the idea of decisive response much better than does an (undefined) start of a road.

55. From the poem *Uphill*.

56. As Martyn Lloyd-Jones says, no-one who *doesn't* say 'Lord, Lord' will enter the kingdom (*Studies in the Sermon on the Mount*, Vol. 2, p.264).

57. For one thing, people are already making life choices *before* they hear any of Jesus' words, and to fit the illustration these 'houses' would all be built on sand; some hearers would then decamp to start from scratch building new houses on solid rock, while others remained on the sand. Similarly, the 'rock' of the foundation does not *in this illustration* correspond exactly to Jesus Christ himself, even though he is so described in Isaiah 28:16. The thrust of the illustration in Matthew 7 is simply that the foundation of our lives determines our ultimate destiny.

58. In the first case, *prosepesan*; in the second, *prosekopsan*.

59. Paul uses a somewhat similar illustration in 1 Corinthians 3:10-15, where the final judgment is likened to fire which will test the quality of a Christian's work. The key difference is that Paul is speaking only to Christians, who will all 'survive' the judgment, even if much of their work may not.

60. Greek *exeplessonto*. It's a strong word.

61. Stott, *Christian Counter-Culture*, p.213.